Law & Literature

Edited by
Daniela Carpi · Klaus Stierstorfer

Volume 3

De Gruyter

Dialogues

Dialogues on Justice

European Perspectives on Law and Humanities

Edited by

Helle Porsdam and Thomas Elholm

De Gruyter

ISBN 978-3-11-026898-0
e-ISBN 978-3-11-026938-3
ISSN 2191-8457

Library of Congress Cataloging-in-Publication Data

A CIP catalog record for this book has been applied for at the Library of Congress.

Bibliographic information published by the Deutsche Nationalbibliothek

The Deutsche Nationalbibliothek lists this publication in the Deutsche Nationalbibliografie; detailed bibliographic data are available in the Internet at http://dnb.dnb.de.

Printing: Hubert & Co. GmbH & Co. KG, Göttingen
∞ Printed on acid-free paper

Printed in Germany

www.degruyter.com

Table of Contents

Helle Porsdam / Thomas Elholm
Preface 1

Daniela Carpi
Prologue. Law and Culture 3

I. Law and Humanities – The Road Ahead

Greta Olson
De-Americanizing Law and Literature Narratives:
Opening Up the Story 15

Jeanne Gaakeer
European *Law and Literature*: Forever Young. The Nomad Concurs . . 44

II. History, Memory and Human Rights

Jay Winter
Human Rights and the Second World War 75

Mattias Kumm
The Idea of Thick Constitutional Patriotism and its Implications
for the Role and Structure of European Legal History 108

III. Forgiveness and Law

Svend Erik Larsen
Forgiveness as a Challenge to the Law: A Literary Perspective 141

Hans Petter Graver
Measure for Measure: On Law and Forgiveness 160

IV. Justice, Culture and Copyright

Mia Rendix
Copyright as Moral Strategy of Reclaiming the Past:
The Return of the Icelandic Sagas 177

Fiona Macmillan
Rights, Culture, Property: In Search of a New Design for Intellectual Space 193

Helle Porsdam
Epilogue. Cultural Heritage and Law: The Case of Cultural Looting . . 219

List of Contributors 237

Preface

This book is a result of the work done within the Nordic Network of Law and Literature. The Network was established in 2005, when Associate Professor at the University of Aarhus, Karen-Margrethe Simonsen – the main coordinator of the Network – was awarded a large sum of money by Nord-Forsk, Nordic Council of Ministers. The funding was given for the purpose of establishing a network of scholars of law and literature in the Nordic countries and to increase the interest in interdisciplinary research in law and literature from a Nordic perspective.

Since then a number of conferences and doctoral workshops have been arranged, books and articles have been published, and the Nordic Network has paved the way for close cooperation between scholars of law and literature in the Nordic countries (see homepage: http://littrett.uib.no). The last seminar arranged by the Nordic Network was held in the Villa Vigoni at the Como Lake in Northern Italy in October 2009. This book comprises revised editions of some of the lectures given at this seminar.

The title of the book has been copied from the title of the seminar at the Villa Vigoni: "Dialogues on Justice: European Perspectives on Law and Humanities". After a couple of years with seminars and publications on law and literature we thought it was time to expand the concept. The aim is to focus on interdisciplinary discussions on justice in a Nordic and European context. By expanding the focus to justice and humanities – beyond "law and literature" – we intend to embrace different perspectives closely linked to the research and discussions about law and literature, for example "cultural studies".

We have chosen four main themes, each of which is described from different angles. For each theme we have asked a scholar with a background in the humanities and a scholar with a legal background (or lawyer) to elaborate on the topic. The four themes and the authors are:

I) Law and Humanities – The Road Ahead (Professor Greta Olson and Professor Jeanne Gaakeer)
II) History, Memory and Human Rights (Professor Jay Winter and Professor Mattias Kumm)
III) Forgiveness and Law (Professor Svend Erik Larsen and Professor Hans Petter Graver)
IV) Justice, Culture and Copyright (Assistant Professor Mia Rendix and Professor Fiona Macmillan)

Framing the four themes, Professor Daniela Carpi has written the Foreword and Professor Helle Porsdam the Epilogue. Both of these essays try to capture the *reason d'être* of the interdisciplinary research on law and humanities.

One of the main goals of the Nordic Network has been to create a dialogue between scholars of humanities and scholars of law or lawyers. Hence, the title of the book is "dialogue" and even the editors have a mixed background of humanities and law. Helle Porsdam is a professor of American Studies at the Department of History, University of Copenhagen, and Thomas Elholm is a professor of law at the Department of Law, University of Southern Denmark. Both editors were members of the organizing committee of the Nordic Network.

We are proud to present yet another result of the cooperation within the Nordic Network of Law and Literature and we are sure – as the content of the book will hopefully show – that it marks the beginning of a multi- or interdisciplinary research field with very fruitful perspectives. We believe that the book will be the latest rather than the last result of the Nordic Network of Law and Literature!

Copenhagen, March 2011 Helle Porsdam and Thomas Elholm

Daniela Carpi
(University of Verona)

Prologue
Law and Culture

After a few decades of interdisciplinary legal academic studies centred on law and its interpretation we can in some way speak of the contemporary state of the art and of developments of interpretative jurisprudence. Generally speaking we can debate and define these movements as postmodern in a wide sense, meaning with the word postmodernism an antifoundationalist tendency officially dating back to the eighties. As literary theoreticians have assessed, this new "age of anxiety" has gone hand in hand with the crisis of language and its signification (connected to Saussure's linguistic turn) and with the philosophical sceptic attitudes of American deconstruction, which theorized on the infinitization of interpretation and the impossibility to attain a universal meaning of things. The assertion of the impossibility of expressing theories is a feature of these antifoundationalist theories[1], even if this sounds paradoxical in our hypercritical age where new theories are constantly being devised. This is why we have discerned the widening out of North American jurisprudence to the most varied theoretical themes: we have witnessed a deep cultural transformation permeating the entire Western world. The postmodern turn is rooted in a vaster critical movement called "cultural studies", an interdisciplinary field where certain concerns and methods have converged:

> The usefulness of this convergence is that it has enabled us to understand phenomena and relationships that were not accessible through the existing disciplines.[2]

Therefore if cultural studies define themselves through the disruption of the boundaries between disciplines, the law appears as one of the main *métarécits* which were officially deconstructed by a postmodern sense of fallibility. We have witnessed a pluralist and multicultural interpretative turn, separating

---

1 Gary Minda, *Postmodern Legal Movements. Law and Jurisprudence at Century's End* (New York: New York University Press, 1995).

2 Graeme Turner, *British Cultural Studies* (London and New York: Routledge, 1990), 11.

itself from the belief in universal truths and in the government of a fixed set of rules.

The postmodern turn in jurisprudence set itself as a "law and" system of analysis since its very beginning. In particular, as Gary Minda observes, the philosophical movements of the Eighties paved the way for a new form of juridical criticism by opening a debate between new linguistic and cultural practices, such as law and economics, feminist jurisprudence, law and literature. Law became a cultural object and part of a cultural social discourse in a multicultural society. According to Geoffrey Hartman the latest years of the twentieth century are characterised by so-called "culturalism", that is by the effort to use art to diagnose or affirm particular cultures. He even speaks of "fateful militancy" achieved by culture in the world.[3] He means to restore literature's specificity as a focus for thinking about culture.

The most famous and seminal interdisciplinary enterprise has probably been the law and literature comparison, which has also drawn the attention of professors of literature who managed to apply theories originally purported by jurists in literary examples. The combined efforts of both jurists and humanists has reached the aim of renewing both the study of the law (the literary examples have in some way been seminal in teaching of the law itself) and of literature (offering new perspectives in the interpretation of texts).

But now the original field of law and literature studies has gradually extended to comprise many new "law ands", thus widening out the original interdisciplinary undertaking. We are therefore aware of a proliferation of intellectual practices that have gone well beyond the first seminal approach of law and literature.

> The tendency towards greater interdisciplinarity [...] may ultimately lead to a general reconfiguration of genres in which 'law' disappears as a distinct discipline. In this sense the 'interdisciplinary' is merely evidence of a transition from one matrix of disciplines to another.[4]

Having lost a universal concept of knowledge and having become prey to hyperspecialisms, we must go back to a sort of *ars combinatoria* that at least allows us to compare the different disciplines. Leibniz in fact distinguishes between two sorts of art: *ars inveniendi* and *ars combinatoria*.[5] The former is the

---

3 Geoffrey Hartman, *The Fateful Question of Culture* (New York: Columbia University Press, 1997), 1.

4 Michael D.A. Freeman and A.D.E. Lewis eds., *Law and Literature* (Oxford: Oxford University Press, 1999), XV.

5 Gottfried Wilhelm Leibniz, *Scritti di Logica*, ed. Francesco Barone (Bologna: Zanichelli, 1968), 186ff., 216ff.

art of the sparkling of the idea, of discovery; the latter is the capacity to combine it with the data of experience. Technology best exemplifies *ars combinatoria*: it is the capacity to discover new forms of language. In the law's case it means inventing new juridical languages that are fit for human coexistence. Thanks to *ars combinatoria* unforeseen meanings are discovered. Law becomes an art among the other arts.

> The postmodern legal recourse to other disciplines, to sociology, philosophy, economics, history or literature, represents much more than a simple proliferation of academic concerns [...]. At an institutional level it represents the symbolic collapse of the concept and practice of any singular or sovereign jurisprudence [...] postmodernity recalls the difference and the otherness without which the sameness or precedence of law could not be built. In substantive terms, other disciplines have been the means of representing other experiences and other constructions of law and its impositions.[6]

Among the latest trends in the "law and" fields of research the connection between law and culture has come to the forefront. We speak of a cultural analysis of law, of law as culture and culture as law, of the use of cultural studies methodology to interpret the law, of law as a cultural artifact.[7] The problem is, as Mezey correctly affirms, defining what we mean by culture.

The development of the concept of culture has a long-standing history, that saw the merging together of different fields of knowledge from its very beginning: from Burke's conception of the English Constitution, as opposed to the French Revolution, which foreruns Arnold's idea of a common culture[8], to Carlyle's *Signs of the Time*[9], Coleridge's *On the Constitution of the Church and State*[10], Matthew Arnold's *Culture and Anarchy*[11], Thomas Sterne Eliot's

---

[6] Peter Goodrich and David Gray Carlson, Introduction to *Law and the Postmodern Mind. Essays on Psychoanalysis and Jurisprudence* (Ann Arbor: The University of Michigan Press, 2001), 2.

[7] See for example: Naomy Mezey, "Law as Culture", *Yale Journal in Law and Humanities* 35 (2003): 35–67; Francis Cardinal George O.M.I., "Law and Culture", *Ave Maria Law Review* 1 (2003): 1–18; Roger Cotterrell, "Law in Culture", *Ratio Juris* 17.1 (March 2004): 1–14.

[8] Edmund Burke, *Reflections of the Revolution in France* [1790] (Oxford: Oxford University Press, 1950).

[9] Thomas Carlyle, *Signs of the Time*, in *Selected Writings*, ed. Alan Shelston (Harmondsworth: Penguin Books, 1961).

[10] Samuel Taylor Coleridge, *On the Constitution of the Church and State*, in *Complete Works*, ed. William Greenough Thayer Shedd (New York: Harper and Brothers, 1884).

[11] Matthew Arnold, *Culture and Anarchy* [1932], ed. J. Dover Wilson (Cambridge: Cambridge University Press, 1994).

Notes Towards the Definition of Culture[12], C.P. Snow's *The Two Cultures*[13], F.R. Leavis' "Mass Civilization and Minority Culture"[14], Raymond Williams' *Culture and Society 1780–1950* and *Keywords*[15], and Geoffrey Hartman's *The Fateful Question of Culture*[16], just to mention a few of the many philosophers who have dealt with the question of culture.[17] In the course of time culture has been separated from civilization, as the Frankfurt school with Adorno theorized, so whereas culture is connected to spiritual growth and improvement, civilization is connected to technological progress and material progress in general. The two concepts come to be at variance, as Spengler purported in his *The Decline of the West*[18] when saying that a society can reach the maximum of civilization but the minimum of culture. But all this has been well assessed by critics.

At a certain point anthropology also comes into play with Tylor's *Primitive Cultures* and Clifford Geertz's *Interpretation of Cultures*[19], focusing the analysis on the so-called "thick descriptions", that is on the analysis of material facts and ways of life. And here is where my own discourse comes in:

> [...] cultural studies is an interdisciplinary, transdisciplinary, and sometimes counter-disciplinary field that operates in the tension between its tendencies to embrace both a broad, anthropological and a more narrowly humanistic conception of culture. Unlike traditional anthropology, however, it has grown out of analyses of modern industrial societies. It is typically interpretive and evaluative in its methodologies, but unlike traditional humanism it rejects the exclusive equation of culture with high culture and argues that all forms of cultural production need to be studied in relation to other cultural practices and to social and historical

---

[12] Thomas Stearne Eliot, *Notes Towards the Definition of Culture* (London: Faber and Faber, 1948).

[13] Charles Percy Snow, *The Two Cultures* [1959] (Cambridge: Cambridge University Press, 1960).

[14] Frank Raymond Leavis, "Mass Civilization and Minority Culture" [1943], in *Education and the University* (Cambridge, London and New York: Cambridge University Press, 1979).

[15] Raymond Williams, *Culture and Society 1780–1950* [1958] (Harmondsworth and London: Penguin, 1963); Raymond Williams, *Keywords* [1958] (Oxford and New York: Oxford University Press, 1976).

[16] Geoffrey Hartman, *The Fateful Question of Culture* (New York: Columbia University Press, 1997).

[17] See Daniela Carpi, "Cultura e civiltà", in *In limine. Cultura ed enigma* (Firenze: Alinea, 1997).

[18] Oswald Spengler, *The Decline of the West* (Oxford: Oxford University Press, 1991).

[19] Edward B. Tylor, *Primitive Culture* [1871] (New York: Brentano's, 1924); Clifford Geertz, *Interpretation of Cultures* (New York: Basic Books, 1973).

structures. Cultural studies is thus committed to the study of the entire range of a society's arts, beliefs, institutions and communicative practices.[20]

If this is the aim of the cultural studies movement, we can easily affirm that law falls within this domain and therefore we can talk about law and interpret it in cultural terms. In fact, as some critics have begun to assert, law is inseparable from all the discourses that give shape to society.[21] It is a discourse among the many discourses that form our world. However in the course of time the term "culture" has developed from the agricultural sense of the Latin *colere*, "cultivate" to a metaphorical one indicating the spiritual cultivation of one's soul and mind. In this sense is has evolved from a quasi-messianic sense of sharing and creating a universal common ground in a religious-philosophical perspective to one more based on customs and fashion, which is the sense that prevails nowadays and is intertwined with political undertones. Culture is a way to explain things. Anthropology has modified its meaning: "This important move marks a rejection of the idea of culture as the universal progress of humanity and a shift toward something like 'a particular way of life'".[22] Or also: "Culture can be conceived as the almost unconscious meaning-systems that people inhabit and enact without choice".[23]

Culture is no longer a self-contained whole, but a porous, shifting, interdisciplinary practice that causes intersections in society and its discourses. In fact the intersecting of law with many interdisciplinary discourses declares its belonging to the cultural canvas. Part of cultural analysis consists in fact of a remapping of cultural boundaries, hence the use of particular symbols that become fashionable and may be shared by many disciplines. As an example, let us consider the metaphor connected to the law that has become widely accepted: the blindfolded woman with the scales. We have moved from a stately, Junoesque female figure holding the scales with two dishes to the woman's disappearance and the transformation of the scales' dishes into two feathers. From an image of solidity and assurance we have therefore moved to an image of fickleness, of levity and uncertainty, and of imaginative creativity which after all is the general idea of miscarried justice that characterizes critical legal studies in its denunciation of law's uncertainty. The law comes to partake in the general attitude of crisis of *métarécits* that typifies

20 Lawrence Grossberg, Cary Nelson, Paula A.Treichler, *Cultural Studies* (New York and London: Routledge, 1992), 4.

21 Austin Sarat and Thomas R. Kearns eds., *Law in the Domains of Culture* [1998], The Amherst Series in Law, Jurisprudence and Social Thought (Ann Arbor: University of Michigan Press, 2000).

22 Mezey, "Law as Culture", 41

23 Mezey, "Law as Culture", 42

postmodernism and in the contraposition to the assessed values of the system that is typical of cultural studies which are anti-canonical and anti-academic even if stemming from within the academy. Being law one of the most potent signifying practices, it is a way of being in the world, as Paul Kahn correctly asserts.[24] Law gives form to our way of life, which brings us inside an anthropological perspective where law is a discourse among the discourses of society. By using the term "discourse" I insert the law within the law-and-literature research analysis, while extending the critical comparative connection to other influential discourses.

> Law participates in the production of meanings within the shared semiotic system of a culture, but it is also a product of that culture and the practices that reproduce it.[25]

As a matter of fact law exists in culture: if it shapes the relations of a certain community, law also shapes culture and is in its turn shaped by it. Law creates the conditions of culture to some degree. However the creation of a transnational community is now being formed in a European society, which promotes new shared values. This newly-formed sort of community must be defended against globalisation, so as to maintain the characteristics of the different traditions forming the community itself. Therefore on one hand law defends tradition, but on the other hand it helps reshape it so as to make it progress thus avoiding inertia.[26] Law appears to be a protector of cultural heritage (let us think of the laws of copyright protecting words and creative ideas).

If culture implies the sharing of traditions, beliefs and values which create a common ground for social life, law has the same meaning and deals with the same elements included in the idea of culture.

> [...] a cultural analysis/cultural studies of law not only helps in challenging traditional ideas of culture, it also may help advance new conceptions of law. Among these conceptions are those that call us to attend to the possibility that the proliferation of law in film, on television and mass market publications has altered and expanded the sphere of legal life itself and to consider law as a world of images whose power is not located primarily in their representation of something exterior to the image, but is found in the image itself.[27]

---

24 Paul W. Kahn, *The Cultural Study of Law. Reconstructing Legal Scholarship* (Chicago: Chicago University Press, 1999).

25 Mezey, "Law as Culture", 47.

26 See Roger Cotterrell, "Law in Culture", 1–14.

27 Austin Sarat and Jonathan Simon eds., *Cultural Analysis, Cultural Studies and the Law* (Durham and London: Duke University Press, 2003), 10.

Law is much more than a means of control and containment: it is rooted in all sorts of extra-juridical experiences. Cotterrell asks himself if legal effectiveness is determined by cultural conditions. The concept of culture changes according to the development of society, and law in turn must adapt itself to the changed social conditions.

Life in society is based on constant negotiations and exchanges between different branches of culture, which sets this discourse within cultural studies. This domain covers the social processes involved in the production, transmission and reception of symbols or cultural forms. Greenblatt correctly asserts that a culture is a particular network of negotiations for the exchange of material goods, ideas and people: a certain culture operates as a structure of control, a series of limitations within which social behaviour must be contained, a repertoire of models to which we must conform.[28] Thus ideology is the way in which what we say and believe connects with the power-structure and power-relations of the society we live in.[29]

Cultural Studies bring about the union of the aesthetic and the political: culture is the grounds on which the analysis proceeds, the very object of analysis, as well as the place of criticism and of political intervention. Culture has come to stand for a mode of life, directly involving attitudes, language, institutions and power structures, and a whole system of cultural practices. Law is part of all of this: this is why the comparison shifted from the original one of law and literature to more comprehensive and varied cultural discourses.

> The problem of cultural studies is the difficult task of both acknowledging cultural and human differences and discovering means of creating culture and community where whatever people share with one another is not lost in acknowledged difference. In relation to literary criticism, the problem of cultural studies is the difficulty of linking literary and cultural works to each other to bring particular works out of the neglect and secondariness to which for all kinds of political and ideological reasons they had been condemned.[30]

Lotman speaks of a culturalization of the world that is transforming the world into a text. He says that the main aim of culture is that of structurally

---

28 See *The Polity Reader in Cultural Theory* (Cambridge: Polity Press, 1994); Stephen Greenblatt, "Culture", in *Critical Terms for Literary Study*, eds. Frank Lentricchia and Thomas McLaughlin (Chicago and London: The University of Chicago Press, 1995).

29 Terry Eagleton, *Literary Theory: an Introduction* (Oxford: Oxford University Press, 1983), 14.

30 Robert Con Davis and Roland Schleifer, *Contemporary Literary Theory. Literary and Cultural Studies* (London: Longman, 1994), 599.

organizing the world.[31] Culture generates structures and therefore is a non-inherited memory of society which is expressed in a system of prohibitions and coercions. Being law *par excellence* a regulating system (Foucault's idea of controlling and punishing) it is an intrinsic part of this cultural structure.

If we consider the relation between law and culture from a Catholic perspective, as in Francis Cardinal George's essay, fundamental moral truths are brought into plan. Therefore the relationship appears more problematic. In fact he asserts that the enactments of law are on some institution's authority. Legislation is the primary cure for moral defects. From this perspective the cultural transformation of society calls for new innovative legal norms. "Efforts in each sphere presuppose and depend upon the success of efforts in the other".[32] Cardinal George also observes that the law can shape culture even through its absence. A patent example of this is the technological evolution that characterises our age, in particular the bioethical sphere. New scientific experiments on the human body have transformed the view of man inside society. Such innovations must correspond to new juridical norms that widen the concept of human rights in this new phase toward the post-human or trans-human. The new concept of persona entails taking an evolution of the body and the expanse of its potentialities into consideration. We have to face a transformation of cultural models, which implies a transformation of the juridical and social status of persona. In this example it is evident how law is forced to cope with new unforeseen cultural situations; therefore law is a patent part of the cultural panorama. The absence of an official regulation of the problems solicited by biotechnologies concerning the legal persona can create situations that are difficult to control. As a result in this case the law is called into question by cultural evolution itself. Law becomes the forger of our collective sense of right and wrong. The intersection of law and morality consequentially stems from the dialogue between law and culture.

What I have mentioned so far paves the way for this book's innovative perspective starting with an enlargement of the "law and literature" label to a "law and humanities" one that is more comprehensive of the latest evolution of the field. In particular it concentrates on some very seminal cultural topics, such as copyright, creativity and cultural heritage; history, memory and the culture of law; forgiveness. The original field of law and literature has spread so as to include many new "law ands": law and religion, law and econ-

[31] Jurij M. Lotman and Boris A. Uspenskij, *Tipologia della cultura* (Milano: Bompiani, 1975).

[32] Francis Cardinal George, "Law and Culture", 10.

omics, law and the image, and now law and culture. What emerges is an all pervasive presence of the law in our life, which clearly demonstrates the correctness of the old maxim: "ubi societas ibi ius et ubi ius ibi societas".

> Focusing on the production, interpretation, consumption, and circulation of legal meaning suggests that law is inseparable from the interests, goals, and understandings that deeply shape or comprise social life.[33]

In the ongoing crisis where postcolonialism presents new cultural challenges the circulation of legal meanings has become more fluid. As many critics suggest, we "must read the legal dimensions of cultural productions and the cultural meanings encoded in the popular representation of legal processes and events".[34]

---

33 Sarat and Kearns, *Law in the Domains of Culture*, 6.

34 Sarat and Kearns, *Law in the Domains of Culture*, 7. In fact there is a number of very seminal critical works centred on the connection between law and culture that demonstrate that these studies have become an ongoing process during the latest years. Just to mention a few: Robert Post ed., *Law and the Order of Culture* (Berkeley: University of California Press, 1991); Stuart Hall et al. eds., *Policing the Crisis: Mugging the State and Law and Order* (New York: Holmes and Meier Publishers, 1978); Austin Sarat and Jonathan Simon eds., *Cultural Analysis, Cultural Studies and the Law* (Durham and London: Duke University Press, 2003).

I. Law and Humanities – The Road Abroad

Greta Olson
(University of Gießen)[1]

De-Americanizing Law and Literature Narratives: Opening up the Story[2]

Having come of age in the academy during a period of acute self-consciousness regarding the inherent cultural and historical limitations of the individual's critical perspective, I will begin this essay by placing its author. I am an expatriate American with a background in philosophy, art, and literary studies who has now lived half of her middle-aged life in Germany. I came to the subject of Law and Literature through a research project on law, norm, and criminalization conducted by lawyers, literary scholars, philosophers, and criminologists. In an effort to give our interdisciplinary work a theoretical frame, I read and began to write about the history of Law and Literature research. This initially led to a phase of trepidation about how much scholarship had been done in the interdiscipline and how comparatively little of it I could at first grasp. I then moved on to bulimic reading binges, a period of imitative writing, and, finally, to the now, a sense of discomfort and impatience with what I regard to be limitations in the prevailing narratives of research. (One might call this a *histoire* of phases of learning.) It is from that perspective of discomfort that I write this essay with an interest in moving the stories we tell in our scholarship forward.

My frustration with prevailing models of Law and Literature has to do with my binational and bicontinental identity. I see an inappropriate reliance on American models of scholarship in much derivative European Law and Literature research. This is due, as I will argue, to the relatively recent development of the field. Colleagues adopt the questions, plots, and primary texts of American Law and Literature scholarship while disregarding how these elements are not necessarily in synch with their own very different legal cultures and local literatures. In its most tertiary mode, Law and Literature texts provide yet another reading of equity in Shakespeare, based on a loose analy-

---

[1] My sincere thanks go to Andrew Majeske for suggesting that I submit this essay for review and to the two anonymous reviewers whose critical comments helped to move this story forward.

[2] This article was first published in *Law and Literature* 22.1 (2010): 338–364. It is reprinted here by permission of the publisher.

sis of the motifs of adversarial law. This is a derivative form of analysis, I contend, because law is not law in these texts but a trope for justice, and existing assumptions about law and literature are not challenged. Equity, which is modeled in these texts as the antithesis of law, becomes a way of not talking about legal culture or practice but about an ideal of the just. Moreover, this work assumes that the Anglo-American adversarial trial provides the general plotline for all legal narratives; this is hardly the case.

Conversely, I quibble with much American scholarship because it assumes that it is universal in its approach, whereas from my own dual perspective it appears deeply imbued with current preoccupations of American legal culture. American scholarship assumes the universality of the adversarial trial system, the ubiquity of the debate about how to interpret the Constitution, and the variety of social and civil rights issues such interpretation entails, as well as the common law tradition of arguing through precedent.

At this point this essay might end the exposition of its opening gambits and move into offering examples of the problematic kinds of Law and Literature scholarship named above. Yet this procedure would be reductive and would simply enumerate the negative. Instead, I will take a different path.

To explore the limitations inherent in prevailing modes of scholarship, I want to compare the story lines that inflect three nations' modes of conducting Law and Literature scholarship. This sentence rushes its writer and her potential readers into several areas of controversy. It is controversial to suggest that nations encourage particular types of scholarship to the detriment of others. Such a statement speaks for the balkanization of research and a lack of universality in scholarship; it stresses difference and even raises the ugly visage of potential nationalism. I do not advocate any simplistic essentialist view of nationality or national scholarship. There is great evidence that ideas and scholars travel. As nomads, scholars bring schools of thought to new places where they are in turn adapted and changed. (Consider in this vein: American attorney and law professor Adam Thurschwell, who pursues distinctly continental forms of Law and Literature critique; or Peter Goodrich, a formative thinker in British postmodern jurisprudence, who is now a professor at Benjamin N. Cardozo School of Law and the editor of this journal; or Jeanne Gaakeer, a Dutch judge, who pursues a Boyd-White ethical trajectory in both her adjudicatory and scholarly practice.) Since I will compare only American, British, and German research in this essay, the sentence that begins this paragraph, moreover, speaks for a Western-centric perspective, which ignores the radically different plots of Law and Literature that have emerged elsewhere. This limited perspective arises solely out of the author's limitations: these are the varieties of scholarship about which she presumes to know something. A more comparative view would venture beyond these three legal cultures and their scholarship to discuss other forms of law, as alluded to at the end of this text.

In this essay I borrow some of the tools of narratology to compare Law and Literature plotlines. Narratology – the study of narratives and how narratives, or stories, inform and affect perception – has, according to a preeminent scholar in this field, Monika Fludernik, become a "master discipline."[3] It offers us ways to understand how the elements of storytelling pervade our experience and inform not only law but also medicine, psychology, education, and perception itself. Narratology involves the more general process of how humans make sense of their world through storytelling. Indeed, important research in Law and Literature has been conducted using specifically narratological means. (This includes narrative jurisprudence and, for instance, Peter Brooks's multiple works on confession.) I want to ask, then, what is different about the stories that groups of scholars associated with three nations tell in Law and Literature scholarship and what is similar, and begin to query why this is the case. There is a potential danger associated with my procedure. I will necessarily generalize trends in three types of national scholarship and, in order to offer an overview, leave out significant details.

The American Story: Alternative Ethical Worlds in Realist Prose

Law and Literature is arguably already overdetermined by virtue of the competing histories of its participatory disciplines and the processes by which they became institutionalized. Why then, the reader may ask, bring in yet another methodology to what may already appear to be muddied waters? This need springs from a moment of disciplinary exhaustion that has led to a period of reassessment manifested in a plethora of recent historical overviews. Along these lines is Julie Stone Peters's excellent review of the field published in 2005. She argues that Law and Literature grew out of literary scholars' need to make their work have some material weight in the world, and out of lawyers' wish to re-engage with ethical and humanitarian questions in legal practice, education, and theory. Peters concludes that Law and Literature has outrun the scope of its original questions as well as its binary

---

[3] Monika Fludernik, "Histories of Narrative Theory (II): From Structuralism to Present," in *A Companion to Narrative Theory*, eds. James Phelan and Peter J. Rabinowitz (Malden, MA: Blackwell, 2005), 47.

interdisciplinary character: it may only survive by transforming itself into a variety of more inclusive interdisciplines.[4] Appropriately, she cites Guyora Binder and Robert Weisberg's quite inclusive *Literary Approaches to the Law* as indicative of this trend. In their introduction, the authors describe the move away from opposing the literary to the legal through an analysis of the expressive and the aesthetic aspects of "legal discourse":

> While much Law and Literature scholarship has opposed the literary to the instrumental analysis that dominates contemporary legal discourse, cultural criticism of law rejects this dichotomy. Instead, it implies that far from excluding aesthetic or expressive considerations, such instrumental policy analysis has a constitutively important expressive dimension that literary reading can illuminate.[5]

Peters offers a three-phase history of the field. My mini-narrative differs from hers but of necessity recurs to the past in order to highlight current dead ends in scholarship. In its most recent manifestation, the American Law and Literature movement developed during the 1970s out of a frustration with what was viewed as the social and judicial conservatism of the emergent Law and Economics movement. This conservatism was only heightened by the appointment of William Rehnquist as Chief Justice of the Supreme Court during the Reagan era and what were largely viewed as the Rehnquist court's incursions on more liberal Supreme Court decisions regarding civil liberties and the interpretation of the Bill of Rights.

Thus, in his formative works J.B.White called for a return to ethics in legal education and legal practice. Intrinsic to this was the law's necessary recognition of its inherently literary qualities. White's key terms have included language, translation, rhetoric, and community; and he foresaw a visionary unity of content and form in ethical, performative, legal writing. By embracing the positive rhetoricity of law, he harkened back to Benjamin Cardozo's 1925 essay "Law and Literature," which similarly called for a union of substance and form in legal writing.[6] This includes a positive assessment of Cardozo's and law's general use of metaphor. In a more recent formulation of his intentions, White has reiterated his commitment to pursuing "idealism" in all forms of legal practice. This entails an appeal to an ideal of the just: "The

[4] Julie Stone Peters, "Law, Literature, and the Vanishing Real: On the Future of an Interdisciplinary Illusion," *Publications of the Modern Language Association* 120.442 (2005).

[5] Guyora Binder and Robert Weisberg, *Literary Approaches to the Law* (Princeton: Princeton University Press, 2000), 19.

[6] For a further discussion, see Monika Fludernik and Greta Olson, "Introduction" to *In the Grip of the Law: Trials, Prisons and the Space Between*, eds. Monika Fludernik and Greta Olson (Frankfurt: Peter Lang, 2004), xxxiii–xxxiii.

simultaneous insistence upon law and justice produces a constant pressure to think and rethink both what justice is and what the law requires. It is an engine for opening the law to our deepest values."[7]

Similarly, the cofounder of America's Law and Literature movement, Richard Weisberg, first addressed his legal and ethical critique specifically against Rehnquist's form of adjudication and generally against formalist applications of law, which he sees as both devoid of ethics and reinforcing of modes of social inequity.[8] Not only does literature provide "sense and sensibility"[9] to law in Weisberg's eyes, but his method of reading narratives about the law, such as Melville's *Billy Budd, Sailor* (1924, posthumous), provide law with a poetical or creative ethics, as is mirrored in the title of his third book *Poethics, and Other Strategies of Law and Literature* (1984). Remaining consistent with the aims of his initial scholarship, Weisberg has recently positioned himself in relation to his much commented upon opposition to postmodernist readings of law: "[M]ost of it, I think, is that I preserve (as I claim the novelists do themselves) a reverence for law."[10]

In other much quoted texts in American Law and Literature scholarship, *Love's Knowledge* (1990) and *Poetic Justice: The Literary Imagination and Public Life* (1997), the philosopher Martha Nussbaum looks – like White and Weisberg – to literature, particularly to nineteenth-century novels, to find alternative sources for the study of the good life and ethics. Similar to White, she finds this alternative ethics in the unity of "content and form" that typifies the literary.[11] Literature provides, then, a corrective both to the pretensions of scientificism aimed at by individuals such as Richard Posner and to the nihilistic relativism suggested by Stanley Fish's analysis of interpretive communities. Thus novels provide a moral philosophy that cannot be found in deontological and utilitarian ethical systems.

These formative thinkers in the American Law and Literature movement look to novels, paradigmatically to nineteenth-century realist novels, to re-

7 Jeanne Gaaker, "Interview with James Boyd White," *Michigan Law Review* 105 (2007): 1403.

8 Richard Weisberg, "How Judges Speak: Some Lessons on Adjudication in *Billy Budd, Sailor* with an Application to Justice Rehnquist," *New York University Law Review* 57.1 (1982): 19–31, and Richard Weisberg, *The Failure of the Word: The Protagonist as Lawyer in Modern Fiction* (New Haven: Yale University Press, 1984).

9 Richard Weisberg, "Coming of Age Some More: 'Law and Literature' Beyond the Cradle," *Nova Law Review* (1988) 13: 107, 110.

10 Richard Weisberg, "20 Years of Story-Telling on the Law," *Cardozo Law Review* 26 (2005): 2223, 2225.

11 Martha C. Nussbaum, *Love's Knowledge: Essays on Philosophy and Literature* (Oxford: OUP, 1990), 22.

store an ethical substance and form to law. Important scholars in the American Law and Literature movement, including Brook Thomas (1987), Wai Chee Dimock (1996), Dieter Polloczek (1999), and Robin West (1999), have similarly looked to the novel for those residues of justice or those narratives of victimization that are elided from what are seen as the conventional stories told by law. American scholars react and speak to a legal culture that is centered around the rhetorical and procedural drama of adversarial law. As we know from countless Grisham novels, TV movies, and film thrillers, if not from our own experience, the adversarial trial is at the heart of the American legal ritual. This is in fact a contest, a theatrical rule-driven production in which the competing stories told by the prosecution and the defense are articulated and in which only one story, whether true or false, can ultimately prevail. Accordingly, emphasis is placed on rhetoric; the judge acts as a referee who ensures fair telling and good conditions for audience reception through observing appropriate procedure. Given the common law tradition, legal argument evolves on the basis of precedent from decisions made about earlier similar cases, although there are many unresolved arguments about how to interpret the doctrine of stare decisis.

Thus questions endemic to the study of fictional prose narratives such as the reliability of the narrator, here the witness or witnesses, and the conditions and methods of the storytelling are central concerns. Moreover, queries about intention have importance. Intentionality is invoked when describing the culpability of perpetrators, as well as in the interpretation in civil law of wills, contracts, and legislation. Most centrally, the perpetual discussion about the proper interpretation of the American Constitution, whether in the alleged originary sense of its authors or in an evolving form to fit current circumstances, involves notions of intention and remains central to U.S. legal culture.

Why is it important that the alternative stories that are sought in the American Law and Literature movement are found in the nineteenth-century realist novel? Mentioned above, *Billy Budd* is arguably the paradigmatic literary text in American Law and Literature, having a value in the interdiscipline not unlike the Constitution in American legal debate. Not only was the novella central to Weisberg's first critiques of formalist and legally blind applications of law, but it was also central to Richard Posner's penning a book that many of us love to hate, the best-selling *Law and Literature: A Misunderstood Relation*,[12] a textbook that wholly dismisses the usefulness of Law and

---

[12] Posner eviscerates Weisberg's and West's readings of *Billy Budd* and critiques the muddied quality of Cardozo's use of metaphor in his early essay. He also assures

Literature to legal practice. *Billy Budd* also was the basis for Posner's debate with Robin West.

The choice of nineteenth-century novels as the model for the literary in Law and Literature bears importance because this type of novel solidified the norms of what we call literary realism and became the model of what readers expect novels to be. Realist novels convince readers of the believability of their complex stories as well as of the societies and social struggles they represent; characters portrayed in them are moreover like people we might meet in the real world; we can imagine knowing them, and we believe in the changes they undergo within the span of 300 to 600 pages or more. Moreover, realist novels preserve a unified notion of the humanist subject: she has a core that remains constant during the course of the novel's unfolding. Such novels perpetuate what the writer J.M. Coetzee has called "the realist illusion" provided by the "word-mirror."[13] Accordingly, the realist novel, unlike its modernist and postmodernist successors, does not question language or the process of communication. Words in such novels appear to have an inherent and natural connection to the things they represent; there is no hint that such relationships are based on paradigmatic relations and the arbitrary assignments of signifiers to what is signified. Moreover, the conventional realist novel begins like *David Copperfield*, *ab ovo*, or at the beginning of the story: it provides an exposition, a series of complications, and ends with some form of closed or satisfactory ending. The storytelling is thus, if anything, more complete than the plots we experience in the real world. As long as the reader is engaged in the lengthy reading process, the possible world presented in the realist novel appears to be an actual alternative world.[14]

Finally, the realist novel is narrated in such a way that the narrative voice – the teller of the story – appears to have an authority over the events she relates: the right to assume this authority is not contested. The realist novel offers a seemingly true, complete world in contradistinction to the problematic one suggested by real life. Actual legal stories show why it may be idealized into a repository of the ethical.

---

his reader of the irrelevance of literary study for the normative work of law: "Law is a system of social control as well as a body of texts, and its operation is illuminated by the social sciences and judged by ethical criteria. Literature is an art, and the best methods of interpreting and evaluating it are aesthetic." Richard Posner, *Law and Literature: A Misunderstood Relation* (Cambridge, MA: Harvard University Press, 1988), 7.

13 John M. Coetzee, *Elizabeth Costello* (London: Vintage, 2004), 16, 19.

14 On possible world theory, see Marie-Laure Ryan, *Possible Worlds, Artificial Intelligence, and Narrative Theory* (Bloomington: Indiana University Press, 1992).

Yet it is just this refusal on the part of the realist novel not to lift the curtain on its own illusion-creating properties that has led many twentieth- and twenty-first century critiques to see the novel as an ideal vehicle for class and gender ideologies. I mention in this vein Ian Watt, Raymond Williams, Nancy Armstrong, and Frederic Jameson, who have saliently demonstrated how the novel conveys dominant cultural norms and naturalizes power relations. Thus for the contemporary literary critic, Weisberg's call for Law and Literature to restore "reverence" to law, or White's appeal to an idealism in legal practice and Nussbaum's claim that an alternative form of ethics can be found in the literary, are problematic. One worries that the call to literature to be the ethical "Other" may be a call to an ideological genre, whose very strength lies in its naturalizing, through realist means, its own political and social claims.

By stopping at this juncture, I am arguably doing a great disservice to the heterogeneity of American Law and Literature scholarship. The above description belies the influence of critical racial theory, feminism, and critical legal studies in order to further, arguably more overtly political, developments within the American Law and Literature movement. Moreover, my thumbnail sketch ignores the contributions of overtly deconstructionist American scholars such as Robin West and Drucilla Cornell. Yet, as I argued at the opening of this essay, when scholars new to the field go to Law and Literature for theory or models of scholarship, they recur to the foundational work of Weisberg, White, and Nussbaum. This leads to imitative work. When their work issues from another geographical provenance this reliance on foundational models also causes a somewhat forced application of the preoccupations of American legal culture to whatever text is being analyzed.

Poetry and Myth as Law's Other in British Critical Legal Studies

Moving to the other side of the Atlantic, the reader of this essay may be surprised that British Law and Literature practice differs substantially from its American counterpart, given the two jurisdictions' common language and common legal history. This is in part, again, due – I want to argue – to pervasive differences in legal cultures and the kind of scholarship these cultures give rise to. Here, I need to further distinguish between the law of England and Wales versus other parts of the UK and general British legal culture. In terms of major structural differences, England differs from the States in that it has an unwritten constitution; periodic movements to codify this constitution have been shot down. This gives English law and jurisprudence, by necessity, a different relationship to questions of writing, interpretation, and legal precedent. The origin of English law, its practicality and flexibility, is then always located in a nonidentifiable text and past: "In effect, the common law knows no origins and has no need of them, since the tradition itself is a sufficiently rich heritage to enable it to draw on its own resources for the authority of its decision-making processes."[15] English law involves an inevitable competition between orality, written records of past judgments, and appeals to tradition. This has also led to a wealth of scholarship concerning how English copyright laws have intersected with theories of authorship and writing.

Besides the difference in the status of the constitutions and the greater obligation of judges under English law to be bounded by precedent, England's common law tradition is currently being challenged by the European Union's rapid codification of legislation. Moreover, British legal culture is preoccupied by its relation to postcolonial discourses originating out of Ireland, New Zealand, Australia, South Africa, and other African nations whose legal systems were created or influenced by England's imperialist past. Thus British legal culture is perforce more inclusive and broader in its preoccupations than its American counterpart.

The most striking difference in British scholarship, however, is that it would never, to paraphrase Groucho Marx, want to belong to any club of Law and Literature that would accept it as a member. Rather, proponents of British scholarship call their work British critical legal studies, critical jurisprudence, or a postmodernist or an aesthetic philosophy of justice.[16] These descriptors are all-important: first, they demonstrate that British scholarship identifies, if at all, with American critical legal studies and not with Law and Literature, even if it employs many of the same methods. Namely, it uses literary texts in the widest sense to perform a critique on the law. An identifying characteristic of much British work is its dismissal of the undertheorized and relatively apolitical nature of American critical legal studies. Thus a sense

15 Costas Douzinas and Ronnie Warrington, *Justice Miscarried: Ethics, Aesthetics and the Law* (Hempstead: Harvester Wheatsheaf, 1994), 90.

16 For histories of British developments see Costas Douzinas, Peter Goodrich and Yifat Hachamovitch, "Introduction: Politics, Ethics and the Legality of the Contingent," in *Politics, Postmodernity and Critical Legal Studies*, eds. Costas Douzinas, Peter Goodrich, and Yifat Hachamovitch (London and New York: Routledge, 1994), 1; William Lucy, *Understanding and Explaining Adjudication* (Oxford: OUP, 1999); Costas Douzinas and Adam Gearey, *Critical Jurisprudence: The Political Philosophy of Justice* (Oxford and Portland, OR: Hart Publishing, 2005), 230–47; Costas Douzinas, "Oubliez Critique," *Law & Critique* 16 (2005): 47; and Bronwyn Stratham, "Postmodern Jurisprudence: Contesting Genres," *Law & Critique* 19 (2008): 139.

of self-congratulatory positive political difference runs through much British work. However, this sense of positive difference is arguably a regular feature of European intellectual life during the late-Bush era; it entails the risk of masking opportunities for exercising self-critique.[17]

Critical legal studies involve the explicit practice of questioning and undermining the monumental image of the law: "law is criticised as the reification of the world;"[18] it involves creating false images of itself, which are then mistaken for the reality of law. It implies the history of Kantian, Marxian, and post-Marxian critique; it involves a questioning and undermining of assumptions about law as a form of knowing. As "a political philosophy of justice,"[19] jurisprudence goes beyond law to specifically address the object of injustice under law. Finally, postmodernism – a contested word – implies a break with the rational certainties of the Enlightenment and modernity and a break with a belief in any overriding teleological narrative of human history such as Christianity or Marxism, as well as an awareness of the problematic and arbitrary nature of communication and language.

Costas Douzinas, the director of the Institute of Humanities at the Birkbeck School of Law, a center for critical jurisprudence in the UK, has offered a history of British critical legal studies: it took off during the 1980s and continues as a strong critical practice today. Like American Law and Literature, it has enjoyed three phases: in its first deconstructive phase during the 1980s, practitioners followed the post-structuralist practice of treating law as a text – or a field of significations – rather than a monumental system or rules; this entailed demonstrating the text's various omissions, margins, and unconscious qualities, and involved showing that law rested on no ultimate origin or foundation; this was followed during the 1990s by an "ethical turn" in

---

[17] In this vein, Costas Douzinas has written that the cause of the demise of American critical legal studies was due to the problematic nature of American legal and academic culture: "They [the reasons for the American obsession with judicial reasoning and interpretation] include the acute *nomophilia*, the centrality of law, litigation and judges in American culture; the constitutional tradition, which has staked the legitimacy of the polity on the claims of reasoned consistency and historical loyalty of judicial discourse; and, last but not least, the desire of academics to be accepted as privileged participants in public discourse and as valuable commentators of current affairs ... It has been said, rather unkindly, that America moved from barbarism to decadence without passing through civilization. It is more accurate to say that it has moved from constitutionalism to terminal legality without passing through (self) critique." Douzinas, "Oubliez Critique," 59, 60.

[18] Adam Gearey, "Ozymandias," in *Law and Aesthetics* (Oxford and Portland, OR: Hart Publishing, 2001) 1, 1.

[19] Douzinas and Gearey, *Critical Jurisprudence*, 40.

scholarship;[20] a new focus was placed on the elided Other in legal practice. In a quote from one of Douzinas' texts from this period, he writes with Ronnie Warrington that "[t]he law is necessarily committed to the form of universality and abstract equality; but it must also respect the requests of the contingent, incarnate and concrete Other, it must pass through the ethics of alterity in order to respond to its own embeddedness in ethics."[21] The third phase of critical legal studies, as described by Douzinas, responds to the present era in which phenomena such as human rights and democracy have been exported by force. Thus Douzinas writes: "Law as an empty signifier that attaches to everything from pavement walking to smoking and Iraqi liberation is autopoetically reproduced in a loop of endless validity but is devoid of a sense of signification."[22] One notes the enormous difference in emphasis as compared to American scholars. Rather than revering law, or practicing it with idealism, Douzinas proposes to unmask its very emptiness.

Importantly, the phases that Douzinas describes correspond to phases of contemporaneous literary criticism as well as, in part, to the evolution of the late Jacques Derrida's philosophy. Whereas White and Weisberg initiated the Law and Literature movement in the United States using the novel as a locus of the ethical, Jacques Derrida's 1989 essay "Force of Law: The Mystical Foundation of Authority" was seminal for the British movement. Here, Derrida historicizes the circumstances under which Walter Benjamin wrote his "Critique of Violence" (1921) in order to demonstrate, one, how philosophy constantly attempts to lend its arguments authority with a logos outside of itself and, two, to demonstrate law's indissoluble connection to violence, a violence that takes place both in language and in deed – in how the powerless are treated within law. Uncovering these relationships becomes the possibility of and for justice. Thus, the sound bite that is most often quoted from this text is: "Deconstruction is justice."[23]

Derridean deconstruction dominated critical theory during the 1980s. Deconstruction functions through dismantling categorical certainties by comparing binary terms, for instance, writing and speech or absence and presence, and demonstrating how these terms can only function in relation to each other: they exist only by virtue of their complementary and supposed difference. Deconstruction shows these terms to be arbitrarily related and

20 Douzinas, "Oubliez Critique," 65.
21 Douzinas and Warrington, *Justice Miscarried*, 185.
22 Douzinas, "Oubliez Critique," 66.
23 Jacques Derrida, "Force of Law: The 'Mystical Foundation of Authority,'" in *Deconstruction and the Possibility of Justice*, ed. Drucilla Cornell (New York: Routledge, 1992), 3, 15.

without inherent essence or foundation. Initiating and practicing deconstructive criticism was followed by a period of greater political engagement. During the late 1980s, the deconstructionist Paul de Man was discovered to have written articles for a Belgian pro-Nazi publication during the war years, at least one of them overtly anti-Semitic. This was cause, among other things, for Derrida to respond to a charge that has been made continuously against deconstructive criticism since its inception: deconstruction dismantles old metaphysical sureties but leaves nothing in their place. A so-called political turn occurred in Derrida's writings during the late 1980s and "The Force of Law" was part of it. This turn was accompanied by the philosopher's making of explicit political statements and writing more overtly political texts about law and violence, rogue states, globalization, friendship, and war. Finally, Douzinas's reading of law in the phase of the present historical moment is not dissimilar from the French cultural theorist Jean Baudrillard's treatment of the multiplication of images in contemporary life: our culture is so pervaded and dominated by images that they no longer have any meaning other than in themselves; they have no foundation; they no longer refer to the things they represent. This orientation on images speaks for the more aesthetic, rather than literary, orientation of British work. Law is understood to manifest itself not only in legislation, judgments, and public policy but also in images themselves.

Not all British proponents of critical legal studies are as dire in their view as Douzinas is in his portrayal of law as a simulacrum. Moreover, Derrida is hardly the philosopher to which they all refer. Heidegger, Levinas, Blanchot, Lyotard, Deleuze, and Žižek are also important influences. To restore contingency, an awareness of the Other to law, critics challenge or critique it as being without foundation. One of the manners of performing critique involves using literature, in the widest sense, to deconstruct the monolithic supposed positivism of law. Describing the work in a volume of essays called *Law and Literature,* which was written by Birkbeck-based scholars in 2004, Goodrich writes:

> The lawyers in this volume all engage with literary texts as a way of challenging the stylistic, textual, and hedonic limits of law. They argue in variable forms that literature represents a fracture, a crisis, a puncture of the legal restraint of the text.[24]

Since law is viewed as without foundation – as perpetually justifying its own authority – the texts that British critics use to challenge or undermine it are

---

[24] Peter Goodrich, "Endnote/Untoward," in *Law and Literature*, eds. Patrick Hanafin, Adam Gearey, and Joseph Brooker (Oxford: Blackwell, 2004), 159, 161.

poetic and mythic ones, rather than examples of realist prose. For instance, Douzinas and Warren read Shakespeare's Sonnet 87 to show law's continual performance of itself as a form of mortal combat in which the claims of the Other are elided and destroyed. Melanie Williams reads W.H. Auden's poem "September 1, 1939" and its reception history so as to unpack the ideology behind Ronald Dworkin's legal philosophy. Adam Gearey reads Shelley's sonnet "Ozymandias" in order to initiate an "aesthetics of law"; similarly, he juxtaposes Joseph Raz's legal philosophy with Philip Larkin's poetry to suggest that jurisprudence requires a poetics of the Other, and uses Heidegger's understanding of poetry to unpack Derrida's work on the law.[25]

Particularly, Maria Aristodemou has been important in bringing myth and fairy tales to readings of the law. Her *Law & Literature: Journeys from Her to Eternity* (2000) could be read as an alternative textbook to Posner's dismissive *Law and Literature* in that it refuses to privilege law's claim to truth or normativity over literature and fantasy. The text of law she traces is discovered in the evolution of the Oedipus myth through Freud and Lévi-Strauss's interpretations of it to the psychoanalyst Lacan's finding a justification for all law in this narrative: the particular Oedipal conflict is generalized by the individual into the acceptance of an order of abstract rules. In this genealogy she finds the forgotten embodiment of law, its bodily nature and its rejection of women, desire, and materiality:

> The attempt to keep philosophy and law separate from literature is also, as I suggest in my closing chapter part of the attempt to exclude woman from the legal labyrinth ... The male lawyer's preference for abstract language, reason, and intellectuality is also an attempt to deny the tactile, the bodily, and the sensual: to suppress, supposedly by overcoming, but instead by imitating with words, woman's capacity to procreate with her body.[26]

Aristodemou's work, in turn, recurs to Goodrich's argument in *Oedipus Lex* (1995) and *Law in the Courts of Love* (1996), among other texts, that the prac-

---

25 Douzinas and Warrington, *Justice Miscarried*, ch. 7: "'As a dream doth flatter': Law (love, life and literature in Sonnet no. 87)", 242–64; Melanie Williams, "Then and Now: The Natural/Positivist Nexus at Truth and Reconciliation: Auden's 'September 1, 1939,'" in *Journal of Law & Society* 31: 60; Adam Gearey, "Ozymandias," at 1; Adam Gearey, "The Poetics of Practical Reason: Joseph Raz and Philip Larkin," *Law & Literature* 19 (2007): 377; and Adam Gearey, "'Where the Law Touches Us, We May Affirm It': Deconstruction as a Poetic Thinking of Law," in *Derrida and Legal Philosophy*, ed. Peter Goodrich (Basingstoke, New York: Palgrave Macmillan, 2008), 201.

26 Maria Aristodemou, *Law & Literature: Journeys from Her to Eternity* (Oxford: OUP, 2000), 4.

tice of law requires a constant denial of its metaphoric, unconscious, and literary qualities and a denial of heterogeneity, materiality, and women. For Goodrich then, jurisprudence begins with a recovery of the unconscious:

> The other scenes of law – its images, its figures, its architecture, its rites, myths, and other emotions – are potentially the economies of resistance to law. They evidence, I will argue, the possibilities of a jurisprudence of difference, and specifically a genealogy of other forms of law, of plural jurisdictions and distinctive subjectivities, of other genders, ethnicities, and classes of legality and of writing.[27]

As in White and Weisberg's work, British critical legal scholarship involves a moment of retrieval of the forgotten and the repressed. Yet instead of striving for a unity of form and substance that will necessitate a newly ethical realization of law, the forgotten itself is emphasized as an unreachable origin so as to dismantle law's authority and to imagine alternative law(s). Thus the pursuit of the images of law, or its aesthetics, is not a form of law-in-literature, a tracing of how law is reflected in various media, but a form of critique that engages with the various institutions of law by showing how law's authority, truth value, and positivism are all problematic.

The choice of lyric and mythic genres in much British work to complement law is central. Poetry is generally understood to be the only nonnarrative genre.[28] Poetry was originally sung and accompanied by the lyre. As with music in general, the genre is thought to appeal more to the emotions and the unconscious than the ratio. In the Romantic tradition, poetry aimed to reproduce moments of intensely felt experience rather than to instantiate a story. Unlike realist prose, lyric poetry rarely offers mimetic illusion. Moreover, due to its compression, often counter-intuitive syntax, and highlighted use of metaphor, reader investment in understanding poetry tends to be greater than in prose. (For those of us involved in teaching literature, this means that it is often easier to get students to embrace the task of reading an 800-page novel than a poem.) Furthermore, the subject of lyric poetry is less easily identified as a constant unfragmented self. If lyric poetry and myth offer no illusion of reality, no plausible alternative world but a moment of intensity, then their interaction with law differs in effect. The fragmentation of experience, the difficulty of communication, the alienation of the modern

---

[27] Peter Goodrich, *Oedipus Lex: Psychoanalysis, History, Law* (Berkeley: University of California Press, 1995), 15.

[28] Although there have been several compelling recent arguments by narratologists for why this should not be the case: See the works of Eva Müller-Zettelmann and Peter Hühn, and see Brian McHale's recent "Beginning to Think about Narrative in Poetry," *Narrative* 17 (2009): 11.

subject – all qualities of the postmodern condition – are thus arguably better articulated in nonnarrative poetry than in realist prose. Hence, readings of poetry conform more to the "ethics of alterity" that Douzinas and Warrington espouse.[29] This notion of alterity rests on philosophies, such as that of Emmanuel Levinas, that attest that the self can only be realized through the call of the Other.

Consistent with the use of poetry to challenge and critique law is the use of autobiographic, confessional, and journalistic forms in many British Law and Literature texts to dismantle the pretensions of law as rational and positivistic. This form of Law and Literature has a performative character, which Bronwyn Statham dates to Douzinas, Warrington, and Shaun McVeigh's *Postmodern Jurisprudence: The Law of Text in the Text of Law* (1991). The final chapter of this work, "Suspended Sentences: A novel approach to certain original problems in copyright law," enacts the story – in letters and judgments – of the rejection of the authors' essay by an English law journal and a student's claim that his dissertation was the basis for this text and that copyright law was breached; a third text comments on the others.[30]

In a similar vein Douzinas and Gearey conclude each chapter of *Critical Jurisprudence* with a journal entry about events in the lives of the authors, presumably during the writing of the book. Goodrich supplies a highly self-ironic essay to his contribution to the Birkbeck collection of essays called *Law and Literature* that concerns his musings on a highly critical, obscene comment about himself written in the margin of a library copy of his first book. This break with the typical rationalism of scholarship bespeaks, on the one hand, an awareness that personal narratives are an intrinsic part of politicized scholarship; cf. the feminist writings of Rachel Blau DuPlessis, or, more recently, Kenji Yoshino's interspersing of autobiographical episodes in his indictment of the current demise of American civil rights in *Covering: The Hidden Assault on Our Civil Rights* (2006). On the other hand, it recalls Derrida's early experimentalism in texts such as *Glas* (1974) in which the history of metaphysics is questioned through the mirroring of a text about Genet and one on Hegel in two columns of continuous text, with various other quotations interspaced throughout.

To avoid the binarism that deconstructive criticism has taught us to be the crutches of self-legitimating thought, let me introduce yet a third legal system and its attendant legal and Law and Literature narratives.

---

29 Douzinas and Warrington, *Justice Miscarried.*

30 Costas Douzinas and Ronnie Warrington with Shaun McVeigh, *Postmodern Jurisprudence: The Law of Text in the Texts of Law* (London: Routledge, 1991).

From Analytic Drama to Legal Phenomena: The Two Stages of German Scholarship

Continental Europe has a civil law, rather than a common law, tradition. According to this tradition, legal reasoning proceeds through a process of deduction from the abstract norms of codified law to the particular case at hand. Moreover, the inquisitorial system of civil law determines that the court and thus the judge or judges determine the "objective" facts of a case as well as passing judgment over them. Since no jury but rather a judge or judges decide the outcome of a trial, judges have a prosecutorial as well as an arbitrating function. They are merely assisted by lawyers. Trained in Germany according to a legal science tradition to consider every possible legal side of a case, German judges eschew rhetoric and are taught to formulate their outcomes with a maximum of objectivity.

Based originally on pan-European Roman Canonic law, or *ius commune*, the German Civil Code did not emerge until the end of the nineteenth century and was the result of an effort to unify a variety of German territories, city states, and kingdoms. In order to articulate a German civil code, Friedrich Carl von Savigny countered the Germanist tradition that argued for the importance of Teutonic legal traditions. Instead, Savigny advocated ridding contemporary law of its local accretions and returning to the Digest or *Pandectae* of Roman legal sources in order to articulate an internally consistent and logical system of legal argument. This Pandectist practice, with its effort at completion, remains central to the development of German legal study and practice.[31] It informs the BGB or the Civil Code that was adopted in 1900 and continues to be used today. An exercise in "legal formalism,"[32] the first General Part of the BGB consists of generalized rules applicable to the other four books of law covering contract, obligations, property, domestic matters, and inheritance.[33] Learning how to relate these various parts of law to one another through a process of abstraction is thus a major part of a German law student's training:

The BGB is not addressed to the citizen at all, but rather the professional lawyer; it deliberately eschews easy comprehensibility and waives all claims

---

[31] Reinhard Zimmermann, "Characteristic Aspects of German Legal Culture," in *Introduction to German Law*, eds. Mathias Reimann and Joachim Zekoll (Munich: Beck, 2005), 5.

[32] Zimmermann, "Characteristic Aspects of German Legal Culture," 11.

[33] Gerhard Danneman and Basil Markensis, "The Legacy of History on German Contract Law," in *Making Commercial Law*, eds. Royston Miles Goode and Ross Cranston (New York: Clarendon Press, 1997), 1.

to educate its reader; instead of dealing with particular cases in a clear and concrete manner it adopts throughout an abstract conceptual language that the layman, and often enough the foreign lawyer as well, finds largely incomprehensible, but that the trained expert, after many years of familiarity, cannot help admiring for its precision and rigor of thought.[34]

The Civil Code has faced two kinds of substantial revisions. The first of these was caused by the adoption of the *Grundgesetz* or Basic Law in 1949. This constitutional document was not called such because Germany was divided at the time, and composing a constitution was put off until after reunification. Responding directly to legal abuses and the horrors of the Nazi period, the Basic Law guarantees civil liberties, including first and foremost the inviolability of human dignity (a Kantian concept). Another change in German legal culture and a potential challenge to its traditional hermeticism has been caused by the country's integration into the European legal community. Both the Council and the Parliament of the EU communities' directives and the European Court of Justice's decisions have challenged the preeminence of Germany's legal system and have brought about modifications in contract law. Although the principle of subsumption from codified law remains central to German legal practice, judges also now refer to precedents and to commentaries on statutes in their judgments. Hence German law has become more of a mixed case.[35] Whether Europe will eventually return to an *ius commune* remains to be seen.

German Law and Literature scholars proudly cite a long tradition of interdisciplinarity. This includes the Grimm Brothers, who are famous for their philology and fairy tale collections. Unlike Savigny, the Grimms stressed the importance of Germanic legal traditions during debates about codification. Jacob Grimm wrote that "law and literature arose from the same bed."[36] Moreover, he coined the term *Germanist* (or German scholar), which meant, in contradistinction to a Romanist, both a teacher of German law and a scholar of the German language. Proud mention is also frequently made of the many *Dichterjuristen* who have written in the German language.[37] This term translates roughly as legal scholars who are also poets or who write

---

34 Konrad Zweigert and Hein Kötz, *An Introduction to Comparative Law*, 2nd ed. (1992), 150; quoted in Danneman and Markensis, "The Legacy of History on German Contract Law," 14.

35 Zimmermann, "Characteristic Aspects of German Legal Culture," 25.

36 Jacob Grimm, *Von der Poesie im Recht* (1816) (Darmstadt: Hermann Genter, 1957), 8.

37 Eugen Wohlhaupter, *Dichterjuristen*, 3 (Tübingen: Mohr, 1953–1957).

literature. *Dichterjuristen* include – to name only a few of the most prominent examples – Goethe, Novalis, Kleist, E.T.A. Hoffmann, Heinrich Heine, Kurt Tucholsky, Franz Kafka, and most recently, Bernhard Schlink. Schlink's novel *The Reader* (*Der Vorleser*, 1997) has become famous outside of Germany due to its recent film adaptation.

Yet despite the emphasis on historical commonalities between law and literature, a first generation of German Law and Literature scholars has been quite dismissive of the importance of literature for law. Perhaps the insistence on the logical rigor of German legal science has given rise to a distrust of the claims made by American scholars for literature's potential to reform law. Legal scholars such as Ulrich Mölk, Klaus Lüderssen, and Thomas Vorbaum have accused literary scholars of inadequately engaging with the rigors of legal practice when they practice Law and Literature.[38] Moreover, by emphasizing law's clarity and normativity versus literature's ambiguity, Heinz Müller-Dietz and Bodo Pieroth stress differences between law and literature rather than points of mutual influence. Summarizing a talk given by law professor Pieroth on Law and Literature, a commentator writes: "In legal science one aims to achieve the greatest possible clarity, whereas literary studies aims to understand different levels of meaning" (my translation).[39] In the first monograph-length study of the influence of the law-as-literature movement on Germany, Birgit Lachenmaier concludes that a general skepticism prevails regarding what are seen as the vague goals of the American movement, its limited usefulness for German juridical practice, and its missing methodology.[40]

---

38 Ulrich Mölk, "Vorwort," in *Literatur und Recht: Literarische Rechtsfälle von der Antike bis in die Gegenwart* (Göttingen: Wallstein, 1996), 7; Klaus Lüderssen, *Produktive Spiegelungen. Recht in Literatur, Theater und Film*, 2nd ed. (1991) (Baden-Baden: Nomos, 2002), 10; Thomas Vormbaum, "Die Produktivität der Spiegelung von Recht und Literatur," in *Produktive Spiegelung. Recht in Literatur, Theater und Film*, 2nd ed. (Baden-Baden: Nomos, 2002), xi, xx; Heinz Müller-Dietz, "Literarische Strafprozessmodelle," *Goldammer's Archiv für Strafrecht* 150 (2003): 269; Bodo Pieroth, "Recht und Literatur befruchten sich gegenseitig. Jurist der Universität Münster untersucht Gemeinsamkeiten und Unterschiede zwischen den beiden Disziplinen" 07.08.2000 – (idw) Westfaelische Wilhelms-Universität Münster, Oct. 15, 2006, available at http://www.uni-protokolle.de/nachrichten/id/61658/.

39 Pieroth, "Recht und Literatur befruchten sich gegenseitig,": "In der Rechtswissenschaft werde versucht, eine möglichst große Eindeutigkeit zu erzielen, während die Literaturwissenschaft darauf abziele, verschiedene Bedeutungsebenen zu erfassen."

40 Birgit Maria Lachenmaier, *Die Law as Literature-Bewegung – Entstehung, Entwicklung und Nutzen* (Berlin: Wissenschaftlicher Verlag Berlin, 2008), 26, 228–30.

Traditionally, German Law and Literature scholarship has stressed the dramatic genre. Paradigmatic texts include Friedrich Schiller's family tragedy *The Robbers* (*Die Räuber*) from 1781, in which an unjust society drives a good man to anarchy and crime, and Heinrich von Kleist's comedy *The Broken Pitcher* (*Der Zerbrochne Krug*) from 1806. Here, a much-admired local judge is shown to be the criminal in the case he is investigating and presiding over. Without a clear narrating presence, plays forefront conflict and place their audiences in the role of the judge (in the inquisitional system).[41] *The Broken Pitcher* is also an example of a so-called analytical play; this type of play mirrors the courtroom situation by reconstructing a decisive action, which took place before the play began. These plays fascinate German Law and Literature scholars because they were instigated and initially performed during a period when the disciplinary boundaries between law and literature had not yet become rigid and contending legal systems were being actively debated. *The Broken Pitcher*, for instance, demonstrates tensions between traditional German law and contemporaneous efforts to achieve unified codification.[42]

In what I want to term a second, post-deconstructionist phase of German Law and Literature scholarship, deconstructive analysis has been embraced, as has Foucauldian analyses of how discursive practices affect one another. This turn was in part initiated by Anselm Haverkamp's analysis of Derrida's work on Walter Benjamin and its importance for deconstructive legal philosophy.[43] Post-deconstructionist scholars include Cornelia Vismann, Thomas Weitin, Michael Niehaus, Florian Hoffmann, Peter Schneck, Manfred Schneider, Anke van Kempen, and Gert Hofmann, among others. Typical of this scholarship in English is Peter Schneck's recent application of Derrida's work on legal and literary genre to an analysis of how literature insists on the superior legality of its own evidence.[44] Vismann and Florian Hoffmann have published a special issue of the *German Law Journal* on Derrida in 2006 as well as co-edited *Derrida and Legal Philosophy* (2008). A translation of Vismann's German-language monograph from 2000 concerning the meaning of archives and archival techniques for legal systems and legal cultures has just appeared in English (Files: Law and Media Technology, 2008). Given the German Democratic Republic's practice of keeping extensive files on the supposedly subversive activities of its inhabitants and the continuing contro-

---

41 Anke van Kempen, *Die Rede vor Gericht* (Freiburg: Rombach, 2005), 24.

42 Van Kempen, *Die Rede vor Gericht*, 67.

43 Anselm Haverkamp ed., *Gewalt und Gerechtigkeit. Derrida – Benjamin* (Frankfurt: Suhrkamp, 1994).

44 Peter Schneck, "The Laws of Fiction: Legal Rhetoric and Literary Evidence," *European Journal of English Studies* 11 (2007), 47.

versy about how these files should be treated, this is a particularly pertinent relevant topic in the now unified Germany.

It is noticeable that many of the authors mentioned above analyze and deconstruct legal phenomena in large historical studies, such as ones on judging, interrogating, promising, witnessing, as well as forensic speech. On the one hand, this breadth of scholarship bespeaks the particularities of German academia: in order to be eligible for a professorship in Germany one must write monumental historical studies. On the other hand, the change in emphasis from plays to legal phenomena speaks for the movement in Law and Literature away from an analysis of a given literary text to a larger interest in aesthetic texts as elements of legal culture. Thus the paradigmatic literary text in German Law and Literature is no longer the historical play but the legal process itself. German scholarship differs from deconstructive British work in that it is less overtly performative. Scholars generally retain a serious tone and eschew the autobiographical.

Dead Ends and Open Closures

Having described differences in aims, forms, and sample literary texts in American, British, and German work, I wish to turn now to some recent trends in Law and Literature scholarship that are common on both sides of the Atlantic. This would suggest that Law and Literature can be regarded as a historical movement. On the one hand, this movement displays some common general developments. As the last sections have shown, however, this movement has, on the other hand, been variously interpreted depending on where it is being practiced.

One scholarly dead end that persists and arguably weakens the interdiscipline is the reproduction of essentialist visions of law and literature made in the attempt to critique the law. I have already written about American Law and Literature scholars' commitment to a traditional vision of literary narrative as the locus of ethics. Reiterating this commitment, Weisberg has recently commented on how Schlink's *The Reader* demonstrates how novels uniquely create a space in which judgment over a crime can be made while allowing for the comprehension of the perpetrator's actions: "But narrative, *The Reader* proves, *is* the locus of accountability joining a tradition in our novelistic culture that provides where little else does a space in which human behavior can be both understood and (where culpable) accurately judged."[45]

---

[45] Richard Weisberg, "A Sympathy That Does Not Condone: Notes in Summation on Schlink's *The Reader*," *Law & Literature* 16 (2004): 229, 233.

This positive review suggests the overwhelming importance of narratives to human comprehension of the world and thus verifies the findings of much recent cognitive research. It should thus be gratifying to scholars, such as myself, who are committed to narratological readings of literary texts. Yet Weisberg's view reifies an understanding of literature as the good and the ideal in contradistinction to rough-and-ready law and the everyday.

This attitude is by no means exclusive to American scholars who rely more often on realist prose works to interrogate law. In postmodernist British work, a tendency to treat the mythic or the poetic as a Levinasian Other that may call law to a better self also prevails. In the following quote, Douzinas and Gearey allude to Shelley's claim in his "A Defense of Poetry" (1821/1840) that poetic language remakes the world and poets legislate over it: "By reminding us that writers and artists have legislated, while philosophers and lawyers (some celebrated, others forgotten) have spoken poetically, we suggest the possibility of new ways of thinking and living the law."[46] Arguably, a neo-Romantic idealization of the poetic as a reformative force occurs here. Such a view ignores the insights of cultural critics such as Raymond Williams, Michel Foucault, and Fredric Jameson that literature and the literary also reproduce and naturalize prevailing power relations, good and bad. Arguably, the idealization of literature in Law and Literature critiques occurs more readily among lawyers than literary scholars.

Moving from the other direction, a tendency persists, particularly among literary scholars, to equate law with material history, politics, and the real, meant here in the non-Lacanian sense. This is in part due to literary scholarship's having retreated from an embrace of high theory and deconstruction that marked 1980s criticism. This was followed by a renewed interest in historical conditions and materiality as the specific context in which a text arises and into which it is received. While in themselves sound, these developments may also lead to essentialist thinking about law and literature as opposites. Florence Dore, an Americanist working at Kent State University in Ohio, has traced the trend in American novel studies to address legal history as intrinsic to literature and vice versa. She argues that what was once seen as the novel's relation to the political has now been reformulated "as a relation between literature and law."[47] This trend is marked by "an aversion to linguistic ambiguity"[48] that tends to reify traditional ideas about literature and the law:

---

46 Douzinas and Gearey, *Critical Jurisprudence*, 34.

47 Florence Dore, "Law's Literature, Law's Body: The Aversion to Linguistic Ambiguity in Law and Literature," *Law, Culture & Humanities* 2 (2006): 17, 24.

48 Dore, "Law's Literature, Law's Body," 19.

> [R]ather than bringing the critical practices that derive from literature's linguistic richness to studies of the law, literature scholars surprisingly tend to reproduce rather than complicate the assumption that laws present us with hard "truths" that "ring through the literary … It is this turn, it seems to me, that has led to a sense among literature scholars that law can return us to a "hard" historicity that preceded theory.[49]

In the move to the historical and the material, it appears as though the insights of postmodernism and deconstruction have been forgotten. The law is projected as a concretized absolute. Regarding law as a signifying practice goes forgotten. Law becomes a synonym for violence; law's contribution to the furthering of civil rights, for instance, goes unheeded.

These mutual trends lead to a gendering of law and literature that is counterproductive for interdisciplinarity: literature represents an intersubjective ethics of care, which may cure law of its violence; it is figured as contiguous and ambivalent. Law is normative and concrete, historically embedded, and without rupture. One finds this gendering of the two disciplines from early on. Indeed, it is implicit in Jacob Grimm's hetero-normative comment that poetry and law arose from the same bed. It has been commented on by critics such as Jane Baron (1999), Aristodemou, Peters, Martin Kayman, and myself (2007), among others. Yet despite repeated commentary, this tendency remains. Christine Künzel has written explicitly about the conceptualizations of the two parts of the interdiscipline along the lines of gender difference. She contends that without an explicit analysis of this metaphorization of law as masculine and literature as feminine, with all of the attendant cultural baggage this division entails, Law and Literature cannot move forward.[50] The most traditional binarism in Law and Literature is the juxtaposition of law and literature as analogous to the difference between law and equity or law and mercy. In countless readings of *The Merchant of Venice*, *Bleak House*, and other now canonical texts, "mean" positive law is contrasted with an ethics of care that is suggested by alternative literary storytelling. Law is masculinized and literature or myth is feminized in an essentialist manner. For a contemporary student of literary studies, this is highly problematic, as literature has been shown to be a vehicle for class and gender ideologies. It is not innocent; it is not in any sense wondrously material, feminine, and contingent. It informs and stems out of a cultural mo-

---

[49] Dore, "Law's Literature, Law's Body," 19–20.

[50] Christine Künzel, "'Aus einem Bette aufgestanden'. Anmerkungen zum Verhältnis' zwischen Recht und Literatur," in *Figures of Law: Studies in the Interference of Law and Literature* (Tübingen and Basel: A. Francke Verlag, 2007), 115–32.

ment; moreover, as Derrida and others have pointed out, literature enforces, like all genres, the laws of its production, dissemination, and exegesis.

What Dore sees as a trend in literary scholarship to want to disambiguate law may in fact be an instance of a larger cultural movement – a new tendency towards concretion and a mistrust of ambivalence in general. Martin Kayman, a British scholar who has worked extensively on Law and Literature, copyright, as well as the cultural politics of the English language, has noted the increasing preeminence of forensic linguistics in British legal education.[51] Rhetorical study is then being replaced by the priority of a material analysis of language and articulation. Kayman traces this tendency further in an interest in a new empiricism, which affects many aspects of legal culture. Thus the fascination with forensic science made manifest in a plethora of television series is replicated in a desire to return to a body of evidence.

The neofoundationalism that concerns me here is built around a return to the body. This is not any longer the sensual humanist body of empiricism that had been a privileged object of the earlier critique. The body of empiricism was at least one whose sensations required processes of interpretation and validation that, since David Hume, have always been bound to forms of skepticism. In contrast, the body I am referring to would be more accurately called a body of truth, a *corpus verum*, to use the expression of the Eucharist, a body that commands belief.[52]

Departing from the dead ends, I would like to highlight more forward-looking developments in the study of Law and Literature. The first of these is a change from a binary discipline to a triadic or multiple one. The second is a move from understanding the literary to be a realist novel or a poem to conceiving it as a larger aesthetic text. Both indicate a modernist or postmodernist emphasis on open endings rather than neat closure.

Regarding the former development, I wholly agree with Peters's assessment of the current state of scholarship in the States. She describes the plethora of recent histories of the discipline as "signifying law and literature's transformation into something bigger and necessarily more amorphous."[53] Common to both sides of the Atlantic is, then, a move beyond an interdiscipline based on the interface and dialogue between two well-established dis-

---

51 Greta Olson and Martin Kayman, "From 'Law and Literature' to 'Law, Literature and Language: A Comparative Approach,'" *European Journal of English Studies* 11 (2007), 1.

52 Martin Kayman, "The Body of Law, the Corpus, and the Return of the Real," in preparation, quoted here in kind agreement with the author.

53 Peters, "Law, Literature, and the Vanishing Real", 451.

ciplines, to a triadic or a plural venture. Exemplary of this trend is the fact of this essay having first been delivered as a paper at an MLA session on Law and Narrative. Literature was implicitly a part of the session's topic, and indeed readings of literary texts were the basis of analysis in two of the three papers delivered there. Similarly, in collecting calls for papers for the European Network of Law and Literature, it has proven increasingly difficult to locate the appropriate forums by simply typing the key words "law and literature" into search engines. What was once called Law and Literature is now entitled Law, Culture, and the Humanities; or Law, Literature and Culture; Law, Literature and Language; or Law and Semiotics. If "literature" remains in the title of new permutations of the interdiscipline, it is understood as something beyond the traditional written literary text.

Thus a move can be detected away from the supposedly dichotomous, or complementary, projects of law and literature to a more inclusive practice of regarding law as a cultural practice.[54] Recent scholarship that works along this line includes Paul Raffield's excellent *Images and Cultures of Law in Early Modern England* (2004), which demonstrates the symbolic pertinence of the Inns of Court for an emerging common law culture, or Sue Chaplin's *The Gothic and the Rule of Law, 1764–1820* (2007), which delineates the presence of the Gothic in Blackstone's *Commentaries* and contemporaneous novels. Less accessible to English-language readers but quite similar in intent is the recent German collection of essays, called *Bildregime des Rechtes* (2007), which might be roughly translated as "Law's Regime of Pictures." As the title implies, the collection explores the connections between law and images and theorizes whether the loss of monumentality of law has led to a greater meaning of images.[55]

The other move in current scholarship is to embrace the visual and the aesthetic in a more generous notion of the literary than has been typical in Law and Literature. For many of us working in literature departments, this will be a familiar development. Our discipline is now as much about cultural development and the practices of signification as it is about close reading. Writing about this change in a seminal essay from 1989 called "Towards Cultural History – in Theory and Practice," Catherine Belsey describes the move towards "signifying practice" and the difficulties that inhere in this. As she

---

[54] See Guyora Binder and Robert Weisberg's introduction to *Literary Criticisms of the Law* (Princeton: Princeton University Press, 2000) for the theoretical background of these developments.

[55] Jean Baptiste Joly, Cornelia Vismann, and Thomas Weitin eds., *Bildregime des Rechts* (Stuttgart: Akademie Schloss Solitude, 2007).

jocularly states in an attempt to cheer up an imagined disgruntled reader: "But if we can interpret Shakespeare, we can surely learn to interpret fashion and music – and privies."[56] Thus while we may – and we do in Germany – still lecture students on how to recognize zeugma and periphrasis in Pope's *Rape of the Lock*, we also teach courses that focus on representation and ethics using photographs of torture in Abu Ghraib prison. For those coming from an orientation in the law and an education in the legal, the embrace of the visual and the aesthetic as endemic to law may be a less comfortable endeavor.[57]

No Grand Narrative

This essay reviews the plotlines and narratives of some varieties of Law and Literature. In describing three types of scholarship, I have relied implicitly on a differentiation the legal sociologist Lawrence Friedman once made that I continue to find useful in describing some of the cultural issues involved in how we regard law and literature individually and in conjunction. He calls legal culture "the ideas, values, attitudes and opinions people in some society hold with regard to law and the legal system."[58] Furthermore, Friedman differentiates between so-called internal and external legal cultures, points out that borders between them are porous, and suggests that law centrally depends on the opinions about it generated in the larger culture in which it is made. His work also implies that legal cultures are ideological, and that external manifestations of law are just as important for internal legal cultures as individual judgments. Moreover, he suggests that despite topical similarities between legal systems – e.g., American and English Law – differences in legal cultures may be far larger and have far greater cultural ramifications than might be initially supposed.

My descriptive critique of how legal cultures structure the subjects, plots, and development of their Law and Literature scholarship has been performed due to what I see as moments of blindness in various types of re-

---

56 Catherine Belsey, "Towards Cultural History – in Theory and Practice," *Textual Practice* 3 (1989): 159, 166.

57 Peter Goodrich has written on this topic in these pages: "Now indeed law and literature seems a distant illusion, a remote and unreal academic parlor game, Sunday afternoon conversation. It is equally retro, definitely old school. No question here. Literature survives as part of something more." "Screening Law," *Law & Literature* 21 (2009): 1, 20.

58 Lawrence M. Friedman, "Is There a Modern Legal Culture?" *Ratio Juris* 7 (1994): 118.

search. I cannot conclude now with any grand narrative because I am convinced that such a narrative is no longer tenable in a period that no longer believes in organizing historical stories that attempt to explain everything. Thus let me close with several *petit récits* or simply suggestions for further thought.

Regarding the cultural politics of Law and Literature practice, I wish to suggest to my sister and fellow American colleagues that we be conscious that the adversarial, common law legal system with a constitution that is interpreted in the Supreme Court is not the only basis for legal cultures. We need to be careful of a tendency to universalize our scholarly narratives when talking about Law and Literature in general and remember that particular preoccupations are in fact endemic to the American setting. Moreover, I would caution against idealizing the realist novel. This does not mean dismissing the novel from its place in Law and Literature altogether, but being canny about the representational techniques and political agendas that the realist novel tends to render invisible. There are novels that problematize the way in which they are told and seek to undermine the authority of their narration. J. M. Coetzee's novels are a case in point. Law and Literature scholarship on these texts exemplifies a new, more critical engagement with novelistic prose.[59]

In a complementary fashion, I would call to my European colleagues to remember that the Law and Literature movement arose in its most recent manifestation out of a frustration with legal training, interpretation, and practice in America. This movement represented an effort to return a performative ethics as well as an idealism and reverence to law. Copying the forms of this scholarship by adopting an adversarial scenario or by assuming similar struggles between, for instance, law and equity within other legal cultures will only lead us into imitative scholarship. Rather, the peculiarities of our own legal systems and legal histories need to be kept in mind as we contest law with the aesthetic and use law to query the literary.

Finally, I need to point out the inherent weakness of my own argument. A recent debate in Britain concerns the validity of adopting sharia law in some situations. My own work evinces a limited familiarity with just three legal systems and legal cultures and a complete lack of knowledge about many others. It also points towards a larger issue of to what degree a populace's faith in its legal system determines the kind of questions its practitioners will critically

---

[59] Melanie Williams, *Empty Justice: One Hundred Years of Law, Literature and Philosophy – Existential, Feminist and Normative Perspectives in Literary Jurisprudence* (London and Sydney: Cavendish Publishing, 2002).

ask about the law. It is with this limitation and question in mind that I conclude with the wish that we both contextualize and open up scholarly stories in Law and Literature.

* * *

Since this article was first published in June of 2010 it has received a fair amount of critical comment. This fact and the knowledge that it will be reprinted in a volume intended in the first instance for a European audience have led me to venture to suggest a few recommendations for researchers who are interested in furthering the project of European Law and Literature scholarship.[60]

1) I advocate the pursuit of comparative work for two interrelated reasons. One, American research paradigms and American legal culture have, in fact, provided the background for much of the Law and Literature research being done today; thus it is vital to name explicit differences in various European legal cultures and literatures and then to actively explore how these points of contrast shape our understanding of how literature and law interact with each other and inform our perception. Pointing out areas of linguistic, juridical, aesthetic, and cultural dissimilarity will create useful interventions in a world where globalization increasingly forces different legal paradigms and their source languages and legal traditions to interact. Two, European countries are in the process of integrating their own laws, legal systems, and courts with those of the European Union. This process is rife with conflict. Consider the controversial decisions by the European Court of Human Rights regarding voting rights for prisoners in the UK or preventative detention in Germany; alternately, criticisms by the German Constitutional Court of the European Court of Justice's overstepping its jurisdiction reveal that European people and sovereignties are not of one mind regarding where the locos of law should be. Our research can help to articulate sources of and reasons for these conflicts.

2) Scholars working within various intellectual and legal traditions across Europe need to address the issue of our different languages. For better or worse, English functions as a *lingua franca* in much international peer-reviewed research. Moreover, English also constitutes the working language in

---

60 My great thanks go to Martin A. Kayman for his critical comments on what follows here.

many European legal institutions as well as in much international litigation.[61] One response to this trend is to publish poly-lingual work with summaries in English; this enables those who are less at home in English to reflect on their local legal cultures and literatures. Another strategy is to work in English on non-Anglophone texts, literatures, and legal issues thus making them accessible to a larger readership.

3) For those of us who wish to write about literature in the traditional sense, it may – in the spirit of much political criticism – be important to turn to genres other than realist prose fiction and/or strongly narrative poetry. If we do choose to work with the former type of texts, we need to be canny about their representational techniques and the ideologies that shape them.

4) We need to question the "literary" per se. Similar processes of selecting, highlighting, and narrating or arranging occur in non-verbal texts as in literary ones. The moves to address mediality, visuality, digitality, and popular culture as well as the social processes these phenomena partake in represent, for me, the most vital areas of research today. Yet in undertaking this work, we need to be wary of perpetuating facile interpretations of law and justice that have been undertaken in some traditional *law-in* literature scholarship. Naming the manners in which different modalities affect our perception and refusing to regard multi-media texts as mere reflections of a prior content in law, justice, and the legal but as active participants in legal culture are integral to this project.

5) While the discussion of what the new multiplicity of law-related scholarship should be called may be fruitful and might lead to a more articulate concept of where research is going, 'Law and Literature,' 'Law and Culture,' 'Law and the Humanities,' and 'Law and Media,' 'Law and the Visual,' or 'Law and Art' are in fact related fields. In attempting to promote European work, it may be strategic to also honor our points of likeness.

6) Making our scholarly, political and institutional aims as explicit as possible will, I believe, help further European Law and Literature scholarship. In writing the article printed here I followed several aims: The central one was to point out what I perceive as a reliance by some scholars on a short-list of canonical Law and Literature texts written in English as primary source material and the attendant adoption of American legal concepts and paradigms.

---

[61] María Ángeles Orts Llopis, "The Untranslatability of Law? Lexical Differences in Spanish and American Contract Law," *European Journal of English Studies* 11 (2007): 1, 17–18.

This appeared to me to be to the detriment of an analysis of Europe's variety of legal cultures and literatures. It has also fostered a hesitancy to address the current conflict between local and traditional legal cultures and emerging European Union and global ones. A second motivation was to highlight what may be two erroneous tendencies in much Law and Literature: The first of these is to assume that law is identical with justice or equity. By contrast, I regard law as a social practice. The second is to feminize, idealize or essentialize literature as a panacea to law. Literature is not innocent. It is also involved in social practices and is caught up in the defense and perpetuation of various forms of capital.

With these recommendations and with the article they grew out of, my hope has been to move the conversation about European Law and Literature forward. And this can only happen with you, in dialogue.

Jeanne Gaakeer
(Erasmus University Rotterdam)

European *Law and Literature*: Forever Young
The Nomad Concurs

1. Introduction on a Personal Note

It was not until the day that I became a judge that I fully understood the importance of what my doctorate research in the field of Law and Literature taught me, i.e. that success in practicing law depends to a large extent on the legal imagination in its various guises. I specifically mention the legal imagination because my view on the bond between law, language and literature is informed by the works of James Boyd White, important as they are for legal practice because White has remained true to the original aim of Law and Literature, i.e. to provide nourishment to the legal practitioner, and that is precisely what, in my view at least, contemporary scholarship has lost track with.

Nevertheless, as I continued my parallel education and began to find my own topics for further research in the expanding field, I began to see the implications of the fact that as European scholars' interest in literary-legal studies developed, homage was paid almost exclusively to American models and topics, disregarding the European roots of the bonds between law and literature and perpetuating the canon(s) given by Anglo-American scholarship.

So it should come as no surprise that I wholeheartedly agree with Greta Olson's observation in her contribution to this volume that American Law and Literature scholarship tends to present its research on American politico-legal and cultural issues as the images to be mirrored.

While over the years I have kept finding many exciting things in what is being done in American *Law and Literature*, I do not turn a blind eye to the impossibilities when it comes to importing the results or translating the recommendations found there to European *Law and Literature*, given the specificity of the (historical) development of law in what we now call Europe. The agonistic structure of the American legal process[1] and the political aspects of

[1] Or, as Greta Olson and Monika Fludernik wrote in their "Introduction" to *In the Grip of the Law: trials, prisons and the space between*, eds. Monika Fludernik and Greta

constitutional interpretation are prime examples in this respect when compared to the inquisitorial approach dominant in most civil law countries, one that favors a process of verification of evidence. So Greta Olson is right to rattle the cage a bit.

Having said so, I aim to explore some topics pertaining to the project of 'Europeanizing' our way of engaging in *Law and Literature*. In doing so I cannot – and will not as the literary-legal nomadic judge that I am who has internalized the principle of 'hear the other side' – always escape opposing the European situation to the American. There is good reason for that, too, because, on the one hand, American *Law and Literature* scholarship definitely invites cherry picking, not only given the wealth of strands or approaches but also when it comes to discussing essentially European canonical works with classical Greek tragedy as the case in point, and, on the other hand, given the tendency perceived in European civil law countries today, in criminal law at least, to move away from a predominantly inquisitorial trial in the direction of distinctly American and/or common law adversarial features, such as equality of arms with respect to hearing expert-witnesses.

So, paradoxically perhaps, this speaks for a thorough study of and a dialogue with American *Law and Literature* if only when it comes to (implicitly) importing features of other legal systems to preclude the repetition of mistakes made. This is especially pertinent because European Union member England shares with America the common law system while the rest of the European countries are civil law countries and, as Greta Olson so rightly observes, now that England is part of the European Union it has to deal with the influence of European supranational law, and subsequently, with the continental tradition of codified law.[2] And then we have not even spoken about such aspects as the demarcation of political and geographical space – what is that thing called Europe? –, the idea of a national history (in the example of England: the development from England to England plus Wales, and later on Scotland to the United Kingdom of Great Britain and (Northern) Ireland), the differences as far as (written) national constitutions are concerned, or the effects of the delegation of national sovereignty to "Brus-

Olson (Frankfurt am Main: Peter Lang, 2004), xiii-xiv, 'The battle to define literature's significance to law may reflect the adversarial nature of Anglo-American law itself' (xxxi).

2 The question whether England looks upon itself as a part of Europe is closely connected to this issue. An advertisement for a Bradford UK-based poetry magazine in the *London Review of Books* (5 August 2010): 26, distinguishes between domestic subscriptions, "Europe" and "rest of the world". Note: not domestic and "rest of Europe".

sels". These things speak for more attention within European Law and Literature to differences and similarities.

Now that interdisciplinary movements originating in the Unites States have these past few years been incorporated in European legal education and embraced by European scholarship, with *Law and Economics* as its most prominent example to date, I want to emphasize that this development occasions at least two lines of research. First, an investigation of the various forms that disciplinary co-operation may take, from the trans-disciplinary via the multi-disciplinary to the inter-disciplinary, i.e. one more thorough than has been the case to date, for all too often the terms are mixed up or used indiscriminately without giving the conceptual implications any further thought. Secondly, and building on the former, this development speaks for an elaboration on the methodological aspects of law itself, especially if we also consider that legal methodology and hermeneutics inescapably have to deal with the influx of modern technology, e.g. in the form of results of blood or DNA tests on a defendant's body materials, and with other disciplines in various fields of law, varying from the behavioural sciences to environmental sciences, and, last but not least, with the broad range of studies of law in the humanities.

Arguably this also pertains to the ongoing debate about the place of law as an academic discipline on the spectrum of the sciences, i.e. the question whether law as a verbally oriented discipline is part and parcel of the humanities or whether it should be considered one of the social sciences on the view that law is (also) a technique of problem solving at the individual and the societal level and a means to create social structures. This debate is as much guided by the morphology of the legal system that is brought to the discussion, as it is by the methodological dispute in the social sciences themselves, i.e. whether their methods focus on explaining human behaviour in terms of the natural science model or on understanding human behaviour in the manner of the humanities. Its outcome or, more modestly, the scholarly position taken, of course directs and delineates disciplinary co-operations.

2. American and European Law and Literature: Two Cultures?

2.1. Prolegomena on the Rise and Fall of American *Law and Literature*

When Owen Fiss voiced the fear that the disintegration of public values he perceived in society would threaten law, he pointed to *Law and Economics* and its presumed negative effects given its instrumental view on law as a tool to bring about a specific goal decided beforehand. Fiss warned that law 'without inspiration' would mean the death of law, as we knew it.[3] His proclamation was not directed so much against the development of interdisciplinary legal studies *per se*, but rather against the emergence of the economic model as the exemplary model for law with wealth maximization, calculation, risk assessment as the main elements of the process of exchange as the method of determining (human and legal) value. Fiss later challenged *Law and Economics*' claim for the centrality of the market and lauded the restoration to legal studies of 'a proper place for the question of values'.[4]

Law, though perhaps not the autonomy of doctrinal law, survived the rapid growth of interdisciplinary legal movements that marked the 1980s and 1990s, and *Law and Literature* flourished, also as a counter movement to *Law and Economics*. Today, the institutional evidence indicates that *Law and Literature* has gained prominence over the years. The fact that its position is now under critique, if not under attack, both from the side of legal and literary studies, is proof of its maturity.

Paul Heald recently even proclaimed the death of *Law and Literature*, albeit in an optimistic vein.[5] Distinguishing between the strands of 'law as literature as language' with James Boyd White as its pioneer, 'law in literature', 'law as cultural movement', and 'law and literature as ethical discourse', Heald dismisses the first three. He claims that the legal profession yawns at the first two for lack of normative content given their focus on legal argument, rhetoric and narrative, and because such research is usually done by non-lawyers and obviously law has a natural resistance to outside influence. The third entails the risk of reducing law to a mere cultural product and that challenges the authority of law as far as dispute resolution is concerned. The litmus test Heald applies is the citation index. The result? James Boyd White, to name just one, is cited over 2500 times in academic articles, but only four times in judicial opinions, and thus he fails to make the grade. The fourth strand, brought to prominence by Martha Nussbaum, is the one espoused by Heald

3 Owen M. Fiss, "The Death of the Law", *Cornell Law Review* 72 (1986): 1–16, 14. In this essay I draw from materials in Jeanne Gaakeer, "O negócio da Lei e da Literatura: criar uma ordem, imaginar o homem", in *Direito e Literatura. Mundos em Diálogo*, eds. Helena Buescu, Cláudia Trabuco, and Sónia Ribeiro (Coimbra, 2010), 13–47; "On the Study Methods of our Time": methodologies of *Law and Literature* in the context of interdisciplinary studies"; "The future of literary-legal jurisprudence: mere theory or just practice?" (forthcoming 2011).

4 Owen M. Fiss, "The Challenge Ahead", *Yale Journal of Law & the Humanities* 1.1 (1988), viii-xi.

5 Paul J. Heald, "The Death of Law and Literature," *Comparatist* 33 (2009): 20–28, see also University of Georgia Law School Research Paper Series no. 09–006, May 2009, http://ssrn.com/abstract=1407698 <accessed 4 August 2010 >.

himself. Its central argument is that judges should read fiction because the lessons it teaches can directly be applied to decision making.[6] The reason I mention Heald is that his analysis and dismissal of much of what *Law and Literature* aims at is set in the key of any possible influence of any academic field on law. His conclusion that a lack of influence will herald the death of the field, on the one hand, and his conviction that literature itself can have a beneficial influence on the legal professional, on the other hand, merit further thought from the interdisciplinary perspective. His argument is timely for the European context as well given the shift it suggests, i.e. the move away from the original scholarly and pedagogical aim to read literature as a way to understand law toward the idea of the contribution of literature (or the humanities, generally) to legal practice.

So the discussion on whether or not *Law and Literature* needs a fixed agenda or strategy continues. Some rejoice in its pluralistic openness, others aim at more normative and hence possibly more influential projects. All it would seem agree as far as *Law and Literature*'s critical function is concerned. For whether or not one looks upon *Law and Literature* as the starting point for the achievement of the pedagogical aim of learning to do law well (the Whitean project), or as the field to offer new ways to criticize law and its authority, both depart from a distinct view on law's function.

Important to note, if we look at the rise of American *Law and Literature* is that the pragmatic reason for it was said to lie in the fact that a constricted job market for graduate students in the humanities in the 1970s led many to seek refuge from unemployment by entering law school.[7] This obviously did not have a great impact, initially at least, as far as their bringing a clearly outlined view on literature to the field. A focus on the humanizing aspects of literature for law prevailed. Furthermore, or perhaps as a consequence, it took a while before literature departments began to take a serious interest. So Heald may be right in that the plurality and openness of research topics can be seen as a lack of direction and that may well be (one of) the reason(s) of a continued reserve on both disciplinary sides.

Another personal note may illustrate the point. When in 1991 I paid a visit to the English department of Utrecht University where I received my MA in

---

6 See also Paul J. Heald, "Law and Literature as Ethical Discourse", in *Literature and Legal Problem Solving*, ed. Paul J. Heald (Durham [North Carolina] 1998), 3–13.

7 See Harold Suretsky, "Search for a Theory: An Annotated Bibliography of Writings in the Relation of Law to Literature and the Humanities", *Rutgers Law Review* 32 (1979): 727–739, 727; Richard Posner, "Law and Literature: A Relation Reargued," *Virginia Law Review* 72 (1986): 1351–1392, 1353.

1980 and explained that now that I also had my law degree I would like to write a doctorate thesis on that fascinating, and to European eyes new topic called *Law and Literature*, I was hounded out as a traitor to the humanities, for we all knew, didn't we, that law had absolutely nothing to do with (the post-modern study of) literature. So what had gotten into a girl with an MA in British and American literature to see literary interrelations with law? Fortunately, the law department in Rotterdam offered me the opportunity to pursue my goal, but even today I sometimes have to defend my chair in literary-legal studies and explain how important the humanities are to lawyers. This goes to show that even though law and legal theory in the European context are traditionally classified as belonging to Letters – e.g. by the Belgium Royal Academy of Letters, Sciences, and Arts, and the Royal Netherlands Academy of Arts and Sciences –, this classification is not uncontested. As early as the 1940s the famous Dutch jurist Paul Scholten had to defend law against the attack that it did not really belong to the Academy precisely because of its linguistic characteristics.

With the growing influence on law, in the late twentieth century, of instrumentalism of the kind originally promoted by *Law and Economics*, and on the premise that is high time to address matters from a more Eurocentric point of view, I would first like to highlight, somewhat eclectically, a number of elements in the development of law as a background for some proposals for the direction European *Law and Literature* might take.

2.2. European Roots of *Law and Literature*: Unity and Diversity

My starting point is the history of writing, linked as it is to the origin of law, as we know it. The scope of this article forces me to forego the details, but suffice it to say that in the High Middle Ages, the role of the *literati* and *clerici* who were able to read the rediscovered Justinian *Corpus Iuris Civilis* was significant. Philological studies inaugurated at Bologna University formed the basis of the new discipline, as marginal glosses became independent texts aimed at systemizing law.

A *litteratus* possessed letters; he was able to read and write. Here is the root for both the original identification of literature with literacy and the interrelation of letters and the legal profession. This also reminds us that law and literature are cognate human practices although their goals in society are different. Stephen Greenblatt addresses an acute issue for our contemporary discussion on European *Law and Literature* when he says, 'I am not at all sure that we have made much conceptual progress beyond Francis Bacon who notes, in the expanded Latin version of *The Advancement of Learning*, that "the

History of *Literature* is wanting".'[8] His main reason for offering this reminder is that Bacon, given his epistemological project, 'appears to envisage a comparative study', and that on this view the study of literature must not only be, 'cross-disciplinary … [but] also cross-cultural; there is nothing to be gained by staying within one's own national boundaries because a culture's fitness for a particular discursive practice can only be grasped by setting it against another's', and that would include cultural tolerance.[9]

The perfection of the scholastic method of dialectic debate, originated in theology and later prominent throughout academia, was eventually instrumental in incorporating into law elements originally oral and poetical, with the ordeal as a case in point. This verbal orientation also shows in the original symbiosis of law and literature in practice. Thinking of the development of law since then, it is easy to grasp the importance of Bloch's observation that, 'We are used to a sharp distinction between the language of literature and that of law, associated historically with separate and sometimes conflicting spheres of human endeavor. The former has, since the Renaissance, become increasingly synonymous with a discourse emanating from and belonging to a personalized self: the product variously of inspiration, imagination, genius, desire, neurosis, and dream. The latter has, since the age of Montesquieu and Rousseau, come to represent the collective discourse governing the relations between individuals or between the individual and the state.'[10] Furthermore, Bloch also points to an important feature of medieval literary and legal life, if we think of the contemporary development towards *Law and Culture* and/or *Law and the Humanities*, and that is that these were much more than to date perceived as the expression of the collective thought of the community rather than the individual expression of consciousness. Bloch also points to morphological affinities between literary and legal language, for example in language of poetry in comparison to the wording of the legal figure of the 'customal'. Given the formulaic aspect of legal language especially when it came to the accusation in criminal law proceedings, jurists sought refuge in the story in order to give the formula more body.

The etymology of legal terms offers comparable insights. We only have to look at the variety of terms used in Middle English for the function of the ad-

8 Stephen Greenblatt, "What is the History of Literature?", *Critical Inquiry* 23 (1997): 460–481, 470 (endnote omitted).

9 Greenblatt, "History of Literature," 472.

10 R. Howard Bloch, *Medieval French Literature and Law* (Berkeley: University of California Press, 1977), 1.

vocate, with 'narrator', and 'counter', i.e. someone who tells a story (counter as sergeant-in-law can be traced back to the French 'countour' from the verb to count, i.e. to plead in a court of law) as the most prominent.[11] Centuries later Jacob Grimm also mentions the etymology in 'Von der Poesie im Recht'[12], so Greta Olson is quite right to refer to Grimm's observation that law and literature arose from the same bed,[13] although I must quibble a bit with her in that she mentions this observation in one breath with the advent of the term Germanist coined by Grimm and the class of Dichterjuristen (poets who also have a law degree), whereas Grimm himself emphasizes the medieval tradition of poet-lawyers, claiming that 'Richter' (judges), are 'finders', i.e. of their decisions just like 'Dichter' (poets), are finders of the right words, 'trobadores, trouveurs' or 'poetai', the ancient Greek term for 'makers', constructors, here, of texts.[14]

When the scholastic method was taken to its logical extreme, and the fifteenth and sixteenth centuries brought the onset and subsequent expansion of the *studia humanitatis* now known as humanism, the rigid division between logic (the reign of theoretical or scientific knowledge) and rhetoric (favoring practical knowledge and context-depending reasoning) dissolved and the result for law was not only the integration with the *artes liberales* in general but also the unity of theory and practice.

The reception of Roman law and its transformation into a *ius commune* in medieval Europe as well as its subsequent development from the classic *mos italicus* to the French, more local case-oriented *mos gallicus*, are also highly pertinent topics for our current understanding of law in context. Furthermore, the explicit emergence of common law in England and civil law in other European countries as 'literatures', before the latter became rule-oriented, deserve more than just the attention of legal and literary historians. My point here is that what today is heralded as contextualisation and interdisciplinarity has a long tradition that has undeservedly been neglected in contemporary literary-legal studies, in my view because of the dominance of the epistemo-

---

11 See also Anton-Hermann Chroust, *The Rise of the Legal Profession in America* (Norman: University of Oklahoma Press, 1965).

12 Jakob Grimm, "Von der Poesie im Recht," in *Zeitschrift für geschichtliche Rechtswissenschaft* [1816], repr. in *Kleinere Schriften* 6 (Hildesheim: 1965), 152–191.

13 Greta Olson, "De-Americanizing Law-and-Literature Narratives: Opening up the Story." in *Law & Literature* 22.1 (2010): 338–364, 353.

14 Grimm, "Poesie," par. 3. See also Lorenz Frank, "Digitales Fundheft 'Recht und Literatur'," http://lorenzfranck.de/dokumente/litrecht.html <accessed 4 August 2010> for an overview of research on 'Dichterjuristen und (Rechts-)philosophen'.

logical *Wissenschaft* model developed in nineteenth-century Germany for the classification of academic fields.[15]

When we turn to literature, the history of the rise of the novel as a genre is important, given that it was first distrusted as the equation of fiction and lies whereupon writers defended themselves by pretending that their novels were histories, i.e. works with a truth claim, as Kieran Dolin has recently argued.[16] It is not for nothing that the rise of the novel as a literary genre coincides with the rise of historiography as an academic discipline. Barbara Shapiro has convincingly shown that historiography became imbued by the concept of 'fact' as developed in the English legal tradition and subsequently spread to the natural sciences. The distinction between matters of fact and matters of law, a *factum* being an action or event in which individuals participate, as contrasted to a *datum*, a given in and by nature, came to the fore in the way common law dealt with the issue of the evaluation of the truth or falsity of evidence by the jury, leaving the facts to the jury and legal doctrine to the judge. Eventually, reciprocity became the key word, 'Fact oriented surveys, reports, and descriptions were so familiar that fictional "matters of fact" imitated real narratives.'[17] The struggle between rhetorical persuasiveness and legal 'truth' as fought out in today's courts, be it in adversarial or inquisitorial criminal law, makes the importance of an inquiry into this part of the history of ideas of law and literature all the more urgent.[18]

This is especially so, because, empiricism and rationalism culminated in a theory of scientific positivism that became instrumental in propounding that law's value lies in its objectivity, and that law as a body of rules exists separ-

---

[15] A notable exception when it comes to addressing aspects of medieval law and literature and legal humanism is Peter Goodrich, in, for example, *Law in the Courts of Love. Literature and other minor jurisprudences* (London and New York: 1996), and, Legal Enigmas – Antonio de Nebrija, "the *Da Vinci Code* and the Emendation of Law", *Oxford Journal of Legal Studies* 30.1 (2010): 71–99. Eric Heinze, professor of Law and Humanities at the University of London, Queen Mary, has written extensively on English and French power politics and law in the sixteenth and seventeenth centuries; e.g. "This power isn't power if it's shared': Law and Violence in Jean Racine's La Thébaïde", *Law & Literature* 22.1, (2010): 76–109. See also 'Literature and Law', *Textus, English Studies in Italy* XXI, eds. Daniela Carpi and Ian Ward (2008), 3.

[16] Kieran Dolin, *A Critical Introduction to Law and Literature* (Cambridge: CUP, 2007), 101.

[17] Barbara Shapiro, "The Concept 'Fact': legal origins and cultural diffusion," *Albion* 26 (1994): 227–252, 238.

[18] See also Peter Schneck, "The Laws of Fiction: Legal rhetoric and literary evidence" *European Journal of English Studies* 11 (2007): 47–63, for a study of the role of rhetorical strategies in law and literature.

ately from those who are called upon to decide cases. In short, once the facts and the rules are clear, the right answer will necessarily be found by applying syllogistic reasoning. Such a view shows an uncanny resemblance to scholasticism's excrescences. It leads to a hermeneutic insistence on the separation of law and morals initiated by the German jurist Rudolph von Ihering's *Begriffsjurisprudenz* and exemplified by legal positivism, both in the Kelsenian version of the pure theory of law and the empiricist variety promoted by H.L.A. Hart. This triumph of the abstract norm, however, can only lead to sterile formalism.

Judges, I would claim, anticipating my argument on the bond between legal theory and practice below in paragraph 4, are like authors in that they select the facts with a view to structuring the world in the decision they take. The epistemological question to be kept in their minds should therefore always be whether there is indeed a chain of circumstance "out there" or whether (some)one carefully fits together the evidence with other established facts. On this view, the notion of the 'laws of evidence' is, of course, a contradiction in terms. This brings us back again to the epistemological debate about the facts and the concept of cognition and knowledge, and the doubtful distinction between the *factum probandum*, the fact which is the subject of proof, and the *factum probans*, the fact from the existence of which that of the *factum probandum* is inferred. Attention to narrative can help us not to forget that claiming truth in law is a way to take on radical human fallibility, in every respect.

If we combine all this with remembrance of the fact that before the eighteenth century the idea of literature as the distinct field was basically nonexistent, the need for a comparative, interdisciplinary angle becomes urgent. Both the terms *letters* and science denoted knowledge and the adjective literary had the connotation of 'the scholarly' including the philosophical and theological in a broad sense. On this view, literature was not thought of in terms of a discourse restricted by national or disciplinary boundaries. English, French or German literature or any other country's literature for that matter, were not looked upon as entities separate from other *letters* as Adam Smith's *Lectures on Rhetoric and Belles Lettres* show. This is important to note in view of contemporary calls for opening up *Law and Literature*.

Put differently, we may say that it was not until the later part of the eighteenth century that local order set in, in the form of a concept of literature as the restricted area of novels, poetry, drama, and essays, and that on the national level. The same goes for law with the formation of nation states all over Europe, after a long period of (civil) wars, turmoil and social upheaval. With the nation state came the demand for national codes of law and consequently, the demise of the *ius commune* as the sole *ratio scripta* for Europe. The culture, or perhaps we should say the cult of positivism began its rule. The question that arises would then be whether the nation state was instrumental in creating national literature, or the other way around. Here the combined research efforts in the fields of law and literature, especially legal history and literary history, which as yet sorely missed at least in this specific combination, would be called for.

Law is also a case in point as far as the process of differentiation of disciplines and social power structures characteristic of the nineteenth century is concerned. Originally, law and the *Kameralwissenschaften* were one in Germany, before the latter formed the basis the independent discipline of economics. In *Ancient Law* (1861) Henry Maine convincingly argued that anthropology was rooted in law. And when Emile Durkheim and Max Weber founded the discipline of sociology, they did so as lawyers who acknowledged the relationship of the mother discipline and its offspring. When law and literature each went their separate ways as academic disciplines, a natural enmity developed between them, as the German legal philosopher Gustav Radbruch claimed,[19] and concepts that they long shared, such as justice, punishment, and guilt or culpability, began to diverge, and with that their professional languages generally.

Despite this divorce of law and literature, however, traces remained of their old allegiance, albeit in a new coat provided by criminologists and literary authors in the late nineteenth and early twentieth century. Remarkably, these European law in/as literature *avant la lettre* studies are forgotten while Wigmore and Cardozo are held before us as exemplary of the twentieth-century start of whole movement. To complete this short history of ideas, then, of the European bond of law and literature, I want to mention the debate initiated by Cesare Lombroso in *L'Uomo Delinquente* (1876). Lombroso is best remembered for his methodological insistence on a theory of atavism combined with biometrical research focusing on the supposed criminal's bodily features to found his claim that criminals could be differentiated from non-criminals on a scientific basis. Less known is his argument that his theory also formed an explanation of great works of art in which artists of genius have intuited the archetypical criminal, with Michelangelo and Mantegna as prime examples in the plastic arts and Zola, Ibsen and Dostoevsky in literature. In the same breath, Lombroso argued that those literary works that proved fundamentally criminological in outlook were a valuable object of scientific study. This crude and circular methodological point was taken up

---

19 Gustav Radbruch, *Rechtsphilosophie*, eds. E. Wolf and H.-P. Schneider (Stuttgart: 1973), par. 14, 201, 'einer natürlichen Feindschaft'.

by literary authors such as Zola when writing *La Bête Humaine* (1890), and Dostoevsky who acknowledged criminal anthropology's influence on his work (with Raskolnikov in *Crime and Punishment* as the case in point). Lombroso's disciple Enrico Ferri published a study on criminals in art in 1898, *I Delinquenti Nell'Arte*. In it, he describes the three types of criminals that Shakespeare gave us: Hamlet the insane criminal, Othello the criminal out of passion, and Macbeth the born criminal. When Ferri's book was translated into Dutch in 1905, the Dutch author Querido followed suit, arguing that before Dostoevsky it was only Shakespeare who deeply felt the dramatic beauty and mystery of crime and its origins. August Goll (1866–1936), Danish jurist and criminal law theorist (as well as chief of police in Copenhagen), entered the debate and defined Macbeth as an example of the occasional criminal who deliberately chooses to do wrong.[20] The Dutch theologian and criminologist Van Dijk then took Goll to task for his instrumentalist view on literature. Van Dijk's surprisingly modern premise was that in interpreting Shakespeare we should pay attention to the interrelation of narrative perspectives. Later on the renowned Dutch criminologist Röling concluded the argument when he wrote a literary-legal study of Shakespearean criminals analyzing them against the background of the development of the explanatory science which criminology by then had become.[21]

So while for obvious reasons given the institutional origins of *Law and Literature*, the European focus of attention has almost exclusively been directed towards the US and the UK, I think that that the history of ideas, with divergences and convergences of methodologies in the humanities and sciences, shows that there are reasons enough to address matters from a broader European point of view and at the concrete level of practice(s). This is especially acute given contemporary developments such as the move away as Greta Olson would delineate it, from a binary to a triadic or multiple discipline.[22] Given the European historical development, one might argue that the current move to look upon law as a cultural practice as well as the call to include philosophy and the visual arts including movies as legal "texts" is a return to the diversity of old.

---

20 August Goll, *Forbrydertyper hos Shakespeare*, translated as *Criminal Types in Shakespeare* (Honolulu [Hawai]: University Press of the Pacific, 2004).

21 See Jeanne Gaakeer, "'The art to find the mind's construction in the face': Lombroso's criminal anthropology and literature: the example of Zola, Dostoevsky, and Tolstoy," *Cardozo Law Review* 26.6 (2005): 2345–2377; "Strange Matters, Macbeth and Dutch criminology," *Shakespeare Yearbook* 15 (Lewiston [New York]: 2005), 251–266.

22 Olson "De-americanizing" 359.

Furthermore, the question behind any definition of law as a cultural discipline presupposes an inquiry into the societal and conceptual conditions of law and legal practice, and such cultural inquiry is in itself a practice guided by the epistemological characteristics of an era. On this view, we need to be able to combine both the internal and external standpoint, i.e. we are in and of that practice as much as we investigate it from the outside. We need to address such aspects of our venture, for not only does the development of the humanities as academic disciplines show that the human connection, originally at the heart of these disciplines, has in itself become problematic, the term culture too suffers from a semantic ambiguity that makes it suspicious to many jurists today in that it is easily linked to the ethnic arguments – it's *my* culture, stupid – in controversies about the role of multiculturalism (including religious issues) in contemporary societies.[23]

3. The Nomad Concurs

My proposal for our further conversation is comparable to Greta Olson's. Rather than remaining derivative of American scholarship European *Law and Literature* can and should reflect European cultural and legal preoccupations. I would also argue that simultaneously we should enter upon a dialogue with American *Law and Literature*, not in order to imitate, as Greta Olson quite rightly warns against, but in order to probe its qualities to find inspiration for future development of European *Law and Literature.*

I say so given the development at the supranational level of the European Union, one that transcends national law. Furthermore, we would all do well to learn to think more comparatively in *Law and Literature* and be mutually informed, if only to clear away possible mutual misunderstanding. Serving as a judge in a continental European civil law system, I would disagree with Greta Olson where she says that 'legal reasoning proceeds through a process of deduction from abstract norms of codified law to the particular case at hand'[24] and that the judge partly has a prosecutorial function. To start with the latter,

---

23 The current politico-legal debate on whether or not to accept visible features of Islam in the form of the traditional female dress in the public sphere is a case in point. Here too a venture into the rich European past would be called for. Think of the influence of Islamic culture via the philosopher Averroes (Au'l-Walid Ibn Rushd 1126–1198) whose importance for law is that he unlocked Aristotle's *Nicomachean Ethics* with its concepts of *epistèmè* (scientific knowledge), *phronèsis* (practical wisdom) and *technè* (practical art). Averroes' influence on Christian thought reached well into the fourteenth century, as Dante's *De Monarchia* shows.

24 Olson "De-americanizing," 352.

the position of the judge between the prosecuting government official and the defendant in criminal cases, or as the arbiter of the dispute between two civilian parties, is that of the neutral third who indeed connects the relevant statutes and principles of law to the case at hand (I am hesitant to use the term 'rule application' given the expectation it raises of an unproblematic existence and use of norms *in abstracto*) and who functions as a check, either against the abuse of government power in the asymmetrical relationship between the state and the citizen, or against a comparable abuse of power between civilian parties. But she does so, ideally at least, not by means of a deductive methodology (only), but, as I will discuss in more detail below, by a combined effort of grasping together what may be called relevant facts and the legal norms. And what is more, she is able to make law. Or, as the website of the Dutch judiciary says under the heading 'The Judge', 'In case the law is not clear and decisive [i.e. on a specific question of law], then the decision of the judge generates the new rule.'[25]

Another aspect that comes to the fore in supranational law is that the word law itself leads to a semantic issue within the European Union and shows the relevance of our attention to the problems of translation. In the legalistic, nineteenth-century idea of law as the sum total of a nation's codified rules in statutes, 'law' is just that. That is to say, law in the sense of just decisions or justice is identical with law as rules, denying the possibility that there may be legal principles that do not have the binary quality of the legal rule but work by giving weight to specific arguments, and refusing to incorporate elements of morality. Contemporary concepts of law within the European Union and without, i.e., at the national level, all include legal principles.

Think also of the semantics of the combinations of 'law and the laws' in English, 'Recht und Gesetz' in German, and 'het recht en de wet' in Dutch. The same aspect of semantic ambiguity crops up in the official texts of the European Convention on Human Rights (EHCR), for example in the immensely important article 6, the right to fair trial. In English it reads, ' … everyone is entitled to a fair and public hearing …', but the French text has, 'toute personne a droit …'. So we have 'entitled' rather than 'everyone has a right' in English and 'droit', 'a right' in French, and not only are these concepts dissimilar as far as the place in their legal systems are concerned, they are also culturally dissimilar in that the idea of a legal right in French thought is deeply connected to the history of the demise of the *Ancien Régime* and the French Revolution.

---

25 www.rechtspraak.nl <accessed 1 September 2010>, my translation.

A remembrance of things past in the form of renewed attention to the importance of literature to legal practice is what I would advocate for European *Law and Literature*. In doing so I acknowledge our human tendency to select from available and/or culturally determined alternatives, and realize that the hermeneutic position from which to offer such proposal is inescapably formed by the circumstance that without some fore-understanding of history we can make no sense of the past while our fore-understanding itself is constructed from our present understanding of the past, and that the same goes for our view on legal practice. There is always the danger of our partisan perspectives. But, put differently, perhaps we should be more like Molière's monsieur Jourdain in *Le Bourgeois Gentilhomme* who, in middle age, suddenly realizes that he has been speaking prose all his life, i.e. we should do more of what the bond of law and literature has shown for so long. I draw support for my argument from the proceedings of the symposium The Power of Stories: Intersections of Law, Culture and Literature (Gloucester, 2005). Melanie Williams argued that a dominant connection of narrative with critical race and psychotherapeutic approaches 'undervalues the practical application for narrative in jurisprudence', claiming that what matters most in literary-legal studies is ' … not necessarily the quest for a particular political outcome but the knowledge that the natural challenge posed by different epistemological sources is in itself a quiet political critique', and Ian Ward pointed to the importance of *Law and Literature* for legal education.[26] Both arguments are closely connected to legal practice.

4. The Importance of *Law and Literature* for Practice and Education

4.1. The Literary Judge

I would argue – and beg to differ from Greta Olson perhaps – that the value of the word remains *Law and Literature*'s unique selling point[27] to legal practitioners, because jurists have always been and are still today verbally oriented. The impetus for the legal turn to literature originally found in the observation that the legal profession was in need of a broader cultural foun-

---

26 Susan Ayers, "Where is Law&Literature Headed? Roundtable Discussion, participants: Susan Ayres, Michael Hyde, Susan Sage Heinzelman, Ian Ward and Melanie Williams," *Texas Weslyan Law Review* 12 (2005): 485–495, Williams 490 and 491, Ward 494.

27 Early on Robin West pointed to the fact that as a movement *Law and Literature* lacked 'a *point*' ("The Literary Lawyer," *Pacific Law Journal* 27 (1996): 1187–1211, 1187).

dation in the humanities, to me, means that a combined study of legal and literary theory and practice in the European context would be called for. Not with a focus on the abstract Herculean judge that Ronald Dworkin holds before us, or Lon Fuller's Rex, but rather with a reflective one on what real judges actually do, i.e. without ending up in an empirical, sociological study.

On the view that the jurist's perception of the case at hand is neither purely deductive nor inductive but rather a combination in the sense of going to and fro, from the act of deciding what can justifiably be called 'the facts', to the legal rule(s) and principles applicable, legal methodology always necessarily focuses on the combination of norm and fact. Such methodology acknowledges that both the norm as it is given by the lawgiver and theoretically cultivated (that is to say that the norm includes theory in the sense of legal doctrine or the academic propositions made for law), and the perception and assessment of the facts are never 'just there' but are always in need of interpretation. That interpretation itself is, of course, guided by existing interpretive frameworks (that are themselves subject to ongoing debate as law responds to new societal, environmental, and technological developments and challenges), theoretical knowledge and the individual jurist's practical experience. This characteristic feature of legal methodology is at the same time the opening to critique in that by its very nature the language of the law is open-textured and legal meaning therefore can always be challenged. In short, the primary object of legal interpretation is never the legal text only.

Now that the intertwinement of theory and practice has its focal point in adjudication of which the judge is the exponent, this speaks for the combined study of law and the humanities generally, and law and literature more specifically. Why? Because, first of all, judges configure. They grasp together the facts and circumstances of the case and decide what is relevant and what is not. In law as in literature, constructing a plot is not just arranging events in a (dramatic) sequence. It is determining what (and who) is to be included and what will be left out. That act is already a judgment and because it should be the result of thorough judicial reflection rather than an automatism, it needs to be informed. That is essential for a just outcome because, secondly, judges are the producers of sentences in at least two meanings: they decide the lives of others and in writing down their decisions they have to state the grounds the decision is based on, so that others can form an opinion about its correctness.[28] As in narrative fiction, a story is presented in a judicial deci-

---

[28] For an early European reference to *Law and Literature*'s potential as legal methodology, see Christian Armbrüster, "'Law and Literature – Movement' in den USA – eine Herausforderung von 'Law and Economics'?" *Juristische Rundschau* 2 (1991):

sion in that someone tells us as readers that something happened, and what it means. It is therefore imperative for judges to gain insight in how narratives work in the world. Attention to narrative can also be translated into a meaningful vantage point from which to resist the reification that is the result of a one-sided, positivist attention to the language of legal concepts. Furthermore, narrative knowledge can also be thought of in terms of self-knowledge, i.e. knowledge of the activities of which the judge as the knowing subject is the author. This in my view is an important feature for professional ethics. For if the judge's deliberation is oriented at choosing the correct legal ends and means, and at translating these into the appropriate legal action, this implies judicial integrity that transcends the obvious demands of clarity and coherence of the judicial decision in that it includes the ethical aspect in the sense of the judicial disposition to keep probing her inner motives and to reflect on the tensions that arise when one has to get a grasp of two conflicting views (on the facts of the case or the point of law, or both).

This is especially in order if we think of the inquisitorial approach in civil law countries that favors a process of verification of evidence in which participants run the risk of falling into the trap of the confirmation bias and/or belief perseverance.

If at the end of the chain of gathering evidence, the case comes to trial, what a judge does is go through the process of verification of evidence rather than the falsification process that Karl Popper would have us do. It is here, then, that insights in narratology can make an important contribution to judicial practice, because the legal professional is not exempt from the psychological processes that he or she is called upon to interpret and judge.

Recent findings in the behavioral sciences, as well as the interdisciplinary field of Law and Psychology suggest that our psychological make-up cannot but fail to live up to the idea of recognizing all incongruities in the case at hand. As humans we are inclined to search for or interpret (new) information and evidence in such a way that it confirms our existing convictions, even in the face of contrary evidence. As a result, there is always a tension between the reconciliation of contraries and our psychological make-up. When in a specific case this leads to cognitive dissonance, the solution most often sought, once cognitive dissonance is literally felt as a problem, consists of explaining and reasoning away these opposites and then the trap of the confirmation bias is wide open, as is that of belief perseverance that reinforces it, for sometimes humans misjudge what they see, or they miss part of

---

61–62. See also Christian Hiebaum, "Recht-Schreiben. Über das Wahre, Schöne und Gute in den juristischen Begründung," *Juridikum* 1 (2004): 52–55.

the information before them. When the judge has read the file, it is the information of that file that will direct her attitude during a trial, during an oral hearing. So what do you do as a judge when chunks of evidence diverge, and, as is the case in law, the environment is always dialectical? The dangers to judicial emplotment are obvious.

All this speaks for a reflection on our evidentiary standards, our interpretive assumptions, the nature of motivation and the grounds stated in judgments, the weight of hearsay evidence, physical and eyewitness evidence, in short, the power of a variety of epistemologies, the visual included, to prevent miscarriages of justice. Because resistance to prejudices of the kind mentioned here presupposes recognition and understanding first, the judge needs to be connected to the broader cultural framework of which law is a part. Or, to come back to the disputed idea of *iudex deductor* and the positivist separation thesis: should the outcome of a lawsuit be equated to the result of the deductive process of the application of objective legal norms, why then bother to have judges at all? The lawgiver might as well codify the desired outcomes of specific legal disputes and/or assign the act of deduction to an automaton. Such line of thought would suggest that human attention is to be dispensed with when it comes to saying what the law is. This would have dire consequences for justice, I would contend.

One recent example of the kind of work I would strongly recommend to judges and *Law and Literature* scholars is that done by Miranda Fricker in the field of philosophical hermeneutics. In *Epistemic Injustice, Power and the Ethics of Knowing* she offers an illuminating discussion of two types of epistemic injustice from which discourses can suffer: testimonial injustice, i.e. when prejudice causes a hearer to give a deflated level of credibility to a speaker's word, and hermeneutical injustice, i.e. when a gap in collective interpretive resources puts someone at an unfair disadvantage when it comes to making sense of their own social experiences. Frick illustrates the problems resulting from such injustice by means of Harper Lee's *To Kill a Mockingbird* and Patricia Highsmith's *The Talented Mr. Ripley.* The idea that judgment is perceptual also holds true for our dealing with testimonial (in)justice because it depends on 'the virtuous hearer's perceptual capacity (be) understood in terms of a sensitivity to epistemologically salient features of the situation and the speaker's performance.'[29]

---

29 Miranda Fricker, *Epistemic Injustice, Power and the Ethics of Knowing* (Oxford: OUP, 2007), 72.

4.2. The Humanities and Legal Education

We should also note the educational differences that influence the enterprise of *Law and Literature.* European universities offer four-year courses in law as an academic discipline, with students starting their studies right after having finished their secondary school. That means that neither the aspect of vocational training prevalent in American law schools, nor the discussion whether law is or should be included in the liberal arts curriculum is on the European agenda to the extent that it is in the US. While continental European higher education since the late nineteenth century was previously modeled on the German system which strictly distinguished between vocational and academic higher education, however, today, after the Bologna Process, we also witness the implementation of the major and the minor after the American model in addition to the introduction of the bachelor-master form of the academic curriculum. Furthermore, the call for the introduction of a liberal arts type of education, with a three-year curriculum that allows students a broad range of choices as far as academic subjects are concerned, has already lead to the foundation of a number of "colleges", for instance, in the Netherlands, University College in Utrecht and Roosevelt Academy in Middelburg.

Nevertheless, the idea of the liberal arts as the means with which to cultivate human values cannot be translated into the European curriculum without further thought of the European background.[30] Here, too, dialogue is in order, if only because the American discussion on the combined teaching of law and the liberal arts dates back to the 1950s and 60s, when Harold Berman argued that law students are unable to digest jurisprudence without a basic knowledge of common law, civil and criminal procedure and legal history, and these subjects should therefore be taught in the liberal arts curriculum.[31]

Anthony Kronman recently voiced a concern comparable to Berman's. His main point is that the question of life's meaning, in a broad sense, was once at the heart of university education, but has now been, 'exiled from the

---

30 See, generally, *Law in the Liberal Arts*, ed. Austin Sarat (Ithaca and London: Cornell University Press, 2004).

31 See Harold J. Berman, *On the Teaching of Law in the Liberal Arts Curriculum* (Brooklyn: The Foundation Press, 1956). For a comparable view that a curriculum for lawyers needs to show the numerous vantage points on the whole spectrum of life, see Kenneth L. Knickerbocker, "Talents for the Study of Law," *Journal of Legal Education* 12 (1960): 534, as cited in 'A Gathering of Poets & Writers' in *The Legal Studies Forum* xxxiv.2 (2010): 449.

humanities, first as a result of the growing authority of the modern research ideal and then on account of the culture of political correctness that has undermined the legitimacy of the question itself and the authority of humanities teachers to ask it.'[32] Subsequently, or so he claims, the humanities have been put on the defensive. On this view, the further development of *Law and Literature* would also demand a change of heart in the humanities, or at least, a clarification of their aims, lest our scholarly discussion can be caught only in the metaphor of ships passing in the night. Think also of matters terminological: the liberal arts in the American sense, are they the same as the *Geisteswissenschaften* in Germany, the moral sciences, or humanities in England, or the *sciences humaines* in France? Here too (in)translatability remains an issue we should not hesitate to address given the move away from *Law and Literature* traditionally conceived toward *Law and Humanities* a.k.a. *Law and Culture.*

A good starting point, in my view, for such a discussion is Costas Douzinas' answer to the question 'What are the Humanities?', i.e. that they are '... either a set of academic subjects that typically consists of Classics, Philosophy, History, and Literature (the disciplinary approach) or an attitude toward teaching and learning that could be extended to all types of subjects (the humanistic approach).'[33] To him, the very idea of the humanities is a '... consummately modern and decidedly American invention', and as an academic institution typical of American education.[34] He criticizes Martha Nussbaum for looking upon the humanities as what he takes to be a mere palliative, for example in her *Cultivating Humanity: a classical defense of reform in liberal education*, in that calling for external help accepts the poverty of legal education. To Douzinas, the limited view of an auxiliary function of the humanities is restricted in its disregard of the historical and cultural background of the idea of the human and humanity.[35] His sketch of the develop-

---

32 Anthony Townsend Kronman, *Education's End, why our colleges and universities haven given up on the meaning of life* (New Haven and London: Yale University Press, 2007), 7 and 45ff.

33 Costas Douzinas, "A Humanities of Resistance: Fragments for a Legal History of Humanity," in *Law and the Humanities. An Introduction,* eds. Austin Sarat, Matthew Anderson, and Cathrine O. Frank (Cambridge: CUP, 2010), 49–72, 49.

34 Douzinas, "Humanities of Resistance," 49–50.

35 But see her recent *Not For Profit: why democracy* ***needs*** *the humanities*, Martha C. Nussbaum (Princeton and Oxford: Princeton University Press, 2010), in which she voices concern that given the profit motive pervasive in modern societies, science and technology seems to have gotten the upper hand and claims that while there is no objection to science and technology other abilities equally crucial may get lost in the competition: 'These abilities are associated with the humanities and the arts:

ment of the word *humanitas* in the Roman Republic (a translation from the Greek *paideia*) as *eruditio et institutio in bonas artes*, i.e. the organized education in the arts and sciences, or *Bildung*, to modern uses of the words humanism and humanity is important for opening up new vistas on the combined effort of law and literature to make an actual contribution to stem the tide of all kinds of instrumentalism on a global scale, hence his call for a 'Humanities of Resistance'.[36] Such matters are indeed too important to leave them to the European Cultural Convention of the Council of Europe. While fortunately we have progressed since C.P. Snow made the (in)famous distinction, or so his critics claim, with F.R. Leavis as the most prominent, between the scientists and non-scientists, and grouped under the latter heading those working in the humanities, thereby diminishing the culture they stood for (given their perceived inability to contribute, at least directly, to a solution of global problems such as the lack of human welfare in developing countries), controversial ideological issues, as well as in 'disciplinary' terms remain and the value of literature and the humanities for the constitution and reaffirmation of our humanity is not uncontested.[37]

5. Sources of Tolerance

My conclusion would therefore be that there is more work to be done, not only in order to remedy law's current lack of attention to the myriad possibilities that the humanities offer, but also to clarify underlying methodologies and epistemologies so that we gain more insight in our disciplinary joint ventures at a foundational level of each contributing discipline. In 1992 Brian Leiter warned us to avoid the risk of 'intellectual voyeurism', i.e. 'superficial and ill-informed treatment of serious ideas', that results from a lack of interest in and mutual understanding of the (philosophical) concepts

---

the ability to think critically; the ability to transcend local loyalties and the approach world problems as a "citizen of the world"; and, finally, the ability to imagine sympathetically the predicament of another person' (7, note 2 omitted).

36 See also Peter Brooks, "Literature as Law's Other," *Yale Journal of Law & the Humanities* 22.2 (2010): 349–367, for a reflection on how the interpretive humanities may stand in relation to law, claiming that ' … the movement [i.e. *Law and Literature*] has more often than not strayed from its most productive paths of inquiry' and suggesting that ' … the humanities can perhaps teach people to read with a fine and necessary suspicion' (350). This view is most congenial to me because Brooks speaks of law as a praxis, a way of doing things, and that, as I argue, is what Law and Literature scholarship has forgotten.

37 See, for example, David Howarth, "Is law a humanity, or is it more like engineering?" *Arts and Humanities in Higher Education* 3.1 (2003): 7–26.

at work in a discipline.[38] Jack Balkin's provoking name for interdisciplinary scholars was 'romantic rebels'.[39] These are powerful reminders of the pitfalls of interdisciplinary work. How are we to serve two masters at the same time and be successful in creating a new third?[40] If we are indeed rebels, then with rather than without a cause, I would suggest.

For lawyers, given the institutional and societal aspects of law, there is another argument that speaks for such clarification. 'As lawyers we cannot simply accept the conclusions of others; we must make them our own, and to do that we must step out of the legal culture and into that of the other one. In doing this we are not picking up "findings" but learning a language', wrote James Boyd White in his 1990 book *Justice as Translation.*[41] It is here, I would claim, that the topic of interdisciplinarity can be connected to the perspective of legal methodology, on the view that it will simply not do for law to lump together all 'Law ands …'. Not too long ago, Karlheinz Stierle asked whether, 'mutual translation of cultures [is] possible without the third instance of a medium of translation as lingua franca?'.[42] This is a good question for a further discussion on interdisciplinarity itself, given that the term 'translatio studii' refers to the transfer of learning and the transfer of subjects of scholarly research. Or, as Thomas Beebee more recently put it, the important question is whether the 'and' in interdisciplinarity is actually operative in the sense that one discipline has a bearing on the other and vice versa.[43]

The subject also pertains to the question of how *Law and Literature* authorizes itself through the (hi)story it tells. What beginning did we choose, and

---

38 Brian Leiter, "Intellectual Voyeurism in Legal Scholarship," *Yale Journal of Law & the Humanities* 4 (1992): 79–104, 80.

39 Jack Balkin, "Interdisciplinarity as Colonization," *Washington and Lee Law Review* 53 (1996): 949–970.

40 See also Jane Baron, "The Rhetoric of Law and Literature: a sceptical view," *Cardozo Law Review* 26 (2005): 2273–2281.

41 James Boyd White, *Justice as Translation* (Chicago: University of Chicago Press, 1990), 14.

42 Karlheinz Stierle, "Translatio Studii and Renaissance: from vertical to horizontal translation," in *The Translatability of Cultures, figurations of the space between*, eds. Sanford Budick and Wolfgang Iser (Stanford: Stanford University Press, 1996), 55–67, 55.

43 Thomas O. Beebee, "Can Law-and-Humanities Survive Systems Theory?" *Law & Literature* 22.2 (2010): 244–268. Beebee (246, n,5) refers to Domna C. Stanton's article 'Foreword: ANDs, Ins and BUTs', *Publications of the Modern Language Association* 121 (2006): 1518, in which Stanton seeks a *tertium translationis* to link human rights to the humanities via the historical conceptual connections existing between them in humanism.

more importantly, how are we going to adapt or reconstruct the plot for the future? We must probe our own disciplinary pre-judices lest we present academic simulations based on ideas that we already firmly held before our act of cooperation. I say so because the question of a European perspective returns with a vengeance when we broaden the field to *Law and Culture.* Robin West, for example, has recently argued that while these past fifteen years, *Law and Culture* has overshadowed *Law and Literature*, this has not led to a take-over of the critical function of *Law and Literature.*[44] To date, or so West claims, *Law and Culture* is unfortunately more an outgrowth than a successor of *Law and Literature*, with analogous connections between its two constitutive components.[45] She starts by distinguishing three logically possible relations between law and literature as traditionally explored in *Law and Literature*: first, the literary project in which law is seen as the subject matter of literature as a result of which literature is read for the value of the insights it gives into law; secondly, the jurisprudential project that looks upon literature as the narrative root of law; and lastly, the hermeneutic project in which law is seen as literature as far as interpretation is concerned. To West, *Law and Culture* has developed comparable projects in 'law *as* a form of culture' and 'culture *as* law' (italics mine), but not as yet a cultural analog to 'law in literature'. West deplores that 'There has been no systematic treatment, of which I'm aware, of the possibility that cultural products, no matter how defined or conceived, might actually contain distinctive jurisprudential insights into the nature of law that might significantly inform jurisprudential debates.'[46] In short, *Law and Culture* lacks the *paideic* aim that Law *and Literature* promotes. The examples she gives to illustrate her various points are all taken from American *Law and Culture*, from tv series such as LA Law, CSI, The Sopranos and Ally McBeal, to a rape case at Duke University and Tom Wolfe's *I am*

---

[44] Robin West, "Literature, Culture, and Law – at Duke University," *Georgetown Law Faculty Working Papers* (2008), http://scholarship.law.georgetown.edu/fwps_papers/75 <accessed 5 August 2010>. Also, *Teaching Law and Literature* eds. Cathrine O. Frank and Matthew Anderson (forthcoming).

[45] I tend to agree with West. See, for example, the contributions to, *Law and Popular Culture*, ed. Michael Freeman (Oxford: OUP, 2004).

[46] West, "Literature, Culture," 15–16. William MacNeil recently filled this gap with *Lex Populi. The Jurisprudence of Popular Culture* (Stanford: Stanford University Press, 2007), a study aimed at recontextualisation of jurisprudence from the specialist to the generalist interpretive community by means of a new 'intertext' in order to rethink the culture of law and the law of culture (2). Not only does MacNeil propose to read popular culture jurisprudentially, he actually shows that and how jurisprudence is read by popular culture, i.e. different from legal methodologies. Here is the *paideic* aspect that West claims is missing.

Charlotte Simmons. One may argue, of course, that such cultural artifacts are well known in Europe, but here too American *Law and Culture* is held up as normative.[47] So Greta Olson's advocacy of interdisciplinary studies geared to the European background and context deserves equal application in this new field, if we agree that popular culture contributes to the mental frames through which we perceive our (his)tories.[48] At the same time we should both cherish, as Montaigne told us to, the art of seeing things from different perspectives, and, at least as far as I am concerned, think of culture in the way that James Boyd White throughout his works has consistently argued, i.e., as a form of thought and life that deserves our serious dialogue rather than fierce contestation.

On this view, Helle Porsdam who as a cultural historian advocates broadening *Law and Literature* into *Law and Humanities*, offers a timely argument when she asks us to 'wonder what 'Law and Literature' looks like in a civil-law context. What happens when the texts discussed are Scandinavian, Dutch or Polish, and what happens when these texts interact, not with the common law but with the civil law?'[49] In saying so, she opposes common-law to civil-law methodology, but she too runs the risk of reaffirming a false opposition when she continues her argument saying that 'C]ivil law starts with certain abstract rules, that is, which judges must then apply to concrete cases', whereas common-law adjudication focuses on specific cases and emphasizes the judge's practical wisdom. As I argued above, this is an extremely

---

47 The same goes I would say for Richard K. Sherwin, the author of the seminal *When Law Goes Pop, the vanishing line between law and popular culture* (Chicago: University of Chicago Press, 2000) and the architect of the important rising field of law and visual literacy. In his introductory essay on the interpenetration of law and popular culture in the edited volume Popular Culture and Law, ed. Richard K. Sherwin (Farnham: Ashgate, 2006), see also http://ssrn.com/abstract=1004740 <accessed 1 september 2010>, he sketches the development as one going on in law since the heyday of legal realism and includes as elements of the strand of law and popular culture other fields such as Law and Literature, Critical Race Studies, Critical Legal Studies and Legal Feminism, as well as the interrelation between law and journalism, sports, and music. Such an all-encompassing outlook on law and culture is typically US-based – and how can it be otherwise, given Sherwin's cultural contexts? – and it cannot be translated to the European context without modifications.

48 Precisely because, as William MacNeil points out, cultural legal studies have inaugurated 'a free-for – all … in its hitherto decorous law-and-lit debates' (*Lex Populi*, at 6). Why, I would suggest, not take as our scholarly topic films such as the French *L'ivresse du poivoir* or *La dixième chambre*?

49 Helle Porsdam, *From Civil to Human Rights, Dialogues on Law and Humanities in the United States and Europe* (Northampton: Edward Elgar Publishing, 2009), 174.

oversimplified and partly incorrect view on what judges do in civil-law countries. Her discussion of the move from *Law and Literature* to *Law and Humanities* ends on a very intriguing note that may well prove to be a good starting point for our continued discussion, because it deals with justice rather than (just) law: 'Were I to hazard a guess as to what the future may bring … I would say that we will be seeing more research on legal positivism and its possible effects on culture (and vice versa) coming out of European law and humanities circles.'[50] Porsdam says so in the context of the source of inspiration that (the success of) the European Court of Human Rights and the European Court of Justice can be to scholars who are 'inspired by their American colleagues to see in law the possibility for making the fight for a better world more effective.'[51]

I fully agree with her observation that the case law of European Court of Human Rights is a source of self-understanding.[52] When we address the problems of the unity and diversity of societies and legal systems within the European Union together with those arising from globalization in other ways, from the digitalization of human life to terrorism and everything in between, we are invited to reflect on the demands of legality, the legitimacy of law and judicial decisions and what better way to do that in the European context than by reading the decisions of the Court of Justice of the European Community or the European Human Rights Court as proposals for the shape and contents of the European community at the supranational level, allowing, of course, for local variety within reasonable range.[53] And we can also read how people locate themselves by means of stories, and consequently, what their narratives can mean in law. When a national court refers to the European Community Court for a preliminary ruling under one of the articles of the EEC Treaty, it asks a question on a point of European law, the answer to which will not only be normative for the national court in question, but for the European community at large. And exactly because deci-

---

50 Porsdam, *From Civil to Human Rights*, 180.

51 Porsdam, *From Civil to Human Rights*, 181.

52 Porsdam, *From Civil to Human Rights*, 69.

53 Think, for example, of the different interpretations of the term 'family life' under the articles 8 and 12 of the European Convention for the Protection of Human Rights, including a variety of human relations, not merely the traditional marriage bond, and compare these to art.41.1 of the Irish Constitution which recognizes the family as 'the natural primary and fundamental unit group of Society' and art.41.3.1 which protects the institution of marriage 'on which the Family is founded', thereby dismissing family units consisting of homosexual or unmarried couples.

sions of these supranational courts are proposals for the European community, the question after the judicial ethos that permeates the decision becomes even more relevant when a decision in a specific case is experienced not only as a legal mistake in the technical sense, but as one that is morally doubtful. So research into historical cross-sections of a field of law, both nationally and internationally, will prove most interesting also for purposes of comparative law. Here too a dialogue with American *Law and Literature* is called for if we acknowledge the tendency, perceived as early as 1991 by Mary Ann Glendon in her *Rights Talk: the impoverishment of political discourse*,[54] of American courts to take a turn in the direction of a more dogmatic stance, whereas European courts are well on their way to develop a new and truly European common law. The rise of such a common law strongly suggests its foundation on equitable standards.

Porsdam's sketch of the future project of *Law and Humanities* then ends by suggesting that such development may lead the legalist camp to harden its fight against beliefs in natural law, a fight for which *Law and Humanities* may provide the forum. I would be somewhat hesitant to connect a renaissance, if any, of natural law thought to a theory of law that includes morality generally, even more so given, on the one hand, the development of EHCR case law with an increase of decisions pertaining to the values and ideals of law (think only of the effects of the Salduz decision (EHRC, 27 November 2008, *Salduz v. Turkey*) on the principle of fair trial as expressed in article 6 of the EHRC in democratic societies under the rule of law, combined with the different ideas on what the rule of law contains, depending on the common law or civil law perspective) and, on the other hand, because with the Hart-Fuller debate on the separation of law and morals long behind us, the number of card-carrying diehards of legal positivism in the field of legal theory has dramatically decreased. Nevertheless, Porsdam's suggestion may be an incentive to re-address the topic of how we imagine European identities, legal and other.

Contemporary pluralism in law and society strongly suggest the need for a study of unity and diversity at different levels, with attention to the traditions that brought us where we are. To this end, *Law and Literature* and/or *Law and Culture*, or *Law and Humanities* for that matter, may function as an umbrella concept in that it can function as a heuristic device of translatability of disciplines and cultures, one that allows a contextualist rather than universalist view of human responsibility. In order to reflect literary, legal, and cultural preoccupations, *Law and Literature* would therefore do well learn to think

[54] Mary Ann Glendon, *Rights Talk: the impoverishment of political discourse* (New York: The Free Press, 1991).

even more comparatively on the theoretical and the practical level of interdisciplinary findings. For this project I advocate that we take the title of Learned Hand's often quoted address literally and think of the humanities as sources of tolerance',[55] arguing, as Ian Ward does, for a legal humanism which offers 'a narrative supplement in the various practices of law and jurisprudence.'[56] A revival of humanism, whether within or without *Law and Literature*, is indeed called for in my opinion, and the same goes for our continued effort to understand interdisciplinary movements.

A broad project of cultural inquiry encompassing the whole range of humanities therefore seems the best option. I say so also given the current politico-legal issues concerning the way in which to deal best with religious and/or cultural differences within Europe, bringing to mind that behind the foundation of 'Europe' since 1648 there was and has always been the trauma of overcoming religious differences. One form this may take is an interdisciplinary approach with a historical focus in order to enhance our knowledge and understanding of our national past and that of our partners in the treaty that is the European Union, and to provide a space in which cultural translation can take place.[57] Such an approach also leaves ample room for methodological integration and collaboration on the subject of practice(s).

To give just one other example of the kind of research we may embark upon: in the Netherlands, a development of broadening Renaissance literary studies to include interdisciplinary research is in full swing. I had the good fortune to be invited to participate in such a project on the subject of the Dutch playwright and poet Joost van den Vondel. I found that there is a valuable starting point for further comparative literary-legal studies in the civic tradition of research on how literary texts contribute to the foundation of a nation, one that has recently been augmented by Brook Thomas in *Civic Myths, a Law-and-Literature approach to citizenship* where he while, 'not claiming that law is the key that will unlock all of the mysteries of works of literature

---

[55] Learned Billings Hand, "Sources of Tolerance" *University of Pennsylvania Law Review* 79 (1930): 1–14.

[56] Ian Ward, "Narrative Jurisprudence and Trans-national Justice," *Texas Weslyan Law Review* 12 (2005): 155–187, 185. In doing so he refers to William Twining's argument that the challenge of globalization drives us towards a revitalized notion of *ius humanitatis*, one that deals "with the common heritage of mankind," (157, note 18 referring to William Twining, *Globalisation and Legal Theory* (Cambridge: CUP, 2000), 50–51).

[57] See also Brook Thomas, "National Literary Histories: Imagined Communities or Imagined Societies?" *Modern Language Quarterly* 64.2 (2003): 137–152, on how the idea of a cultural nation with a sense of national identity is not restricted to sovereign states.

or that literature is the key that will open up a full understanding of the law', convincingly shows how the '"the Founding fathers of American literary nationalism" created a usable past for a nation that lacked one.'[58] Thomas also shows the importance of a critical attitude towards the past, given the danger of reading teleologically and thereby preserving the very myth that is in need of clarification. A literary-legal interpretation is not supposed to be a denial of the rule of law either; it should dramatise various conflicts citizens subject to law have to confront, explore dilemmas, and interweave legal and literary analysis. And he is right when he says, 'the increased fluidity of national boundaries does affect citizenship.'[59] Especially now that territorial boundaries dissolve, by legal measures or by technological innovations such as the Internet, a shared politico-legal culture can provide the cement for modern nations, moving beyond criteria such as ethnicity or shared religious roots. Furthermore, we lack an overarching discussion of European sovereign power so far, i.e. one comparable with discussions on national sovereignties.

So how, for example, does the literature of a period further exercise the public imagination? Blair Worden's recent study on Milton would suggest a comparative study of Lucifer in Milton and Vondel, the historically salient issue of religious and legal dispute being present in both authors' works.[60] For British law and literature of the Stuart era, Elliot Visconsi has recently taken up the subject of the fictionalisation of law, or *mythopoesis*.[61] He aims to show how a playwright like Dryden helped fashion the nation. Visconsi's suggestion that emotional identification is central to most early modern models of political obligation may be of interest for further research on the narrative ethos of early modern writers, when law and literature are integrated in a cultural moment, as is the case in Vondel. I would also suggest research on the theme of the *auctoritas poetarum*, the authority in matters of truth and fact that the humanists ascribed to poets as much as to philos-

---

58 Brook Thomas, *Civic Myths, a Law-and-Literature approach to citizenship* (Chapel Hill: University of North Carolina Press, 2007), i and 20, endnote omitted. Also of interest is Penelope J. Pether, "Comparative Constitutional Epics," *Law & Literatur*, 21.1 (2009): 106–128. See also Friederike Alvermann Ronge, *To write in defense of the legal constitution* (Hildesheim: Georg Olms Verlag, 1993) on how jurists played a crucial role in fashioning the modern nation in eighteenth century Europe.

59 Thomas, *Civic Myths*, 1.

60 Blair Worden, *Literature and Politics in Cromwellian England. John Milton, Andrew Marvell, Marchamont Nedham* (Oxford: OUP, 2007).

61 Elliot Visconsi, *Lines of Equity, Literature and the Origins of Law in Later Stuart England* (Ithaca and London: Cornell University Press, 2008).

ophers and scholars. The unity of law, literature, and historiography, once presumed to exist, can be an interesting subject for consideration in interdisciplinary studies today now that we are faced with new questions of authority and authorship in the digital world where the idea of 'text' as the product of explicitly volitional authorial design seems to become obsolete, with obvious consequences for such concepts as copyright. This suggests a joint effort to address the broader theme of the dominant epistemology and history of ideas of a period. It also opens up the possibility for a further sophistication of the traditional strand of 'law *in* literature' in the form of attention to the law of fiction in both law and literature and to the fiction of the enterprises of law and literature themselves, so that law *in* literature can be studied not only for its descriptive aspect – an indication of how the law is perceived by those external to it – but also for its prescriptive aspect. In short, we should take to heart that lessons from the past can be taken as *paideic* when it comes to establishing unity and solidarity in Europe and act on that notion in our combined studies in law and the humanities.

II. History, Memory and Human Rights

Jay Winter
(Yale University)

Human Rights and the Second World War

One of the most important consequences of the Second World War was the emergence of a new European approach to the balance between the state and the individual. In this essay, I want to highlight the way in which exile politics in London between 1939 and 1945 provided the framework for this new approach to rights. Out of protests by governments and individuals in exile over the crimes being committed daily on the Continent from 1939 on, there emerged a set of war aims which placed human rights at the heart of the post-war international order. The men and women who drafted these documents did so at a time when no one could have predicted an Allied victory in the war. And yet during those desperate hours, during the Blitz, and against the backdrop of Nazi crimes, a new human rights regime was born.

Such an outcome was unprecedented and to a large degree unanticipated. And yet it gives a new meaning to the notion that the Second World War was a war of liberation. Not in Poland, not in Czechoslovakia, not in Hungary, caution historians of Eastern Europe. One form of imprisonment succeeded another. But if we adopt a longer time horizon, perhaps the notion of the 1939–45 conflict as a war of liberation can be defended, and not just for the remains of the Jewish population of Europe who survived the Final Solution. Theirs was liberation pure and simple. The human rights regime of the 1940s was both an over-ground and an underground river; on the surface it froze during the Cold War. But there were other slower, more indirect ways in which human rights liberated Europe. May 1968 was a plea in many registers for liberation, from South America to Vietnam. The Prague spring of the same year gave liberation a human (and socialist) face; even after it was suppressed, Charter 77 resumed the struggle, without socialism. So did Solidarity in Poland, and so did the Helsinki accords of the 1970s, yielding a tradeoff between the recognition internationally of the Soviet Union's western borders and Western surveillance of human rights violations in the Soviet Union itself. It would be absurd to claim that human rights brought down the Soviet empire, and yet the courage of Soviet dissidents was part of a much wider process begun, I believe, decades earlier. The *longue durée* does matter in international history, as the story of the unfolding of the human rights movement in the mid-twentieth century and after shows.

Who were the carriers of this message? Who were the human rights activists of the generation of the Second World War? Some were ex-soldiers, veterans of the Great War who found a way to continue the struggle they endured in one war in the harsh conditions of another. Among them was the French jurist René Cassin, whose contribution to this story is at the core of this essay.

It may be surprising that I focus on the role of old soldiers. The primary reason for proverbial raised eyebrows at this claim is the tendency of scholars to work from an American or from a German perspective to probe the political outlook and pressure of veterans group over the last century. In that optic, veterans are overwhelmingly patriotic, conservative, or reactionary. Their experience of war or of preparation for war makes them authoritarian, illiberal, or natural supporters of right-wing or extreme right-wing political parties and movements.[1]

What happens if we choose a different optic, a French one, and juxtapose it to the conventional view? In some respects, there is evidence of right-wing or extreme right-wing tendencies among some French veterans, like Jean Marie Le Pen of the *Front National*, or the inter-war *Croix de feu*, or among the O.A.S. assassins who tried and failed several times to kill de Gaulle after his *volte face* on Algerian independence in 1959. But in other respects, French history provides a long and well-documented alternative narrative that today remains in the shadows. It tells a story of a different kind, that of a mass movement of pacifist veterans, millions of them, who from the 1870s to 1940, saw military service as the shield of the Republic.[2] It arises in the late nineteenth century in the cry of Jean Jaurès for *La nouvelle armée.* It moves to the left in revulsion over the anti-Republican and Catholic cabal to convict, imprison and forget Colonel Dreyfus. It rails against the use of troops as strike-breakers, but virtually to a man, answers the call-up of 1 August 1914 and fights to the bitter end. Thousands of 'trouble makers' on the left to be arrested so that mobilization can go forward peacefully in 1914 could not be found. Why? Because they had already joined up.[3]

---

1 The literature on veterans movements is vast. For a start, see "War generation: veterans of the First World War," ed. Stephen R. Ward (Port Washington, N.Y.: Kennikat Press, 1975).

2 On this subject, the *locus classicus* is Antoine Prost, *Les Anciens combattants et la société française, 1914–1939*, 3 vols. (Paris: Presses de la Fondation nationale de la science politique, 1977).

3 Jean-Jacques Becker, *Le carnet B; les pouvoirs publics et l'antimilitarisme avant la guerre de 1914* (Paris: Klincksieck, 1973).

During the war itself, many of these men worked to create a veterans movement with two central objectives. The first was decent treatment for the wounded and a decent pension for the demobilized. The second was the abolition of war. Perhaps 60 percent of the roughly eight million men who served in French forces joined these organizations. These were not the voices of parliamentary politics, but of an extra-parliamentary movement, the membership of which came from small market towns and villages – what we call *La France profonde.* Their voices were heard throughout the inter-war years and beyond, and while they were never univocal, they carried an unmistakable pacifist message.[4]

In the short-term, their cause failed miserably. Betrayed by their own illusions, by their belief in reaching out to ex-servicemen in Italy and Germany, even to Mussolini and Hitler themselves, they were left in 1940 with a taste as of ashes. Their story is one of political bankruptcy, to be sure.

And yet, that is not the end of the story. Out of the veterans movement to outlaw war came another crusade, one privileging the rights of soldiers, of the wounded and the unemployed, within the framework of human rights. Drawing on elements of the French revolutionary tradition, and the Universal Declarations of Human Rights of 1789 and 1793, French veterans created a new form of the human rights message, one which arose out of the catastrophe of the Second World War. The passage from the struggle for dignity in and after one world war to an even more profound and long-lasting commitment to human rights after a second world war is the subject of this paper.

The defeat of inter-war soldiers' pacifism was a prelude to their longer-term victory. In the post-1945 period and beyond a number of First World War veterans found ways to reconfigure successfully their message. There is a line that connects the pacifist movement arising from the First World War to the Universal Declaration of Human Rights to the Helsinki accords to Charter 77 and to the fall of the Berlin wall and the Soviet Union. It was not the work of one man but of many men and women who affirmed that the defense of human rights was the best way to preserve peace. One such individual was the French jurist and Nobel laureate René Cassin. I want to use his story to illuminate a broader one, a paradoxical story of failure and transcendence in the period of the two world wars and beyond.

---

4 See Antoine Prost, "Combattants et politiciens: Le discourse mythologique sur la politique entre les deux guerres," *Le Mouvement social* 85, Langage et idéologies: Le Discours comme objet de l'histoire. (October-December 1973), 117–54.

Most accounts of the emergence of today's international human rights regime locate its emergence as a response to the barbarities of the Nazi regime.[5] There is much truth in this assertion, but it is not the whole truth. In some respects, the core idea of human rights – that state sovereignty is not unlimited – emerged in response to the First World War and provided a point of departure for those finally persuaded after 1945 that *raison d'état* is not and can never be the *ultima ratio* or the *prima ratio* of the international order. The message of this earlier human rights movement, driven by veterans organizations, is that Leviathan states which trample on the rights of their citizens are a threat to peace. Sooner or later they will trample on the rights by trampling on the territory of other states. Wherever and whenever the notion of state sovereignty is treated as an absolute, there lies a threat to the dignity of ordinary people and a threat to peace.

Consider this paradox. A war to defend territoriality in 1914–18, in response to the Austrian invasion of Serbia and the German invasion of Belgium and France, set in motion forces which, 25 years later, helped undermine the notion that territorial states are each a law unto themselves. The resolution of the apparent contradiction is that total war created the conditions which brought into being an idea of limited state sovereignty, sovereignty limited by a human rights regime superior to national law. During the Second World War, this idea moved from the realm of the utopian to the realm of politics and in particular the politics of retribution for Nazi crimes. The preparation while the fighting was still going on for war crimes trials and for a successor to the moribund League of Nations framed both innovations within a commitment to base the peace to come on a commitment to human rights. That commitment was embodied in the Charter of the United Nations and adumbrated in the Convention on Genocide and in the Universal Declaration of Human Rights, approved by the United Nations assembled in Paris sixty years ago, on 9 and 10 December 1948.

Before 1933

How did veterans contribute to this set of events? I will tell this story in three parts. The first is located within the 1914–18 conflict. The second is a feature of the inter-war period. The third is an element of wartime resistance and post-war planning during and after the Second World War.

---

[5] Mary Ann Glendon, *A world made new: Eleanor Roosevelt and the Universal Declaration of Human Rights* (New York: Random House, 2001).

First the Great War. During the 1914–18 conflict, and especially at the outset of the conflict, soldiers who bled for their country were maltreated in ways hard to believe today. Part of the source of their misery was military incompetence of the kind recently documented in Walter Reed Hospital. No preparation, no forethought, nothing but callous bureaucratic ineptitude.

It is worth pausing for a moment to locate this problem in a longer timescale. When the Great War broke out in 1914, the International Red Cross was already 55 years old. Founded by Henri Dunant, who was horrified by the sight of wounded men left to suffer or die on the Battlefield of Solferino in 1859, the Red Cross had created codes of conduct which gave to the wounded the right to be treated and cared for. These rights extended to prisoners of war as well, and were human rights. They did not arise out of citizenship or other affiliation. They were the property of all men. The code of conduct drawn up by Francis Lieber in 1863 for the Union armies was based on the same set of assumptions.

International humanitarian law emerged from the nineteenth-century battlefield. The laws of war were codified in the Geneva Convention of 1864 for the amelioration of the condition in armies in the field and in the Hague Conventions of 1899 (Convention II) and 1907 (Convention IV). These conventions drew on earlier currents in the abolitionist movement to deepen a natural rights human law tradition. In this tradition, we have duties to the wounded not as a function of citizenship but as a matter of humanity.[6]

In the First World War, this set of obligations was in place, but it did not apply to the wounded of your own side. Let me illustrate this point in the case of René Cassin, who founded the French veterans movement to ensure that the wounded received decent treatment and later a decent pension from the state that sent them off to battle.

In August 1914 René Cassin was a 26-year old lawyer, born in Bayonne to a prominent Jewish family living in the south west of the country. The outbreak of war found him in Paris, from which he immediately journeyed south to join the 311th Infantry Regiment in Aix.[7] In September he was promoted to the rank of corporal and served near St Mihiel. He remained in this sector, where on 12 October, he was ordered to take a squad of 16 men and advance towards a German strong point near Chauvencourt on the outskirts of

---

6 Geoffrey Best, *Humanity in warfare* (New York: Columbia University Press, 1980).

7 Souvenirs de la campagne 1914–1915. (Paris) Archives Nationales. 382AP/1. These memoirs were composed about a year after the outbreak of the war. Cassin wrote that they constituted a "Temoignage vécu, à l'histoire d'une campagne d'un de ligne au cours de la guerre franco-allemande".

St Mihiel. German emplacements made such a probe suicidal. All 16 men in his unit were hit by flanking fire from well-entrenched machine guns and artillery. He himself was hit in his side, his abdomen and his left arm. He knew that a stomach wound was almost always fatal. Cassin refused evacuation, but told a passing soldier to inform their commander of the strength of the German positions in his sector. In addition he begged this man, Sergeant-Quartermaster Canestrier, to write to Cassin's father that he had died painlessly (which was a lie) and to send to his family a leather cigarette case, two gold pieces of 100 francs and some small bills. Canestrier vanished, and so did Cassin's valuables.

Clearly Cassin thought he would never survive. He asked a priest if someone could say Hebrew prayers with him. The priest replied that his prayers were for everyone, and gave him the benefit of his company.[8] Somehow, he got through the night, and was then handed over to the French army medical services.

The way these units were organized in the early days of the war almost killed him. The rule was that on mobilization you reported to your regiment, in whatever region you were assigned. After battle, you returned to *that* site, either intact, wounded, or in a coffin. Cassin would not be treated in the north east of France, but in Provence, 600 kilometres away. He was sent by wagon and then by train south, and after a journey of 2–3 days arrived in the regiment's hospital in Antibes on the Mediterranean. There surgeons were astonished to see that he was still alive, despite the fact that his abdomen had been torn to shreds. Cassin had been wise enough to drink virtually nothing on the trip. They then told him that his case was critical, and that they did not know if he would survive more than a few hours. That meant they did not have time to anesthetize him, but needed to operate immediately. This Cassin accepted, and somehow endured an hour under the surgeon's knife. He later said he was fortunate that the operation was on a less than sensitive part of his anatomy.

While in convalescence, he wrote the story of his service, and framed it in terms of a conventional French patriot and a Jew. One of the Jewish men with whom he served had told him that a Jew had to be more courageous than others in order to evade accusations of cowardice. This bravery was Cassin's trademark. But for our purposes what is intriguing in his own narrative is how laconic it is. He nowhere dwells on the hideousness of being wounded, of the incompetence of his own medical service, of the appalling cruelty inflicted on him by it. His train journey alone, holding his intestines

---

8 382AP/1, Guerre 14–18, Souvenirs de la campagne 1914–1915.

in his stomach with great difficulty, is a middle passage which might have broken many other men. He saw and felt what battle was, and yet managed to frame his part in it without feeling that it had undermined his own identity.

The courage of his war service was palpable, but so was the miserable treatment he received. This was hardly exceptional among the wounded or among those disabled and discharged. What followed his convalescence was a fight not against the enemies of the French state, but against the callous, inhuman bureaucracy of the French state itself. He was a founder of the French veterans movement, and worked tirelessly to assure that men who had been wounded in the service of their country would have a decent pension, or that the orphans of the men who did not return would be given a start in their lives.[9] This work brought him up against recalcitrant and indifferent authorities. These rights were earned, not only by military service and the shedding of blood, but thereafter by harsh political struggle. French veterans, like others in Europe, were given their pensions grudgingly, not as a right but as a privilege, wrested from the hands of unfeeling administrators and the physicians who served them.

This struggle for natural justice for the lame, the halt and the blind, for men who had answered their countries' call, but then found that few were prepared to heed the voices of the wounded, created something new in European affairs – a pacifist veterans movement. The notion of soldier pacifists may seem like a contradiction in terms, but in inter-war France it was not at all oxymoronic. French Republicans like Cassin saw it as their life's work to ensure that their sons would not have to enter *la boucherie* – the slaughterhouse – of modern warfare. They knew what it had been like and were determined that the young would be spared the fate they had suffered. In striking contrast to the myth of the war experience and lies about the nobility of armed conflict conjured up by the Nazis – veterans too – the French *ancien combattant* movement made war on war. On 11 November they marched to the war memorials in every tiny village; they did so in civilian dress and deliberately out of step. They had been civilians in uniform, and they bore a message from their comrades who had died to the young: war must never return.[10]

This political program was crippled from the start. The focus of the veterans movement in France was justice for their brethren, and for the widows

---

9 382 AP/10 Anciens combattants.

10 Marc Agi, *De l'idée d'universalité comme fondatrice du concept des droits de l'homme d'après la vie et l'oeuvre de René Cassin.* Thèse pour le doctorat d'État, Université de Nice, 10 December 1979. (Antibes: Éditions Alp'azur, 1980).

and orphans they had left behind. But their mission extended into the field of international relations as well, and that meant struggling with and through the League of Nations.

As a leader of the French veterans movement, Cassin had much to do with the International Labor Organization (ILO), headed by Albert Thomas, the successor to Jean Jaurès, assassinated leader of the French Socialist party. This association, building on welfare work in munitions factories in wartime, was committed to ensuring the right to work of all those disabled in the war. On 2 September 1921, Cassin was present at an international veterans discussion of work for war invalids. The meeting was sponsored by the ILO in Geneva. Cassin represented the largest French veterans movement, *l'Union Fédérale*, with one million members, and it was at this venue that he and his colleagues met for the first time enemy veterans from the defeated Central Powers. Such contacts convinced Cassin that veterans had to work together with their former enemies and within the League of Nations if their voice was to be heard in international affairs.

Here is Cassin's point of entry into politics of a very peculiar kind. It was a kind of non-political politics, filled with contradictions that ultimately destroyed it. Cassin was among a host of French veterans who felt that their vision was *above* politics. These were angry men, men who had formed what they termed the generation of fire, and were not prepared simply to let the old merry go round of politics go on its way. Politics was a word they used as an insult, and they played with it and mutated it into a host of venomous rhetorical forms, all filled with vitriol: *politicaille, 'politicailler', 'politicaillerie' 'politicaillon'*: roughly translated as the following: political scum, criminal rabble, wily, shady, scandal-ridden, little piggies at the trough, vulgar, partisan, blood-sucking shits. The vulgarity of this language is not to be missed: we are dealing with ex-soldiers here, and however high-minded their motives, their anger descended to the gutter where they believed their opponents, the politicians, were to be found.[11]

How to get around them without joining in their miserable game was an open question. Cassin refused the offer of a post in the Cabinet of Herriot who came to power as head of a left-center coalition in 1924. Instead, Cassin was glad to join the French delegation to the League of Nations, as the representative of the veterans movement, as if that institution were free of all the faults of politics at home.

At the same time, he took the initiative in establishing an international veterans organization, CIAMAC, which met for the first time at Geneva in

---

[11] Prost, 'Combattants et politiciens', passim.

September 1926.[12] This body emerged from earlier discussions among veterans from both sides in the war, men who were committed to coming together to discuss matters of common interest. The German delegates from the *Reichsbund* affirmed their commitment to Republican values. They accepted the need to pay reparations and to contribute to the reconstruction of devastated regions, all as steps to reassure allied ex-servicemen that they too wanted to preserve the peace. Italian, Polish, Austrian, and British delegates joined them, and went on in later meetings to share information through the ILO on questions of pensions, work placement, and on medical and orthopedic assistance for veterans. Belgian and Yugoslav veterans joined in these discussions. When the Dawes plan regularized reparations payments, the political conditions were ripe for more formal discussions about the formation of an international organization of veterans associations. Initially 80 delegates from 10 nations and 20 associations came to the inaugural meeting, and committed themselves to working for the principle of mandatory arbitration of international conflicts. Here was a body unattached to their governments, able to speak out with the moral authority earned by military service and sacrifice.

Annual meetings were held in the later 1920s in Vienna, Berlin, Warsaw, and Paris. They had no difficulty in integrating German delegates, whose commitment to peace was unquestioned. It was harder to bring Soviet veterans to the table, since the war had been entirely eclipsed by the 1917 revolution.

This set of initiatives was part of the political culture surrounding the League of Nations. Veterans like Cassin argued that repairing the physical damage caused by the war was a first step towards repairing the moral damage it caused. Their task was political education at home and the lessening of enmity between former enemies. They were committed to making the League of Nations as powerful as possible an obstacle to war. That is why their distance from foreign offices was essential: these men spoke over the heads of governments to the millions of men and women whose lives and families had been disfigured by war. They spoke to youth who did not know what war was, and urged them to join in their international crusade for peace.

Their main aim was what we have come to term moral rearmament. By that Cassin meant that those who knew war had to educate the public as to the horrors of violence and the absolute necessity to save the new generation from the catastrophe of another war. This could not be done within the boundaries of one country alone, or solely among the victors. That is why he

---

12 382AP/10, Cassin's report on the Commission de la Paix sur la CIAMAC.

bypassed the more conservative Inter-allied Veterans Federation (FIDAC), which had no truck with the idea that German and Austrian veterans had to be brought into the conversation. Bridges had to be built, but with prior agreement on certain clear principles about the way to preserve the peace.[13]

All these efforts were marked by both the strengths and the weakness of the League of Nations. Cassin's first speech was on international intellectual cooperation, and wearing his hat as a Professor of Law in Paris, he worked to transform the League of Nations from a forum for world peace into a quasi-juridical assembly.[14] One starting point in this effort was the construction of a center for international intellectual cooperation, an idea sponsored by Henri Bergson, and the direct antecedent of UNESCO. The mid-point was the construction of a protocol for the peaceful resolution of international disputes through arbitration. Once drafted and approved, the League would reach the end point, as a kind of high court of international justice, a tribunal, whose moral authority would rest in large part on the support of tens of millions of veterans, who knew a thing or two about war. "A world marked by the blood we shed would do well to accept the imprint of our ideas", he noted.[15]

Disarmament was one of them. Cassin served on the French delegation to the League of Nations for 14 years, from 1924 to 1938, and much of his work in this body concerned arbitration and disarmament. "It isn't enough", he wrote in 1929, that veterans are represented at the League. What mattered more is that "in each nation burned by the war, organizations develop public opinion and that of youth to struggle against the mundane and the murderous language" of armaments and national defence. Only then can they "stand for the principles of Geneva: the defence of peace and security".[16]

It was during his service at Geneva that Cassin began to formulate notions which ultimately bore fruit in the Universal Declaration of Human Rights. In Geneva Cassin had a front-row view of the fragility of an institution which challenged the supremacy of state sovereignty as a principle of international political order. He saw how entrenched were conventional approaches to unbridled state power as the *ultima ratio* of international affairs. No one could question his patriotism, but he had no time for what he termed

13 382AP/14 Rapport de René Cassin à la Commission de la Paix sur la CIAMAC, 1931.

14 382AP/14 League of Nations. Speech on disarmament to League of Nations, September 1929.

15 Marc Agi, *René Cassin, 1887–1976. Prix Nobel de la Paix* (Paris: Perrin, 1998), 54, 57.

16 AP382/14 League of Nations, René Cassin, La xè assemblée vue par un ancien combattant, *Le Journal*, 13 October 1929.

"the ordinary obstinacy of old ideas which, in the name of the absolute sovereignty of states flow directly into the construction of armaments, to the politics of prestige, and then to war".[17]

Cassin discerned that there was an immense gap between the thought of conventional nationalists like Clemenceau or Henry Cabot Lodge and the notions of those like Briand or Wilson, who were prepared to sacrifice some elements of state sovereignty to the League of Nations, if that were the necessary price to erase war from the international political agenda. In the first round, Lodge won the argument, and older notions of state sovereignty prevailed. If a more robust League of Nations it or any similar venture would ever succeed, it would do so only after a sea change had occurred in both academic and popular notions of the indivisible sovereignty of the state, and of the power of the duly elected statesman, acting like a *châtelain dans son château.*

Two major events led to the undermining or refashioning of this older definition of sovereignty. The first was the Nazi constitutional and lawful seizure of power in 1933; the second was the transformation of the French state in 1940 legally under Pétain and Laval. These episodes would open the door to a new kind of thinking on state sovereignty, and we will arrive at these developments in a moment. But for our purposes, it is important to note how Cassin – among others – was active long before these two political earthquakes in the effort to provide an alternative view of state sovereignty. And that view ultimately bore fruit in the 1948 Universal Declaration of Human Rights.

Cassin made the argument explicit in the course of a series of lectures he gave in 1930 at the Academy of International Law in The Hague.[18] His title was 'The new conception of domicile in the resolution of conflicts of law'. His aim was to 'desacralize' claims of state sovereignty. Only thereby, he believed, was it possible to create an environment in which the all powerful state cannot by its own fiat and with impunity trample on the rights of the individual.

Before turning to the structure of the argument, it is useful to note the echoes of Cassin's earlier battles. He joined up in defense of a state whose meanness to the disabled men it had sent out to fight had to be resisted through a vigorous campaign originating in civil society. That struggle first for and then against the state is a stance to which Cassin returned throughout his life. It ensured that he would resist conventional views of political

---

[17] AP382/14 League of Nations, Speech on disarmament, September 1929.

[18] René Cassin, "La nouvelle conception du domicile dans le règlement des conflits de lois" (*Académie de droit international, the Hague. Receuil des Cours*, 1930), 658–809.

authority and state sovereignty and look to revising them in order to establish a just order.

In The Hague, he sketched out how such a new system might operate. To this end he juxtaposed the right of domicile to the right of citizenship and argued that each has merit as a basis of political rights:

> The tie of nationality is not a primary or a unique bond among the members of a nation: there are other more elementary ones … the home, the town, the city. It is precisely because the right of domicile rests on a universal and permanent fact, the concreteness of a place where one lives, a place where families reside, that it has been taken into consideration everywhere to determine the point of juridical attachment of persons and to order more or less completely the status of the individual.

Regimes change, but (with luck) domiciles remain. People remain attached to their homes whatever happens at the political level. This has always been the case among minorities and refugees, as long as they respect the laws of the land. The right of alien residence (while obeying the laws of a land) in a host nation is therefore based on the prior and superior force of domicile over nationality. One reflection of this principle, Cassin argued, is that married women in France could have more than one nationality; in deciding which applies, her domicile could be the point of reference. Cassin here cites explicitly the plight of over one million Russian and Armenian refugees whose personal status was thrown in doubt by war and revolution. Their standing, he insists, must be based on a right of domicile independent of nationality.

To Cassin, the choice between nationality or domicile had evolved over time. Throughout the later nineteenth century, in an era of state building, those standing on claims of nationality grew in number. By the third decade of the twentieth century, most European states took this approach; in contrast about the same number of people lived in state where domicile trumped nationality. These were the Anglo-Saxon countries and Latin American states, in which immigration played a powerful role. Cassin's point is that it was time for the pendulum to move back towards the claims of domicile over nationality in a Continent riven by powerful political and ideological quarrels exposed during the Great War. Jurisprudence had to follow events, in order not to be overwhelmed by them.

The implications of the argument are far-reaching. Domicile over nationality describes the bonds of the veterans of different countries who came together to work with Cassin in his international veterans organization. Domicile over nationality is the principle defense of vulnerable minorities stalked by powerful nationalist movements in states worried about their ethnic composition. Domicile over nationality helps correct the imbalance in then current international law "which confers to the sovereign nation a competence which is too exclusive, simplistic, and ill adapted to satisfy the complex needs of international life ..."[19] What is worse, despite having done its job well in the period of state formation, "the principle of nationality has exhausted its beneficial effects and has become a germ of doctrines destructive to the international community and oppressive to the individual". And finally, by privileging the concept of domicile over nationality, Cassin points the way to establishing the standing of the individual within international law itself. This same line of argument was adopted by the Institute of International Law in New York in October 1929, when it drafted a 'Declaration of the international rights of man'.[20]

Note the date of Cassin's disquisition. Three years before the Nazis came to power, and used sovereign law to destroy every single trace of natural justice, Cassin constructed a powerful argument against the extremes of state sovereignty then still unrealized. How much more powerful then, his argument against the all powerful state once that state under Hitler had made war first on millions of his own citizens, and then on the rest of Europe.

After 1933

Between 1933 and 1945, the balance between human rights and state power shifted radically. Nazi power and Nazi crimes – alongside those of Stalin – pushed to the limit the notion that a state is unconstrained in its treatment of its own citizens. And through the Italian invasion of Ethiopia in 1935, the Japanese rape of Nanking in 1937, the Nazi annexation of Austria in 1938, and the dismemberment and then destruction of Czechoslovakia in 1938 and 1939, the link between states' human rights abuses and their propensity to court the risk or the reality of war became evident for all who had eyes to see. The fascist assault on liberalism was an assault on the entire human rights tradition.

And yet the international effort to translate the suffering of the men of 1914–18 into a political barrier both against war and against the trampling of individual and minority rights failed miserably. It was not only that the League of Nations was hampered by its own structure and the weakness of a policy based on sanctions never carried out. It was also that the veterans movement itself tended to lose sight of the link between human rights and

---

19 Cassin, 'La nouvelle conception', 771.

20 Cassin directly cites this declaration in 'La nouvelle conception', 770.

pacifism. In doing virtually anything to appease Italian and German aspirations, and in placing the need to avoid war above every other consideration, the international veterans movement broke apart. One wing moved towards the position that war was terrible but necessary. Another carried on to the bitter end its belief that men like Hitler and Mussolini who had served in the Great War were men of peace who would step back from the precipice.

In April 1934, Cassin – now honorary president of the organization he helped found, the *Union Fédérale* – joined 450 members of CIAMAC on 'Un voyage de souvenir et de l'amitié' to Italy. These men marched into the heart of Rome, where Cassin met them. There they were greeted by what the *Cahiers de l'Union* Fédérale called 'toute Italie le plus noble et le plus sympathique qui vient de rendre les honneurs à la France Combattante'. Mussolini himself received the delegation, some of whom expressed a starry-eyed admiration of *Il Duce:* he spoke to them, so the *Cahiers* noted, in a "powerful and simple manner, giving the impression of the physical force of a worker or an athlete; poised and impatient for action, his thumbs in the pockets of his jacket … His strength was in his gaze". He spoke in French and assured them of his solidarity, "as head of state, as a veteran, as an Italian, as a fascist". Later that day Cassin joined others in Vatican City, where they were met and greeted by Pope Pius XI.[21]

Why was Cassin there and how did he stomach these empty gestures of solidarity? Italy was still a member of the League of Nations in 1934, though Germany had withdrawn the year before. To preserve the international character of CIAMAC, Cassin accepted this kind of diplomacy, well known to him from his years of service in the League of Nations. But after the Italian invasion of Ethiopia, after the dignified appeal of Haile Selassie for effective League Sanctions, and after the failure of those sanctions, Cassin began to wonder whether his commitment to veterans internationalism was a mistake. The fact that after 1933 Germany was a pariah state was one thing; CIAMAC could not hope for help from German veterans groups any more. Besides, Hitler had taken Germany out of the League of Nations in 1933. But what of Italy? If the League could not act in the case of blatant aggression, and if the veterans movement (like the League) put its faith in solidarity with ex-soldiers before its commitment to human rights, then all that he had done for two decades in this field was futile.

---

21 Bernard Secret, "Un voyage du souvenir et de l'amitié," *Cahiers de l'Union Fédérale des Associations Françaises d'Anciens Combattants et de Victimes de la Guerre et des Jeunesses de l'Union Fédérale*, iv, 55 (15 April 1934): 6–15.

Cassin was far from alone is seeing that war was both unimaginable, too terrible to contemplate, and yet just around the corner.[22] In 1936, he caught the tragedy of the moment in a testament he wrote before undergoing an operation which, his doctors told him, might take his life. They were attempting to repair damage to his intestines caused by the wounds he had suffered in 1914. Thereafter Cassin did not pass a single day without pain. His condition worsened in the mid-1930s, and required major surgery. The envelope enclosing the note Cassin wrote before the operation is labeled 'Open only in the case of death. This is not a will'.[23]

Instead this document is a political testament. While facing death, he returned to the moment in 1914 when he lay wounded on a battlefield in the east of France. He was proud of having served and of having been one of the founders of the French veterans movement. For him the defense of human rights was part of his old soldier's pacifism. That commitment led not away from confronting fascism but towards that collision of fundamental values. And on that point, in 1936, he had had to part ways with his brethren. For them peace came before everything. Not for Cassin. He knew that he was in the minority in the veterans movement, and that as such, his voice was more and more marginalized. "I will die without realizing my dreams", he wrote. The veterans movement had rallied "the peaceful aspirations of the masses", but at the price of opening "the door to the dictators, the warmongers, and those who prepare new massacres". I wonder, he mused, if the French people were being led to a new 'Sedan', a new military catastrophe. The press and the sordid assembly of politicians were preparing the ground. I face death, Cassin wrote, in full knowledge that my life has been futile, that I have not realized my potential in the law or in politics. "Before the grave, I will not draw back. I would have preferred to die for a reason, at the front or in combat". But that was not to be. His last words before going into surgery were 'Je veux vivre'.[24]

What an extraordinary *cri de coeur*. Here was a man facing what he took to be the emptiness of his life's work. His twenty years of effort in the veterans movement had come to nothing. His colleagues had pushed him aside in their rush to appeasement. He hated war as much as any of them, but he would not sacrifice on the altar of appeasement his sense that fascism had to be stopped.

---

22 Jay Winter, "Ironies of war", in *Remembering war: The Great War between history and memory in the twentieth century* (New Haven: Yale University Press, 2006), ch. 4.

23 382AP1, Note of 19 January 1936.

24 382AP1, Note of 19 January 1936.

I know of no other document as eloquent as this one on the theme of how little we know of the full contours of our lives. Cassin survived the operation, and began a life the shape of which he could not possibly have imagined at the time.

After 1940

He was right, though, about the impending catastrophe. In 1940, he watched the collapse of France from an office in the Ministry of Information. He realized that as an anti-fascist and a Jew, he was a marked man. He returned to his home in the south of France, paid his taxes, and decided to embark on an Australian troop ship to England. He never heard the call to arms of de Gaulle of 18 June 1940, but responded to it on arrival in London on 29 June. He told de Gaulle that he was a veteran, founder of the veterans movement, and a Jew. He put himself, as a jurist and as a Frenchman at the disposal of de Gaulle's embryonic movement. De Gaulle called him a godsend. Why? Because de Gaulle had 36 hours left to prepare a document for Churchill establishing his credentials and that of his movement, *France Libre*, as a French government in exile. Churchill was prepared to recognize and of equal importance to fund de Gaulle's movement if he could claim *de jure* status as the representative in exile of the French Republic. Cassin drew up the document which provided this crucial legitimation, later ratified on 7 August 1940, and the cornerstone of the French Resistance movement.[25]

The significance of this juridical service was of the highest importance, which de Gaulle recognized by making Cassin one of his ministers (or commissioners) in exile. Cassin had responsibility for education and justice, and sat on all the major committees of the French resistance movement in London. He represented de Gaulle on missions to Lebanon and to Africa, showing that the Republic was alive in its empire. He ran the central bureau of *France Libre* throughout the worst months of the Blitz.

Cassin was not a politician; everyone knew that. He was a professor and a jurist. But his standing as a jurist – Professor of Law in Paris and a world authority on civil law – and his work establishing the illegitimacy of Vichy made his name synonymous with the Republican cause. Cassin's position as commissioner of justice opened the door to a new phase of his life. It coincided with probably the worst phase of the war. In early June 1941, the Allied cause in the Second World War was at its nadir. Two months before, both Yugoslavia and Greece were invaded; within one month, both were

---

[25] Diary, 1940 in 382AP27.

under Nazi control. That meant that the entire European continent, from Norway in the north to Sicily and Crete in the south, and from Romania and Bulgaria on the Black Sea to the French Atlantic coast, were under Axis domination. Poland was divided between Soviet and Nazi zones. The neutrals – Sweden, Finland, Spain, and Switzerland – posed no threat to the Nazis nor actively collaborated with them.

The sole obstacle in Hitler's way was Britain. In May 1940, German forces surrounded the British expeditionary force in France at Dunkirk. Hitler issued a pause order, during which peace feelers were passed on to Britain. In return for the evacuation of their troops, Britain would have to join an international conference chaired by Mussolini. The deal was clear: Britain could keep her empire in return for recognizing German hegemony on the Continent. Churchill would have none of it. On 28 May 1940, the British cabinet decided on a policy of no negotiations and no surrender. The 'halt order' was lifted. British forces were evacuated, though without their heavy weapons and equipment. Churchill's coalition government, backed by her Empire, and her Dominions, stood alone, awaiting what seemed inevitable – a German invasion of Britain.

British victory in the air battle over the English Channel and Britain herself in the ensuing months ensured that that invasion never reached further than the planning phase. But it is evident that in June 1941 the British cause was not in any sense in the ascendency. The Soviet Union and the United States were committed to neutrality. Betting men and women would have had to wager that the Nazis would win the war. All the odds were against Britain, standing alone against the entire European Continent.

While American neutrality was still intact, FDR signaled a tilt in his administration's policy by signing a Lend Lease agreement to support Britain in March 1941. In the short term, this was of little assistance to Britain, facing air attack day after day. On the night of 8–9 April 1941, the medieval center of the city of Coventry – including its cathedral – was destroyed. One month later, on the night of 10–11 May 1941, the Luftwaffe launched its heaviest air assault on London. Their bombs started over 2,000 fires; 1200 people were killed, and 1700 injured. All in one night.

No one knew it at the time, but that was the worst of the Blitz for London. Virtually every other major city in the country was hit in this period, forcing the evacuation of tens of thousands of children and the descent into the Underground at night for those who stayed behind. It was a dreary, grey, miserable period in London's history. However defiant the Cockney smile or the tip of their hats, Londoners lived under enormous pressure.

Through their apparently invincible military power, the Nazis had begun the construction of what they termed a new European order, whatever the fate of Britain. This Nazi version of a European Union of the future was composed of a German core and a periphery dominated by collaborators in every occupied country. In most cases, the old regimes were simply overthrown by the Nazis when their troops had crushed organized resistance in 1939–41. Then the new 'Quislings' emerged, the generic term for collaborators drawn from the name of the leader of German-occupied Norway. Here were the outsiders, thugs, adventurers, and renegades who saw which way the wind was blowing and who tied their future to the Nazi project.

The case of France was more difficult still, since the truce arrangements between Germany and France after the German victory of May-June 1940 had been conducted government to government. Pétain had been asked by a duly constituted French government to negotiate an armistice. Suspending the Constitution was another matter, dividing those who saw it as a justified emergency measure from those who, like Cassin, saw it as a *coup détat.* At the time, most people in Britain considered such distinctions to be academic. *Force majeure* had a logic of its own. France had been defeated and had – contrary to treaty commitments – agreed to a separate peace with the Nazis. All signs indicated the leaders of what came be termed Vichy France were willing partners in the emerging new order.

St James's Conference I

To counter the notion that the collaborators were the lawful rulers of occupied Europe and that they, under German and Italian leadership, were forging a new Europe, the British decided to hold a war council of her Allies. This meeting, held in St James's Palace in London on 12 June 1941, brought together representatives of her Empire, her Commonwealth, and her Dominions, alongside leaders of governments in exile from countries under Axis control. Poland, the Netherlands, Belgium, Luxemburg, Czechoslovakia, Norway were all represented at the Prime Ministerial level. General Sikorski spoke for Poland; Jan Masaryk was there as foreign secretary of Czechoslovakia; Trygvie Lie, as foreign secretary of Norway. Paul-Henri Spaak represented Belgium as foreign minister in its government in exile.

Churchill met the participants in the Portrait Gallery of the Palace. There he told them and the world that 'whatever are the movements of the Nazis worldwide, it is in the fortress formed by the British Isles where the final outcome of the struggle between liberty and tyranny will take place'. And alongside him were men and women equally determined to see this monumental struggle through to victory.

Representing France were two men. René Cassin was one; Maurice Dejean, later National Commissioner for Foreign Affairs, was the other. Their place at the table was one of the by-products of the Churchill-de Gaulle accord of 7 August 1940, according *France Libre* recognition as a full political as well as military partner in the anti-Hitler alliance. Consequently, when the Allies met at St James's Palace on 12 June 1941 to reject Hitler's new order and to begin preparing the Allied alternative, Cassin and Dejean were there, alongside other representatives of governments in exile. Cassin was there in his capacity as Permanent Secretary of the Council for the Defence of the (French) Empire.

He addressed this assembly and used terms which appealed to those assembled in London as well as to the American people, whose leaders had as yet to take sides in the war. This speech was carefully vetted by de Gaulle before Cassin delivered it. He was there to speak not for himself but for de Gaulle and for *France Libre*. Here is what he said:

> After hard fought battles the French nation has been captive for almost a year. It has been reduced to helplessness and condemned to silence. French forces, however, which incarnate the hopes of liberation of our nation, are taking part in increasing numbers and strength in the fight against our common enemies on land, sea, and in the air. France came into the war to fight against the aggressor of her ally Poland. She remains faithful to the alliance freely entered into with the United Kingdom, with the British Empire, and with the peoples of the British Commonwealth of Nations. She also remains closely united to other nations whose emancipation she championed and whose development she promoted as well as to all victims of German imperialism whose terrible trials she now shares. France repudiates the monstrous 'new European order' which it is sought to impose upon her and in which she would play the part of her executioners' accomplice. She cannot think of peace without liberty. The French people and the populations of the French Empire will continue the struggle until complete victory has been won by the democracies over Germany and her associates. We mean to cooperate in building up a world which will be safe from all menace of aggression and which will offer economic and social security to all. That is the reason why in the name of General de Gaulle we adhere wholeheartedly to the spirit and the letter of the draft resolution which is now before us. This is why we want to express our admiration and gratitude to the British people and to Prime Minister Winston Churchill who is leading with such great energy this struggle of free peoples against tyranny, at a time when the Germans are attempting to create new order for the profit of one race, one nation and one man against the interests of all other peoples. I would like to recall the words of Abraham Lincoln and to suggest that the new international order which we wish to create should be one of government of the people by the people for the people.[26]

---

[26] Archives Nationales, 382AP68, Cable from Cassin to de Gaulle, 11 June 1941.

Cassin was, of course, speaking to the converted. This was a meeting of defiance, not of deliberation. The accord all the delegates signed affirmed three points. The first was that the struggle will continue until 'victory is won'. There would be no compromise or negotiated settlement. The second was that there will be no peace until German forces cease to oppress or threaten to oppress free peoples, that is until the Nazi regime is destroyed. The third is that "enduring peace" will come only after "the menace of aggression" is lifted, so enabling "free peoples" to "enjoy economic and social security". To this end the signatories promise to work together and with others "both in war and in peace".[27] Cassin echoed all of these points in his address. Once again affirming who was the leader of *France* Libre, Cassin and Dejean signed the agreement as 'representatives of General de Gaulle, leader of Free Frenchmen'.

What was significant about this meeting was that *France Libre* had moved from being a marginal group of individuals to being the recognized French partner in the alliance against Nazi tyranny. The first St James's conference confirmed and reiterated the Franco-British agreement of 28 March 1940 that France alongside every other member of the alliance would not conclude a separate peace, which in the French case was out of the question. Both de Gaulle and Cassin had already been condemned to death in absentia by Vichy. Theirs was a life and death struggle, as it was for everyone at St James's Palace. But perhaps of greatest importance was the simple fact that a French delegation would be party to planning for the future, both during and after the war.[28] This was a crucial turning point in the long voyage René Cassin took from exile in London to the day in December 1948, when he read out to the United Nations assembled in Paris the Universal Declaration of Human Rights. How unlikely such a trajectory must have looked at the time.

Ten days later, the war took a turn which ultimately led both to victory in 1945 and to the implementation of Allied plans for the post-war world. The Nazis invaded the Soviet Union, and despite spectacular victories in the weeks after the invasion, it was clear that Britain was not alone, and neither were the governments in exile who had met at St James's Palace a few days before. It is clear too that the entry of the Soviet Union into the war was a decisive moment in the slow but steady tilt of the United States towards the Allies. On 9 August 1941, Churchill and President Franklin Roosevelt met on

---

27 *Trial of War Criminals before the Nuremberg Military Tribunal under Control Council Law No. 10, vol. XV, Procedure, Practice and Administration* (Washington, D.C.: Government Printing Office, 1946–49), 52.

28 382AP68, Cable of Cassin to France Libre about inter-Allied meeting, 18 June 1941.

board USS Augusta at Naval Station Argentia in Placentia Bay, on the southern coast of Newfoundland, then, still a British colony. FDR let it be known that he was going to New England on a fishing trip. Instead he met his Chiefs of Staff and Churchill for their first, but by no means their last council of war. It was Churchill who landed the biggest fish of all.

There could be no doubt as to the American position, formulated in the document they released on 14 August, when Churchill was back in Britain. The key point was in the sixth of the common principles to which they agreed. This read as follows:

> Sixth, after the final destruction of the Nazi tyranny, they hope to see established a peace which will afford to all nations the means of dwelling in safety within their own boundaries, and which will afford assurance that all the men in all lands may live out their lives in freedom from fear and want; [...][29]

Here, four and a half months before the Japanese attack on Pearl Harbor, the United States effectively declared war on Nazi Germany. When Hitler received a cable with this text attached, he exploded. What followed thereafter is still a matter of controversy, but who could doubt that just as in the First World War, the United States was going to join the Allies, and convert a European war into a world war? Hitler had promised that should the Americans so decide, the Jews of Europe would pay the price. And so they did.[30]

St James's Conference II

The second time René Cassin joined an inter-Allied conference in St James Palace six weeks later the entire political landscape had changed. The war was now one of left versus right on a global scale. In September 1941, it was time to bring the Atlantic Charter to bear on Allied war aims and on preparations for the world after the war and for the war crime trials which would ensue. All the governments in exile had abundant evidence of Nazi war crimes against subject peoples. To announce to their citizens suffering under Nazi occupation that retribution would come one day, they provided both hope to the oppressed and a warning to the Nazis that justice would be done. Here is the first clear sign of Allied willingness to hold war crimes trials after the war. Once again, Cassin's presence here foretold the role he was to play in the rapidly evolving international legal framework for the post-war order.

---

29 *The Atlantic charter; the Roosevelt-Churchill declaration* (London: National Peace Council, 1941).

30 Tobias Jersak, "Die Interaktion von Kriegsverlauf und Judenvernichtung," *Historische Zeitschrift* 268 (1999): 311–49.

Anthony Eden, the newly appointed Foreign Minister presided at this second inter-Allied conference. This change at the top was clearly to the advantage of the Free French. The previous British Foreign Secretary, Lord Halifax, was at best tepid towards de Gaulle, whereas Eden, who had served like Cassin in the Great War, spoke reasonable French and admired de Gaulle. The other major newcomer was Ivan Maisky, representative of the Soviet Union, whom Cassin had known in Geneva at the League of Nations a decade before.[31]

In his address to the conference, Cassin made sure everyone knew that this was not the first time Germany had invaded countries with which it was at peace. 'Hitler', he said, 'has merely revived, in a more monstrous and brutal form, William II's dream of world domination'.

> Invaded three times in less than a century by an adversary bent on death and destruction, France can see no safeguard for this independence and freedom, or for that of maritime communications, outside the framework of an effective organization of international security, an essential element of which is preliminary disarmament, the destruction of the military machine and the limitation of war potentialities in countries which have never ceased to threaten her and are still liable to do so.
>
> The French also consider as necessary to the establishment of a real peace the practical ratification of the essential liberties of man and the concerted utilization, in view of the economic and social securities of peoples, of technical progress creative of fresh wealth.
>
> Indeed when peace has come, constant respect for the law of solidarity will impose itself on all. In the future it alone will enable us to avoid a repetition of those catastrophes which rend the unity of the human race.[32]

'The essential liberties of man' was Cassin's way of pointing towards the need to make human rights a bulwark of peace.

The primary business of the second St James's meeting was to ratify and adapt the Atlantic Charter to serve as a succinct statement of Allied war aims. For Cassin, that meant France, along with all other countries had the right to choose its preferred system of government. It also meant that something stronger than the League of Nations had to carry the burden of preventing war in the future. What would strengthen such a new institution would be a clear and comprehensive statement as to the universality of human rights. It is here, in London in September 1941, long before the war was won, that the quest for a new and practical human rights regime began.

---

[31] 382AP68, 24 Sept. 1941, verbatim account.

[32] 382AP63, Verbatim text of Cassin's speech to the Inter-Allied conference, 24 September 1941.

St James's Conference III

The ferocity of Nazi occupation intensified in the autumn of 1941. Both Churchill and Roosevelt issued statements condemning the execution of hostages. After the Japanese attack on Pearl Harbor on 7 December 1941, and the German declaration of war on the United States a day later, they joined with 23 other nations in signing the United Nations Declaration on 1 January 1942, affirming their commitment to the destruction of the Nazi regime.

The evolution of Allied thinking on the post-war world reveals a strong division between the Britain, the United States, and the Soviet Union, who ran the war, and governments in exile representing occupied populations. The Great Powers wanted to postpone any precise commitments on how such judicial proceedings would operate. Governments-in-exile had no such luxury. They needed to show captive populations that their national sovereignty was still intact and that after the war, there would be a national reckoning on war crimes. Such proceedings did not at all preclude the establishment of an international tribunal, planning for which developed in the second half of the war.

The first step to this end was the St James's conference of 13 January 1942. Sir Anthony Eden, British Foreign Secretary, welcomed the delegates, but stood aside from its deliberations, which were chaired by General Sikorski of Poland. The conference issued a declaration signed by representatives of nine occupied countries. Herewith the text they agreed on:

> Whereas Germany since the beginning of the present conflict, which arose out of her policy of aggression, has instituted in occupied countries a regime of terror characterized in particular by imprisonments, mass expulsions, execution of hostages and massacres,
> And whereas these acts of violence are being similarly perpetrated by Allies and associates of the Reich and in certain countries by accomplices of the occupying power,
> And whereas international solidarity is necessary in order to avoid repression of these acts of violence simply by acts of vengeance on the part of the general public and in order to satisfy the sense of justice of the civilized world.
> Recalling that international law and, in particular, the convention signed at The Hague in 1907 regarding laws and customs of land warfare do not permit belligerents in occupied countries to perpetrate acts of violence against civilians, to bring into disrepute laws in force or to overthrow national institutions,
> The undersigned representatives of the government of Belgium, the government of Czecho-Slovakia, the Free French National Committee, the government of Greece, the government of Luxembourg, the government of The Netherlands, the government of Norway, the government of Poland and the government of Yugoslavia

> 1. Affirm that acts of violence thus perpetrated against civilian populations are at variance with accepted ideas concerning acts of war and political offenses as these are understood by civilized nations;
> 2. Take note of the declaration made in this respect on October 25, 1941, by the President of the United States of America and the British Prime Minister;
> 3. Place amongst their principal war aims punishment through the channel of organized justice of those guilty and responsible for these crimes, whether they have ordered them, perpetrated them or in any way participated in them;
> 4. Determine in the spirit of international solidarity to see to it that (A) those guilty and responsible, whatever their nationality, are sought for, handed over to justice and judged; (B) that sentences pronounced are carried out.

The key point here is the third point: that the framing and carrying out of war crimes trials emerged as a central element in the formulation of war aims. Signing the document for France was Charles de Gaulle, who attended, while Cassin was on special mission in Syria.[33] For de Gaulle, the task was not only to seek retribution; it was also to 'take measures to ensure that a renewal of such crimes should be made impossible'.[34]

It was from this point that thinking about retribution and about the shape of the post-war international legal order came together in a kind of double helix. The liberation of subject people and the punishment of those responsible for monstrous acts during the war presented one key element of what the Allies were fighting for. The other part of war aims was the affirmation of positive principles on which the peace would be secured, and that is where human rights came in.

Here we have reached something of a parting of the ways. On the one hand, retribution for Nazi war crimes united all of *France Libre.* On the other hand, the shaping of a new international order, with human rights at its core, was beyond the political horizons of many within *France Libre,* including de Gaulle himself. The Second World War was fought to restore the territorial integrity of individual states occupied and humiliated by German military power. This was its essential character, be it with reference to France or to the Soviet Union. But the very depredations of Nazi occupation set in motion forces seeking to replace the bankrupt system of the League of Nations with an international order of a different kind. The notion that state sovereignty was inviolable and sacrosanct was contaminated by the Nazis and their allies. No state could be permitted to do what the Nazis had done first to their own citizens and then to the rest of Europe, and then to justify its acts on the grounds that sovereignty was indivisible and untouchable as a

---

[33] 382AP158 Cassin pocket diary, 1942, entries for January 1942.

[34] "Allies In Conference," *The Times* (January 14, 1942): 5.

principle of international life. That is why the Second World War was the occasion for the search for a dual approach to reconstruction after the war. First came the need to restore the dignity of those states whose regimes had been destroyed by the Nazis. Territoriality came first. But secondly, there emerged a growing consensus among the Allies on the need to reconstruct the international order on a different basis, one which rested on commitments which went beyond state sovereignty. Out of that search the United Nations emerged and so did a set of human rights commitments flowing from the adoption of the Charter of the UN in 1945 to the passing of the Convention on Genocide and the Universal Declaration of Human Rights in 1948.

René Cassin was a key actor in both these unfolding facets of the framing of Allied war aims. He was a jurist of international standing. He had been a delegate to the League of Nations, and had served his country and been wounded and decorated for his service. He came to issue of war and peace as a veteran, in both senses of the term.

In addition, the second St James's conference opened on the very date that de Gaulle formed his *Comité National Français.* This was the first fully ministerial cabinet of *France Libre*, and much to his surprise, Cassin had only a minor place in it. He ceased to be permanent secretary of the central organization of *France Libre*, the Council for the Defense of the Empire. Instead, he was not named foreign minister, but instead *Commissaire pour l'education nationale et pour la justice*, a marginal portfolio at the time. Later these subjects would take on greater significance, but given the military situation in September 1941, these were of no immediate importance. It was clear that he was moved to the margins of French exile politics on 24 September 1941, and ironically, he was then free to find an international rather than a central political role to play in *France Libre.*

Cassin's failure to secure a critical ministerial place in de Gaulle's cabinet was both embittering and liberating. As on previous occasions, his interest in holding high political office is evident, but his ability to swim in these difficult waters was open to doubt. De Gaulle made this decision, and though he valued Cassin's work, his integrity, and his loyalty, he believed that Cassin's talents placed him not at the heart of the ministerial forcing house of *France Libre*, but elsewhere. Thus after the third St James's Conference, Cassin's work took on a much more explicitly international character, leading him to Africa, to the Middle East, and to the center of Allied planning on the judicial reconstruction of Europe and the world order.

The Inter-Allied Commission on War Crimes

The period between the third St James's conference and the formation of an inter-Allied commission on war crimes was the time when the Holocaust was at its height. But even though hundreds of thousands of Jews were being murdered daily, it was the death of one man, and the retribution it brought in its wake, that moved the Allies into action. On 27 May 1942, a group of Czech parachutists, trained in Britain, fatally wounded SS General Reinhard Heydrich, head of all security policy and protector of Bohemia and Moravia. In revenge, the Nazis exterminated all the inhabitants of one village – Lidice – near the site of the assassination. Czechs in London demanded that the British formally associated themselves with the January 1942 St James's declaration on punishing war criminals. This they were unprepared to do, though they did issue a formal repudiation of the Munich agreement, hardly an answer to Czech demands for justice.

In June 1942 in Washington, Churchill and Roosevelt discussed the question of setting up a war crimes commission. Harry Hopkins, Roosevelt's special advisor, drafted a paper on the work of such a commission in taking evidence and in reporting to the United Nations on egregious violations of human rights, naming those responsible. He also urged the appointment of commissioners of undoubted international standing, who would not be national representatives so much as representatives of the alliance against Hitler.

Churchill agreed with the plan, approved by the British War Cabinet on 6 July 1942. They were willing to go along, in order to contain public pressure to punish war criminals, a current of opinion that grew with reports of Japanese atrocities against British soldiers in the Pacific theatre. What they had in mind was that those accused of war crimes be tried in and by the countries in which the alleged crimes took place. They wanted the restoration of national courts rather than the creation of an international tribunal. Once again, we see the importance of the restoration of territoriality in the development of war crimes policies, as an alternative to extra-territorial judicial proceedings. The fact that the one prepared the ground for the other was one of the unintended consequences of the war and the monstrousness of Nazi crimes.

The Allies did not choose at this time to define what were Nazi war crimes, preferring instead to fall back on older, commonly accepted definitions of the laws of war in the Geneva Conventions. With this understanding, the Cabinet Committee for the Treatment of War Criminals was established. On 7 October 1942, Lord Simon, the Lord Chancellor, and chief legal officer in Britain, announced to the House of Lords that the Allies would set in motion an inquiry into the appropriate form to bring to justice war criminals 'irrespective of rank'. The same day, President Roosevelt stated that there would be trials of a relatively small number of people, those he termed 'the ringleaders responsible for the organized murder of thousands of persons and the commission of atrocities which have violated every tenet of the Christian faith'.[35]

On 20 October 1943, Cassin was appointed French delegate to the Inter-allied commission on war crimes. He sat with colleagues from those governments-in-exile which had signed the third St James's declaration. This document now became official Allied policy. Once again, London became his adopted home and the site of some of his most important wartime work, this time undertaken on behalf of the incipient United Nations.

Complicating this work was the lack of consensus on the work of this commission. The Soviet Union started trying war criminals as soon as they liberated territory from the Nazis. In December 1943, they held trials and public executions in Kharkov.[36] At the same time, Lord Simon had made in clear in the House of Lords that the Allies intended not mass trials but ones limited to a relatively small number of people in positions of power. British law changed, though, to permit the prosecution of accused criminals whose alleged crimes took place in other countries. French law, Cassin observed, was not as advanced as British law in this respect.[37] Further difficulties arose from American doubts about the nature of the work of the commission of experts, on which Cassin himself sat.

Still on 18 January 1944, Sir Cecil Hurst, the President of the Permanent Court of Justice in the Hague, as chair, convened the Commission, even though the Soviet Union had not named a delegate. With new American backing from Herbert Pell, formerly U.S. ambassador to Portugal and Hungary, three sub-committees were formed. The first committee, chaired by the Belgian jurist de Baer, addressed dossiers on war crimes presented by individual nations. Between 9 and 16 February 1944, they examined the first 16 dossiers presented by France. Several were deemed sufficiently complete to present to the whole commission, which could name individuals as those to

---

[35] Arieh J. Kochavi, *Prelude to Nuremberg: allied war crimes policy and the question of punishment* (Chapel Hill: University of North Caroline Press, 1998), 28–32.

[36] Fonds Cassin, 382AP175, "Répression et prévention des crimes de guerres ennemis. Deuxième rapport du Professor René Cassin, Délégué de la France à la Commission d'Enquête des Nations Unies sur les Crimes de Guerre, 3 mai 1944, 1". Hereafter "Crimes de guerre".

[37] Crimes de guerre, 2.

be handed over to Allied authorities for trial. By May 1944 about 100 such individuals were on this list.

The second sub-committee was chaired by Ambassador Pell, and examined procedural questions. He probed national differences in the definition of war crimes, and their handling by civil or military courts, as well as the politically charged question of the character of an international criminal court. The third commission, headed by the Polish jurist Stephan Glaser, dealt with difficulties in legal thinking on collective responsibility for crimes, as well as the viability of the defense of innocence on the grounds of following higher orders.

The outcome of these deliberations was limited by the chair's reluctance to go beyond his government's position of wait and see on matters of international justice. Still the commission agreed to grant the right of lawyers or others to take evidence under oath in any country for the purposes of obtaining evidence of the commission of war crimes committed in another country. They also noted that the pace of atrocities had actually increased in the period of the commission's work, and renewed their determination to make public the intention of the United Nations to bring war criminals to trial, wherever they may be found.[38]

Cassin summarized his own contribution to this commission in uncharacteristically bold terms. He claimed credit for the convening of the third St James's conference, a claim which could have been contested by the Czech and Polish delegations. He also claimed the leading role in preventing the sidetracking of the Commission into limited technical questions of the law. As French delegate, he turned attention time and again to the urgent matter of framing war crimes tribunals, a position which reflected the way *France Libre* aided the Resistance in occupied France itself.

But there was another, more personal level to this part of his work. Cassin learned on his return to France in 1944 that 25 members of his family, including his 88 year old uncle Samuel, and his sister Yvonne and her husband, had been deported from Drancy and killed. He himself had been stripped of his French nationality by Vichy and sentenced to death in absentia. All his property had been sequestered. He was not outside the problem of restoring the legal order and securing justice for those guilty of monstrous crimes. For the Nazis and for Vichy, Cassin and Jews like him were part of the problem, and now in the months of preparation for the return of the Republican order, he insisted on being part of the solution to the legal and moral morass produced by Nazi occupation.

---

38 Crimes de guerre, 4–5.

In the following months in and out of London, Cassin assembled and framed numerous reports for the Commission on crimes committed in France and against French citizens. These included maltreatment of French prisoners of war, black and white, in Germany; the machine gunning of civilians during the *exode* of 1940; and the role of German soldiers and the Gestapo in the transit camp of Drancy, from which French Jews and other Jews found in France were deported to Auschwitz.[39] Above all, he pressed the commission, and succeeded in persuading them, that they had a responsibility to act on behalf of millions still under Nazi persecution, who awaited the day of their liberation as the first day of judgment.

On 4 April 1944, the Commission received from the constituent member states lists of all men in the S.S., the Gestapo, the army or in other leadership positions in each occupied nation, with the intention of seeing who among them would stand trial for war crimes.[40] This was the key step before setting up trials of those whom the Germans had to hand over to Allied authorities at the Armistice, as suspects in war crimes prosecutions.

What Cassin had helped accomplish here was important in both the French and the international realms. For the *Comité Français de la Libération Nationale*, here was one means to reestablish the Republican judicial order, and to limit the role of *l'Epuration sauvage*, or local vigilante justice. For the Allies as a whole, here was one way to approach the trans-national character of crimes without precedent. The first step was to hand over those guilty of crimes against French men and women in France, and the second was to try those guilty of trans-national crimes, which came later to include genocide, a word only just invented by Rafael Lemkin at the time.[41] What mattered was to see a pattern at the core of the Nazi order, one which used terror and murder to execute a plan of domination of Europe and beyond. This is what made the criminality to be judged after the end of the war a collective act. Individuals were guilty of crimes against infants, children, the elderly, deported from Drancy to Auschwitz or starved or worked to death in other camps. That was true, but the nature of the crime went beyond individual culpability. It reached the German conception that law did not touch them in their new order; indeed, to them, there were no laws of war but only the rule of force. Even if they were to lose the war, their crimes will have so weakened the

---

39 Crimes de guerre, 6.
40 Crimes de guerre, 7.
41 John Cooper, *Rafael Lemkin and the Struggle for the Genocide Convention* (London: Palgrave Macmillan, 2008), 24–47.

countries they conquered, they might have reasoned, that Germany could prepare for the next war from a favorable position even when defeated.

Hence the task was no less than the creation of some kind of common international law to restore the ties that judicial systems provide against injustice and cruelty. That reconstruction had to be both political and legal, since the Nazis destroyed extant legal systems *tout court,* and the kind of national culpability that the Nazis fixed on the Jews could not be fixed on the German race per se, but on those among them guilty of crimes established by the rules of law and evidence. By resuscitating justice through the arrest and trial of putative war criminals, countries like France, humiliated by occupation and collaboration, could thereby recover their political dignity. But the enormity of the crimes committed meant that legal steps had to be taken to restore what Cassin termed 'the laws of humanity', the sanctity of which must be protected against 'future aggressors'.[42]

Part of Cassin's achievement on the international level was to keep up the pressure on Britain, the United States, and the Soviet Union to set up an international court to try the major war criminals. To do so would be to drive home to the world at large the revolutionary character of Nazi crimes, and the way these crimes undermined the concept of the rule of law per se.[43]

In this transitional phase of his life, from isolation and anguish under the Blitz to international renown, Cassin benefited from contact with and stimulation by some of the finest jurists in Europe. The work of the Commission on War Crimes was collective, and it would be foolish to claim that Cassin framed its findings on his own. What he shared with his colleagues was a sense of the gravity of the damage that had been done not only to millions of innocents, but to the principle of the rule of law itself. Once more he turned his attention to healing the wounds of war, which this time extended to the nullification of virtually every principal restricting the piratical tendencies of massively powerful state actors.

There was injury to the international order to repair as well. To reach that goal, the Allies had to consider drafting a trans-national legal code,[44] stating what the laws of humanity are, and how nations which, like Hitler's Germany, systematically violate them domestically are a threat to international peace. Here is the link between war talk and rights talk, between protests against the inhumanity of the Nazis and the construction of a trans-national

---

42 Crimes de guerre, 13–15.
43 Crimes de guerre, 44.
44 Crimes de guerre, 45.

code of behavior limiting what states can do against other states and against their own citizens.

Cassin was very sensitive to the domestic side of the double track strategy he was advocating. National war crimes trials had to be held so that justice not only be done but also be seen to be done. There had to be trials in France, not as a matter of reprisals, but as a matter of justice, and trials not only of those guilty of flagrant violations of the laws of war and the criminal law, but also of those whose collaboration made occupation possible and more cruelly effective than it would have been otherwise. Those who exploited forced labor of French citizens in Germany were guilty of one set of crimes; but industrialists who worked with the Nazis were guilty of another, and both must be addressed. Furthermore, French law had to be (and was) changed to permit the prosecution of foreign nationals who committed crimes on foreign soil against French nationals held there.[45] The same was true for those Germans who profited from the theft of Jewish property as it was for those Frenchmen who did so, consciously or not.

Post-war

Cassin's work on the Inter-Allied Commission on War Crimes prepared the ground for both facets of his work, post Liberation. The first was his participation in drafting the charter and supporting documents of the new United Nations, leading to the Universal Declaration of Human Rights in 1948. The second was work in assuring the return to Republican legality through the *Comite Juridique* of the *Comité Français de la Libération nationale*, which he headed in Algiers, and his appointment as vice-president and effective head of the *Conseil d'Etat.* These two subjects require separate treatment, and will not be dealt with here. Suffice it to say that Cassin's work in the Second World War led to his appointment as head of the highest administrative and constitutional court in France, which was revamped and strengthened during his tenure between 1944 and 1960.

Similarly, his standing in *France Libre* enabled him to join Eleanor Roosevelt, Charles Malik, John Humphreys and others in the United Nations in drafting the Universal Declaration of Human Rights in the period 1945–48. He wrote the preamble himself, and it was Cassin who made the final changes and read out the document to the United Nations assembled in Paris on 10 December 1948.

---

45 Crimes de guerre, 49, 63.

It took some time, but Cassin eventually saw that the opening of the Cold War made it impossible for the United Nations Human Rights Commissions to act with any coherent authority. As a consequence, he transferred his efforts to creating an institution higher than that of state sovereignty within the project of European unification. He helped draft the European Convention on Human Rights, passed in 1950; it had teeth. It was the document any country had to sign and respect in order to join the European community. It still is. To enforce the Convention, a new European Court of Human Rights was created. In 1958 that court opened in Strasbourg, and Cassin was first vice-president (associate justice) and then in 1965 President (chief justice) of the European Court of Human Rights. On his retirement from that post in 1968 he was awarded the Nobel Peace Prize.

Let us consider a thought experiment of a relatively innocent kind. Consider Cassin on the dais in Oslo about to receive his Nobel Prize. Imagine for a moment that with him, at that place of honor, on that evening, were millions of old soldiers, men who were pacifists of a special kind: men who had fought for their country and who knew what war was. Cassin's plea to defend human rights as a way to defend the peace was their plea. It became the cause of others after Cassin. It was at the heart of the Helsinki process in 1974, a process establishing the surveillance of the human rights situation in the Soviet Union as the prize for the legitimation of the western borders of that state. It was the plea of Charter 77 and of the host of organizations which undermined Soviet power by insisting on the inviolability of human rights. It was the plea of those who dismantled the Berlin wall and the Soviet empire behind it.

Cassin, who died in 1976, was not to know this extraordinary passage of the human rights project he helped to found. But he did know one part of it. Just a few months before his death, he asked his new wife, Ghislaine Maréchal, who was a film actress in the 1930s and a member of the Resistance in those darks days in London, to ensure that the text of one of his speeches would lie with him in his grave.[46] It was his salute to his brethren in the French army in 1914, who won the Battle of the Marne, and who suffered with him in the autumn of the first year of the Great War. He delivered these moving words of commemoration on 8 September 1940 on the BBC, with the Luftwaffe literally over his head. In his address, he called his comrades of 1914 by name and added: "Yes, I still see you all":

---

[46] 382AP/181.

> I know you well, Captain Woignier, a Catholic from Lorraine with an ardent soul, whose eyes closed forever contemplating your native soil, and you, Vandendalle and Pellegrino, fearless and without fault, peaceful farmers whose blood was as red as your beautiful flowers. I remember you Garrus, humble laborer from the hills of the Var, poacher, free-thinker, volunteer for dangerous patrols, and you Magistrate Samata, who as a Jew refused to move to a less exposed position. Yes, I see you all, guys from Paris, the east, the south, Muslims from Algeria or Senegalese, who fought together with me on those days ... and whose bodies formed an immovable rampart in defense of France.[47]

It was men like these, Cassin asserted in the dark days of 1940, who would achieve victory again.

Cassin was one of millions of men who never ceased to be *Ceux de '14*, *un ancien combattant de la grande guerre.* Everything he did, everything he achieved, was an expression of that identity. He was a pacifist soldier, a Republican militant who all his life fought war even while waging it.

His legacies are many. In his last will and testament, he noted that while not ignoring the world as it is, he was conscious of his achievements, which in his view merited burial in the Pantheon, that secular cathedral honoring the great men of the Republic. In 1940, he had helped keep Republican France alive and united. Thereafter he knew that he had contributed to international law, and above all to what he termed 'a mystique of human rights' throughout the world which was not there before him.[48] That commitment to stand as a soldier of the right, that spirit, arose during one war, informed a veterans movement which strove to avoid another, and then when war came anyway, these values helped Cassin and his brethren to fight and win yet again. Cassin died in 1976, but 11 years later, his casket was indeed interred in the Pantheon, next to Jean Moulin, the leader of the Resistance. And that was right and proper.

Cassin spent his life in a double quest: in search of peace and of the best means to defend human rights, in full knowledge of the link between the two. That message, a product of the Second World War but of much else besides, is with us still.

---

[47] 382AP/185.
[48] 382AP/181.

Mattias Kumm
(NYU School of Law / Social Science Research Center, Berlin)

The Idea of Thick Constitutional Patriotism and its Implications for the Role and Structure of European Legal History[1]

1. The Idea of Thick Constitutional Patriotism[2]

A sense of cohesion grounded in a common identity is widely believed to be a prerequisite for a functioning democratic European polity.[3] If the European Union is to master successfully the tasks assigned to it in the Constitutional Treaty and, using a non-consensual procedure, decide on policies that concern the security of its citizens or have significant distributive effects, then a sufficiently thick common identity is believed to be necessary both to legitimate and to ensure the functioning of the polity in the long term. There is little doubt that such an identity is currently missing. The question is what such an identity should be[4] and whether the political pre-requisites for the development of such an identity exist.[5] Are there historical experiences and accomplishments that enable European citizens to understand themselves as

---

1 This is a reprint of Mattias Kumm's article in the *German Law Journal* 6.2 (2005): 320–354. It has been abridged and adapted to the citation standards of this volume.

2 I thank Jörg Benedict, Moshe Halbertal, Martti Koskenniemi and Ruth Rubio-Marin, for helpful comments and suggestions.

3 Most recently, see Jürgen Habermas, *Der Gespaltene Westen* (Frankfurt am Main: Suhrkamp, 2004), 68–84. See, also, Jürgen Habermas, "Citizenship and National Identity, Its Achievements and its Limitations. On the Past and Future of Sovereignty and Citizenship," *Ratio Iuris* 9.2 (1996): 125

4 The debate on what European citizenship could mean could be was spurred on by the inclusion of a citizenship clause in the Maastricht Treaty. Helpful contributions include Joseph H.H. Weiler, "To Be a European Citizen: Eros and Civilization," *The Constitution of Europe* 324 (1999); Jessurun d'Oliveira, "European Citizenship: Its Meaning, Its Potential," in *Europe after Maastricht: An Ever Closer Union?* ed. Renaud Dehousse (Munich: C.H. Beck, 1994), 126; *European Citizenship*, ed. Epaminondas A. Marias (Maastricht: European Institute of Public Administration, 1994); Jo Shaw, "Citizenship of the Union: Towards Post-National Membership," *Academy of European Law* 6.237 (1995). See, also, Garcia Soledad, *European identity and the search for legitimacy* (London: Pinter Publishers, 1993).

5 For a sceptical view, see Dieter Grimm, "Does Europe Need a Constitution?" *European Law Journal* 1.282 (1995). For a critical response, see Jürgen Habermas, "A Response to Dieter Grimm," *European Law Journal* 1.303 (1995).

having suffered a common past and which animate them to see themselves engaged in the construction of a common political future? What are the appropriate narratives around which a European identity could, over time, develop? What should the focus of a self-conscious politics of memory be? What are the implications for the role and structure of European historiography, in particular for the European legal and political historiography?

One well-known answer to this question is that the basic principles of the liberal democratic constitutional tradition should be understood as the focal point for the development of such a common identity.[6] The constitutional commitment to human rights, democracy and the rule of law.[7] In short, *constitutional patriotism* could be the basis for a common European identity.

1.1. Thin and Thick Constitutional Patriotism

But as has been pointed out,[8] there are at least two problems with such an idea. First, both as an ideal and as an actual political and legal practice, there is *nothing specifically European* about these commitments. They are already reflected in the national constitutional commitments of all the Member States.[9] They are shared by liberal democracies as different as Canada, South Africa and India. And, as universal principles, they claim to be morally valid everywhere that human beings politically organize their co-existence with one another. Second, it is doubtful whether the political liberal tradition of human rights, democracy and the rule of law is *sufficiently thick* to function as the cement of a supranational political community in light of potentially conflicting loyalties connected to ethically thicker national identities. How can abstract moral principles – rather than collectively shed blood, sweat and tears – be the kit for a political community?[10]

---

6 Habermas, *Der Gespaltene Westen.*

7 Art. I-2 of the Constitutional Treaty states: "The Union is founded on the values of respect for human dignity, liberty, democracy, equality, the rule of law and respect for human rights …"

8 An early example of general scepticism about the possibility for any kind of meaningful European identity to develop is Anthony Smith, *Nations and Nationalism in a Global Era* (Cambridge: Polity Press, 1995), 126.

9 See Joseph Weiler, "In Defense of the Status Quo," in *European Constitutionalism beyond the State*, eds. Joseph H.H. Weiler and Marlene Wind (Cambridge: CUP, 2003), 7.

10 Ulrich Haltern, in particular, laments the neglect of 'the political' by European constitutionalists and thinks the idea of ambitious identity politics to be doomed in a consumerist market culture; see Ulrich Haltern, "The Idea of Thick Constitutional Patriotism 1, Pathos and Patina: The Failure and Promise of Constitutionalism in the European Imagination," *European Law Journal* 9.14 (2003). See,

The response to both these challenges is an account of constitutional patriotism that is thicker than a mere commitment to abstract universal principles. The idea that constitutional patriotism should be understood merely as an attachment to the universal moral principles contained in national constitutional texts and nothing more (call this *thin constitutional patriotism*) has never been an adequate representation of the idea, at least not as it has been presented by its best known contemporary proponent, Jürgen Habermas. Citizens do not simply identify with the abstract norms laid down in the constitution. Instead, citizens appropriate and interpret them in the context of their particular history and in the light of their own ethical and political commitments.[11] This process of appropriation and interpretation of basic political ideals takes place not only and as part of education in national schools. It takes place to a significant extent when political and legal claims are deliberated and negotiated in the public sphere. It also takes place as alliances are forged, programmes are articulated, political and legal battles are fought and choices are made. Thus, universal principles of justice may be textually fixed in the constitution. *But they derive their power to shape identities in the present from the connection with the struggles of the past and the ambitions for the future.* By being connected to the particular history, ambitions and current political practices of a particular community, thick constitutional patriotism reflects the specificity of a particular community.

1.2. Identity and the 'Other'

Thickness and specificity, then, can be achieved without emphasizing the importance of a contemporary 'Other', and without arming the boundaries, both symbolically and practically, to defend an imagined homeland.[12] It can be achieved by focusing inwardly and on self-knowledge. In Europe, it is not necessary to start painting dark pictures of a powerful Islamic fundamentalist threat or to paint the Islamic world as a radical 'Other', whatever the cultural and political differences may be to the internally diverse and highly frac-

---

also, "*Der europarechtliche Begriff des Politischen*" (habilitation thesis Humboldt Universität Berlin 2004). The idea of 'the Political' as a particular intensity of association and dissociation, is central to the constitutional and political thinking of Carl Schmitt, *Der Begriff des Politischen* (1932).

11 In his latest book, Habermas takes at least the first steps to spell out what this could mean in the context of a European polity; see Habermas *Der Gespaltene Westen*, especially Part II: *Die Stimme Europas in der Vielstimmigkeit seiner Nationen.*

12 For an insistence on the importance of boundaries, particularistic identities and irrationality as an constitutive element of 'the political', see Haltern, *The Idea of Thick Constitutional Patriotism.*

tured Muslim world. Nor is it necessary to succumb to anti-Americanism. If the major demonstrations which contemporaneously took place on the 15 February 2003 in London, Rome, Madrid, Barcelona, Berlin and Paris against the US attack on Iraq do mark an important event in the constitution of a European public sphere and a European identity,[13] it can only be hoped that it is an identity focused on a commitment to a particular idea of an international legal order that shuns the unilateral use of force, a commitment which is, at the very least, shared by a strong minority in contemporary American politics. A mature European identity has no need of an American 'Other'.[14] The United States is an 'Other' only in the banal sense that it is not part of the European Union. Whatever the legitimate concerns about the foreign policy of a particular U.S. administration are, an identity constitutively linked to branding outsiders as 'Others' is an immature identity grounded in weakness: for its stability, it focuses on something external to it. These are cheap shortcuts to a European identity, shortcuts that involve intolerably high moral and political costs. The clash of civilizations is no necessary feature of the contemporary social and political world. But it can easily be brought about as a self-fulfilling prophesy by those consumed in resentment or fear, and those who exploit it for political purposes.

In this respect, the American experience may provide the 'old continent' with a lesson. As self-absorbed and parochial as some manifestations of American constitutional patriotism may seem to many Europeans, nobody can doubt its strength. Yet, the stories that are central to it involve narratives about the establishment of an ever more integrative and perfect Union, and the remedying of injustices of the past, injustices related to Native Americans, to Blacks, to women, *etc.* Even when it comes to the 20th century wars, the emphasis in public life has mainly been on celebrating achievements, mourning the dead, and contemplating tragedy, mistakes and disagreement (as in the case of Vietnam). Historically, the emphasis has not been on drawing boundaries to exclude a non-American 'Other', notwithstanding the current official rhetoric. Emphasis is put on the serious reflection on the failures and achievements of the past in order to improve on them in the future.

---

13 See Jürgen Habermas and Jacques Derrida's essay published contemporaneously in various major European newspapers: "The 15th of February or: What Unites Europeans," reprinted in: Habermas, *Der Gespaltene Westen*, 43–51.

14 Neither is it is helpful to think of current European identity defined by differences to the US (e.g.,with regard to the role of markets and of state intervention, the respective enthusiasm or scepticism about the role of technology, or the use of force in foreign affairs). See Jürgen Habermas' careful negotiation of this issue *Der Gespaltene Westen*, 52, 53.

1.3. Identity and Criteria for Membership

What then is the link between the idea of thick constitutional patriotism and the question who should be allowed to join? An identity focused on thick constitutional patriotism provides a basis for the existing law and practice of enlargement. "The European Union shall be open to all European States which respect its values and are committed to promoting them together."[15] It insists that the only categorical requirements for membership are linked to the kind of criteria that the EU does in fact use: According to the Copenhagen criteria, a prospective member must be a stable democracy, respecting human rights, the rule of law and the protection of minorities, have a functioning market economy and be willing and able to adopt the common rules standards and policies that make up the body of EU Law. There is no basis to exclude anyone on additional cultural grounds. Clearly, this does not mean that South Africa or Singapore would be plausible candidates. There is the additional legal requirement that a state should be *European*. But the criterion of European-ness is no reason to launch into deep discussions of the ontology of European-ness. It is best understood as a loose geographical criterion that underlines the idea that the European Union is a *regional* and not a global organization. The universal idea it embodies is an idea of world order in which states are regionally integrated as well as belonging to organizations with universal membership. As a loose geographical criterion its application should be governed by political wisdom of a very practical kind in cases such as the accession of Turkey, Bosnia, Albania or the Ukraine.

The prospect for the future development of a thick constitutional patriotism in Europe depends on at least two variables. The first is the nature of the political process at the European level. It either provides citizens with an opportunity and incentive to engage with these ideals and narratives in the course of an ongoing political practice, or it discourages such an engagement. Without the support of the requisite political practices any politics of memory will amount to little more than EU brand management. At best, it will produce a highly transient consumer loyalty to the EU. At worst, it will produce resentment and backlashes against the misappropriation of a vocabulary that is steeped in significance, while at the same time emptying it of all meaning. Much will have to be said about the current institutional practices and their reform by the Constitutional Treaty as well as the ratification procedure in this regard, but this is not the place to do it.[16] Here, the focus is

---

[15] See Art. 1 II of the Treaty Establishing a Constitution for Europe.

[16] Elsewhere I have argued that the structure of the European political process as it currently exists and as it will continue to exist under the Constitutional Treaty

on the second variable. The second variable is the availability of suitable historical material that both animates and constrains the relevant historical narratives and the possible role of a European historiography.

2. Implications for the Role and Structure of European History

2.1. A Kantian Perspective on European History

One way in which thick constitutional patriotism differs from thin constitutional patriotism is that the former is embedded in a historical narrative about how the European polity developed to become what it is. But what kind of a historical narrative is it? What kind of historiography is of particular value for the purpose of serving as a frame of reference for an engaged European citizenry? The idea of constitutional patriotism is connected to a particular idea of European political and legal historiography. The historiography to which it is connected is not solely European because it takes a European perspective instead of framing the narratives within a national frame of reference. Such a European historiography is currently flourishing (in part, with the financial support of the Commission). Choosing a European frame of reference is a helpful first step to loosen the dominance of a national frame of reference in Europe, but it is not enough. Instead, the kind of historiography required for European political and legal history is one that *focuses on the progressive understanding of what are the basic constitutional principles of today – human rights, democracy and the rule of law – as a focal point that gives a European historical account its structure.* The idea of a historical account with such a structure which aims to provide support for the identity of transnational citizens is related to Kant's "*Idee einer allgemeinen Geschichte in weltbürgerlicher Absicht*"[17] Kant developed the idea of an account of world history that took the political and moral principles of the Enlightenment as the prism through which history would usefully be told. Events would be analysed from the perspective of how they affected the emergence, interpretation or stifling of these very ideals. In Europe, such a project acquires a particular urgency from the fact that there is a transnational European polity that claims to be grounded in these ideals. Such an account would

---

undermines rather than fosters the development of a meaningful European identity see Mattias Kumm, "To Be a European Citizen? The Absence of Constitutional Patriotism and the Constitutional Treaty," *Columbia Journal of European Law* 11 (2005): 481–542.

[17] Immanuel Kant, *Gesammelte Werke*, ed. Wilhelm Weischedel, vol. 6 (Darmstadt, 1986), 33–50.

avoid what may well be two typical features of contemporary historiography that significantly undermine its value for the development of a European identity.

First, European political practices would not be the focus of an account that was *radically divorced* from national narratives. They should not be a mere addition to national histories focusing on the state and the nation, with a final chapter that begins, say, with Churchill's Zurich speech and the Schuman Declaration, and ends with the debates on the ratification of the Constitutional Treaty. Instead, such a historical focus would provide common themes that *integrate* narratives about national and European political and legal practices. Existing national narratives would be placed in a European context and European narratives would both feed off from and be an integral part of the plurality of national narratives across Europe.

Second, a 'European' focus of this kind would not insist on emphasizing the historically distant 'common roots' of classical antiquity or the often idealized or disparaged medieval Christian Europe and give short thrift or at best equal weight[18] to the past two centuries up to World War II,[19] because they are believed to embody an age of divisive nationalism (as well as colonialism and imperialism). Instead, in the kind of account that is required, both Christianity and Nationalism[20] would have a central role to play. But a very differently focused one.

2.2. Excursion: Christianity and Nationalism as a Part of European History

Clearly, Christianity is a historical force of practically unequalled importance for European history. The focus on the Holy See and the Bishop of Rome may well have created the first sense of cohesion for a legal, political and cultural entity called Europe in the Middle Ages. Today, its presence continues to be felt in every city square in Europe where churches occupy prime locations. Its spiritual force today and in the future of Europe should not be underestimated and ought not to be feared, but welcomed. The focus of European history would not be the story of a Christian Europe, but Chris-

---

18 See, for example, Michael Salewski, *Geschichte Europas* (Munich: C.H. Beck, 2000). A remarkable European history is also Norman Davies, *Europe: A History* (Oxford: OUP, 1996).

19 See Gordon Craig, *Geschichte Europas von 1815–1980: Vom Wiener Kongress bis zur Gegenwart* (Munich: C.H. Beck, 1989).

20 For an excellent European history focused on of the role of the state and nation, see Hagen Schulze, *Staat und Nation in der europäischen Geschichte* (Munich: C.H. Beck, 1994).

tianity would have an important role to play in it.[21] For the purpose of a history that is to serve as a common reference point for European citizens an account of Christianity could be helpfully focused on three aspects.

The first concerns the negotiations of the relationship between church and state and the gradual emancipation of public institutions and the public sphere from theological debates, clerical privilege and clerical authority. It is not just that for a Europe consisting of Christians, atheists, agnostics, deists, Jews and Muslims anything else would undermine the function of the narrative as a focal point of a common identity. In many respects, the Europe of medieval times rightly remains a negative model for the kind of society that Europe strives to become. For a Europe that endorses a public philosophy committed to the idea of free and equal citizens, a different focus would be appropriate.

One more recent aspect of Christianity that is of exemplary significance is the remarkable story of the conversion of the Catholic Church to the commitments of constitutional democracy – the transition from vehement opposition to 'modernist' ideas to their partial embrace by the end of the Second Vatican Council.[22] *It provides support for the idea that great religious traditions have the theological resources to reconcile and integrate a serious commitment to a godly life with an embrace of Political Liberalism and its institutions.*[23] The emancipation of the public sphere from theological debates, clerical privilege and clerical authority was a process that helped Christians to gain a *deeper understanding* of religious faith as it relates to freedom of conscience, tolerance and engagement with the world more generally. Even those who mourn the fact that religious practices have lost their hold on a large part of Europe's population and who advocate the re-evangelisation of Europe, have reasons to embrace the emancipation of legal and political life from theological debate, clerical privilege and clerical authority. The heated debates on a refer-

---

21 For a recent argument that Christianity should be recognized and welcomed as a central element in the evolution of European civilization, see Joseph H.H. Weiler, *Un'Europa Cristiana* (Milan: BUR Saggi, 2003).

22 See Karl Heussi, *Kompendium der Kirchengeschichte* (8th ed., 1988), particularly concerning the period between 1878 and 1914, 448–454. For comparable developments in the Protestant tradition, see Perez Zagorin, *How the idea of religious Toleration came to the West* (Princeton: Princeton University Press, 2003).

23 In the U.S., this would hardly seem worth mentioning. Most Americans are both religious and constitutional patriots. Many are constitutional patriots and not religious and some are illiberal religious zealots. For the claim that the necessary theological resources also exist within the Muslim tradition, see the discussion in Noah Feldman, *After Jihad: America and the Struggle for Islamic Democracy* (New York: Farrar, Straus and Giroux, 2003).

ence to God in the Preamble, in which devout Christians were present on both side of the issue, should not obscure this central point. A European constitution that rejects reference to God in its Preamble is not, in virtue of that fact, christophobic. And the inclusion of a reference to Christianity in the Preamble is not necessarily an effective first step of the re-evangelisation of Europe.

Finally, a history not so much of Church institutions, but of the ways of life, struggles and questions it has given rise to in European history could help keep in the public eye the idea that even when a person has fulfilled his duties as a citizen, there are questions he would do well to engage that transcend the realm of law and politics. The realm of law, political justice and economic efficiency do not provide answers to how European citizens should live their lives, nor should they. *But the idea of autonomy and human dignity underlying the political ideal of free and equal citizens is better served in a social world and public culture in which citizens are encouraged to reflect and grapple seriously with questions about how to live their lives*, than a world where everything is geared towards the reinforcement and consumptive gratification of their base desires.

The idea of thick constitutional patriotism is intimately connected to an ideal of a European civilization in which the social world and public culture encourages serious engagement with and autonomous choices made in the awareness of the rich tradition of experiments in living that is Europe's heritage. Alongside the heritage of classical antiquity, the history of Christianity provides a rich treasure chest of questions, examples and narratives that deserve public appropriation. It is not surprising that – notwithstanding internal battles with its own demons – the Catholic Church today has become probably the most influential political and spiritual voice speaking in the name of human dignity against the dehumanizing effects of market fetishism, commoditization, consumerism and a public culture fostering thoughtlessness in Europe.

As far as nationalism is concerned, how can it not be a central theme in any European history? The century and a half from the 1789 to 1945 has to be a core part of a European history that serves as a reference point for European citizens. There is no good reason to give priority or even equal weight to classical antiquity or the Middle Ages. But the focus of that history would not simply be the rise of nationalism and a description of an era of nationalism. Such a focus, no matter how critically motivated, would merely replicate the focus of much nationalist historiography. To focus, instead, on the time between the 18th and 20th centuries provides the opportunity to explore the connections, both empirically and normatively, between Political Liberalism and nationalism as they engaged each other across Europe. The focal point could be on the conflicts between a liberal nationalism that has in fact understood itself as an embodiment of Enlightenment ideals,[24] an ethnic nationalism that has dismissed these ideals, and liberal movements that have competed with and transcended nationalism. Such a historical focus would illuminate discussions on the European constitution and competing ideals and forces that animate it: Sovereigntist or Intergovernmentalist ideals that leave as much as possible of national political practice untouched, Eurofederalism that seeks to establish a strong state in Europe as least as an animating ideal for the future (perhaps as a mid-way stop to a world state) and supranationalism, that sees the European Union as a community whose core purpose is to civilize what Weiler has referred to as the 'erotic forces of nationalism',[25] without substituting or dissolving them.

2.3. Some Remarks on Methodology and Bias

Yet, the suggestion to write this kind of history is likely to be met with skepticism or even to be ridiculed. This is not so much because such an endeavor seriously overstretches any scholar's capacities. The hard source-based work to provide the kind of historical narrative suggested here, has, for the most part, already been done. Innumerable monographs dealing with specific aspects of such a story are already in existence. It is unlikely, then, that an attempt to write such a synthesizing account would encounter difficulties because of the lack of research upon which to build. The novelty would lie only in the arrangement and organization of the narrative. In this sense, the ambition to write such a history, though considerable, is not outrageous.

The charges such a conception of European history would face are likely to be of a different kind. The claim would be that writing history using the kind of prism suggested amounts to an ideological abuse and a political instrumentalization of history – a kind of European propaganda. It would resemble the kind of historiography characteristic of nationalist or Marxist historiography, just with a Europeanist ideology, so the claim could go. But such charges would be misdirected. They confuse the *choice of focus* – the development and understanding of basic constitutional ideals – with a bias that undermines the intellectual integrity of the narrative.[26] Why should the focus

---

24 See Ernst Haas, *Nationalism, Liberalism, Progress* (Ithaca, NY: Cornell University Press, 1997); Yael Tami, *Liberal Nationalism* (Princeton: Princeton University Press, 1993).

25 Joseph H.H. Weiler, "To Be a European Citizen: Eros and Civilization," in *The Constitution of Europe* (Cambridge: CUP, 1999).

26 Kant's proposed account of world history may in fact be prone to such charge. Unlike the proposal here, he suggested reading history as if the purpose of world

on the intellectual, political and legal development of these ideas be ideological and the choice of any other topic, the history of a nation, a biography of a medieval monk, the history of aviation etc. not? All historians have their own reasons to engage in the inquiry they are engaged in and it may be hoped that those reasons do not undermine the care with which they perform their work.

It is undeniably true that the more strongly historical narratives are connected to contemporary political disputes and identities, the greater the dangers of cognitive bias and temptations to scholarly integrity. There have certainly been terrible national and Marxist historiographies and there may well be terrible European histories. But the fact that these dangers exist should not cast a general cloud of suspicion over the enterprise. There are, after all, excellent nationally focused historians and there is first rate historiography by Marxists.[27]

Furthermore, the focus suggested here has nothing to do with self-celebration and a whitewashing of European history. Nor does the idea of general history advocate the historiographical equivalent of the Preamble to the Draft Constitutional Treaty, as originally drawn up by the Convention. Instead of celebrating a continent "that has brought forth civilization", as the original Preamble declared, there would be ample space for the "bitter experiences" that the revised Preamble refers to. *A history that obtains its focus from human rights, democracy and the rule of law in Europe is to a significant extent the history of the fight against these ideals, their hypocritical abuse or their complacent misunderstanding.* Both the ideals themselves as well as histories that focus on them are more likely than not to give support to the self-reflective political and legal culture that these ideals have, over time, fostered in Europe. They

---

history were to bring to fruition globally human capacities and liberal ideals. In this sense his account of history was pre-committed to a progress narrative. The kind of historical writing suggested here would not be grounded in such a premise. The very idea of constitutional patriotism, is however, under girded by the *hope and desire* for of an ever-more perfect understanding of the basic principles of justice and their ever more perfect realization in the polity. But this is a political hope. The rhetorical invocation of such a hope is an integral part, for example, in American political rhetoric at Party Conventions or Presidential Inaugural Addresses – in the idea of a more perfect and inclusive Union.

27 A stellar example for this is Eric Hobsbawm, whose major work includes *The Age of Revolution* (Zürich: Kindler, 1962), *The Age of Capital* (New York: Vintage Books, 1975) and *The Age of Empire* (London: Weidenfeld, 1987) which became a defining work of his chosen period, the "long 19th century", from 1789 to 1914. See, also, *The Age of Extremes* (London, 1994) extending his coverage to the "short 20th century".

do not invite a glib, flat and self-congratulatory *hubris* but counsel moderation and a thoughtful tone. Undoubtedly, any history will be and deserves to be contested and criticized with regard to what it leaves out, and with regard to what it emphasizes.

But, on the whole, the enterprise of writing European histories that obtain their perspective from the constitutional ideals of human rights, democracy and the rule of law is likely to spur the kind of debates and engender the kind of disagreements that are likely to foster the development of a variety of rich and complex European identities that crystallize around the appropriation and interpretation of constitutional ideals.

2.4. From European History to European Legal History

In order to provide a more concrete idea of what such an account might look like, the following provides a brief outline of the core structure of a possible European *legal history* that is committed to such an approach. The history proposed could also be called the HISTORY OF LEGAL THOUGHT AND PRACTICE, to distinguish it from other, more positivist conceptions of law and legal history. By the History of *European* Legal Thought and Practice, I mean a history of the basic legal institutions and the basic legal categories that were thought to be central for mapping and subdividing the world of law as well as the basic ideas that supported these institutions and categories.[28]

Clearly, *legal* history is more narrowly focused than political and social history, and is less apt to play a role in the development of thick constitutional patriotism for EU citizens generally. There are two substantial reasons for focusing on European legal history here.

First, legal history has an important role to play for the development of a common legal culture that shapes the identity of European jurists. Europe's constitutionalization – the development and gradual acceptance of the doctrines of direct effect, supremacy, human rights, etc. – is to a significant extent the work of European jurists. It may be a mistake to imagine a role for lawyers in Europe that replicates Savigny's idea of the legal scholar as the em-

---

[28] The approach to legal history described here has much in common with the approach to Comparative Law developed by William Ewald, "Comparative Jurisprudence (1): What was it like to Try a Rat?" *Pennsylvania Law Review* 143 (1995): 1889. In important respects it merely defines the object of study (Law) in terms of a non-positivist account of law along the lines of those developed by Ronald Dworkin, *Law's Empire* (Cambridge, MA: Harvard University Press, 1986).

bodiment of the legal community. But, in a social and political world in which constitutional patriotism is the social and cultural cement, jurists are likely to continue to play a central role in the future. It would be a failure of European historiography if European lawyers in the future thought of European history as the history of the European Union and its law, plus a disparate number of national legal histories (call this the '*sui generis*' approach to European legal historiography: The European Union not as an integral part of a common tradition of political and legal practices, but as a peculiar add-on that does not quite fit any mould).

Second, outlining the structure of any kind of European history is generally full of dangers. It may seem to border on the ridiculous to attempt to do so in a few thousand words. The impression of flatness, due to a combination of lack of detail and sweeping generalizations may give further support to those who are skeptical about such an endeavor in the first place and may earn the scorn of many a selfrespecting historian. The focus on Germany, France and Britain may confirm the suspicions of those who can see nothing in such a choice but an exercise to silence less powerful voices in the name of great power cultural hegemony. What will be offered here is little more than a list of themes and how they are related – much like the syllabus of a course on the history of European Legal Thought and Practice. Even as such there is a great deal missing in this outline, which, some would insist, should be included, just as some may be surprised at what has been included. *If this brief structural outline is presented here nontheless, it is because, all inadequacies and contestable idiosyncrasies notwithstanding, I hope it will at least suggest one important point to those inclined to read it in a spirit of generosity: much can be gained by taking the perspective suggested here.*

3. Some Ideas on a Structure for European Legal History

What, then, could the basic structure of an outline of an account that aspires to such a function look like? As a *legal* history, it focuses on public institutions, the basic ideas that legitimate and guide their practices, as well as the basic legal categories that are used to map the world of law and to define the discipline's sub-divisions. This approach to legal history is, in some sense, not positivist: it suggests an intimate connection between legal practice and the normative ideals that animate it. It would be the historiographical equivalent of what, in jurisprudence, would be called a 'law in context' approach. It connects the description of formal legal structures with the normative ideals underlying it and the political and social forces that give rise to it, shape it and sustain it.

Such a historical account needs to exhibit two features. First, it would have to address the legal implications of the great ideological and political battles against those who challenged the enlightenment political liberal tradition and its commitment to human rights, democracy, and the rule of law. Second, it would have to provide an account of how those who saw themselves as committed to these ideas translated these ideals into concrete institutional arrangements and basic legal categories in their respective social and political contexts. This implies, of course, that a commitment to human rights, democracy, and the rule of law does not simply translate into a particular constitutional blueprint or a set of basic legal categories, just as it does not immediately translate into a particular set of policies. Instead, there have been extensive and deep changes in the dominant understanding of the institutional and categorical implications of a commitment to political Liberalism. European legal history does well to focus on these transformations.

Perhaps, a plausible starting point for such a narrative might be the early Middle Ages and the Gregorian Revolution with its violent separation between the ecclesiastical and secular polity. As Harold Berman argues, it is after the Gregorian Revolution that the core characteristics of the Western Legal Tradition are all in place.[29] The focus of this part of the story would be the development of specifically legal concepts and techniques that are the necessary ingredients for any conception of 'the rule of law'.

The central focus for such a narrative, however, is provided by the Enlightenment. The American and French Revolutions are the political and legal *Big Bang*. Locke, Rousseau and – most of all – Kant,[30] along with the authors of the Federalist Papers, are the intellectual protagonists of the modern constitutional tradition and of Political Liberalism. The radical nature of this revolution for the understanding of what law is about is not always appreciated. The very foundations and purpose of law were newly defined in a way that still resonates today and that reshaped the understanding of even those parts of the law that are of more ancient origin.

---

29 Harold Berman, *Law and Revolution* (Cambridge, MA: Harvard University Press, 1983). See, also, Maurizio Lupoi, *The Origins of the European Legal Order* (New York: CUP, 1999).

30 It has to be noted, however, that the focus of Immanuel Kant's practical philosophy has generally been neglected among legal and political thinkers. Until the 20th century the reception of Kant's practical philosophy had been focused on his *moral* philosophy (the "*Grundlegung der Metaphysik der Sitten*" in particular) and not his legal and political philosophy. The golden age of the productive reception of Kantian *legal and political* philosophy were the last 30 years of the 20th century.

The central revolutionary tenets are captured in the opening of the second paragraph of the American Declaration of Independence as well as core passages of the French Declaration of the Rights of Man.

The relevant paragraph in the Declaration of Independence reads:

> "We hold these Truths to be self-evident, that all men are created equal, that they are endowed by their Creator with certain inalienable Rights, that among these are Life, Liberty and the Pursuit of Happiness-That to secure these Rights Governments are instituted among Men, deriving their just powers from the consent of the governed [...]"

The core passages of the French Declaration of the Rights of Man read:

> Art. 1: Men are born and remain free and equal in respect of their rights. Social distinctions, therefore, may only be founded on common utility.
>
> Art. 4: Liberty consists in being able to do anything which does not injure another: therefore the exercise of the natural rights of each man has no limits other than those which assure the other members of society the enjoyment of the same rights. These may be determined only by the law.
>
> Art. 6: The law is the expression of the general will. All citizens have a right to concur personally, or by their representatives, in its formation [...]

Here, there are three core ideas that are both complex in themselves and stand in a complicated relationship to one another. They have been the subject of political, legal and intellectual struggle ever since. The first concerns individual rights (or, as Kant insisted, the one foundational human right) and defines the limits and purpose of government: The purpose of government is to secure the rights of individuals, understood as a general right to liberty whose limits need to be circumscribed with regard to other individuals. Lines should be drawn in a way that maximizes the general welfare. The second concerns the idea of the rule of law:

All infringements of liberty – all the line-drawing exercises between competing rights by public authorities in the general interest – have to take the form of law. The third concerns democracy: all laws must be enacted in a procedure that allows for the adequate participation of citizens, generally through elections or referenda.

A further characteristic is the absence of both God and religion (or any other perfectionist ideal) as a point of ultimate reference for legal and political life. Many will find it plausible that the ultimate roots of these rights lie in the fact that God has created persons in a certain way, and that rights are instrumental to human flourishing. Indeed the *invocatio dei* was still a common feature in 18th century constitutionalism. But when the authors of the Declaration of Independence declared the foundational principles of Political

Liberalism as self-evident, it created the possibility of thinking of Political Liberalism as the focal point of a consensus that, for the purposes of organizing public life, *avoided* deeper questions of theological foundations and ultimate purposes. It is the kind of public philosophy that does not require deep theological or metaphysical support for its elaboration *in public life*, even if all kinds of competing theological and philosophical accounts exist that can provide such grounding[31] and do provide such grounding for individual citizens. The tradition of Political Liberalism as a *public* philosophy, then, can be regarded as the most celebrated and politically potent historical example of what Cass Sunstein has called an 'incompletely theorized agreement'.[32]

To an important extent the next two hundred years are all about how these basic ideas were digested and their institutional and conceptual implications assessed. They were resisted and denounced as shallow, incoherent and corrupt. But they were also embraced, interpreted, challenged and then reinterpreted. Painting with a very broad brush and with the usual *caveats* with regard to periodization it is helpful to distinguish between three periods in order to highlight the structure of an account that uses the foundational political and legal values of right, democracy and the rule of law as its focal point.[33] The first is from 1789–1919, the second is from 1919–1992 and the third, which we still live in today, started in 1992 with the ratification debates concerning the Treaty of Maastricht. Each period is differentiated from the previous one by the specific opposing ideology, political and social force that challenges the political liberal tradition wholesale,[34] and a specific understanding of the tradition of Political Liberalism as reflected in the basic

---

[31] The best known account of Political Liberalism as a focal point of an overlapping consensus between reasonable comprehensive doctrines is presented in John Rawls, Political Liberalism (New York: Columbia University Press, 1993). John Locke's and Immanuel Kant's account of Political Liberalism are both anchored in a comprehensive philosophy. For a recent study on Locke in this regard see Jeremy Waldron, *God, Locke, and Equality: Christian Foundations in Locke's Political Thought* (New York: CUP, 2003). An influential contemporary account grounds rights in the transcendental presuppositions of speech, see Jürgen Habermas, *Moral Consciousness and Communicative Action* (Cambridge, MA: MIT Press, 1990) and Robert Alexy, "Diskurstheoric und Menschenrechte," *Recht, Vernunft, Diskurs* 127 (1995).

[32] Cass R. Sunstein, *Legal Reasoning and Political Conflict* (New York: OUP, 1996).

[33] For a different periodization focused on transformations of law and legal thought see Duncan Kennedy, "Two Globalizations of Law & Legal Thought: 1850–1968," *Suffolk University Law Review* 36 (2003): 632.

[34] For an illuminating analysis of the range and structure of these attacks see Stephen Holmes, *The Anatomy of Antiliberalism* (Cambridge, MA: Harvard University Press, 1993).

constitutional ideas and basic legal categories, which were developed as a response to these challenges.

3.1. 1789–1919: The Ancien Régime vs. Classical Legal Liberalism

The first period extends roughly from the French Revolution to the end of World War I. The enemies of Political Liberalism during this time were the forces of Restoration. The monarchs, the nobility and the clergy fighting were all fighting for their privileges in the name of historically grounded and religiously sanctioned legitimacy. The political battles fought by the liberals were against the monarchy, the privileges of the aristocracy and the church. The specific nature of the battles could be revolutionary, as was the case with France going through a number of revolutions and constitutional regimes in the 19th century before achieving relative stability in the Third Republic. They could also take the form of a more gradual development, as was the case in Britain, where Dicey (still a staple reference in much of contemporary British scholarship)[35] articulated the mature constitutional law of the 19th century at a time when the position of parliament against the crown had solidified while the franchise had gradually been extended. Germany, on the other hand, produced a failed and feeble attempt at a liberal revolution in 1848 and was late to establish a modern liberal constitution in the form of the ill-fated Weimar constitution in 1919. By the end of World War One, the old European world – the *ancien régime* – ceased to be a significant political force strong enough to resist the tide of political liberal ideas.

The basic understandings of human rights, democracy and the rule of law which developed in this period are familiar enough. Characteristic for this period are the constitutional struggles for the recognition of the people's consent rather than the sovereignty of the monarch as the basis for political authority, expressed in the process of constitution-giving. Other constitutional themes included the recognition of the centrality of the role of parliament (as opposed to the monarchically dominated executive branch), the strengthening of the first – popularly elected – parliamentary chamber against the second more aristocratic chamber (be it the British House of Lords, the French *Senate* or the German *Bundesrat*) and the extension of the franchise (to those without property, to women and by lowering the age requirement, often from 25 to 21).

Attempts to generally constrain executive authority by law's formalities and the emergence of a field of administrative law were also characteristic of

---

[35] Albert V. Dicey, *The Law of the Constitution* (London: Macmillan, 1885).

this period. Despite this, citizens failed to obtain the kind of protection from courts for acts against officials as they obtained in case of actions against private individuals.

Public law, being so closely connected to struggles against the *ancient régime* during most of the 19th century in many jurisdictions, was regarded as closely aligned to politics. It could only get a foothold in universities and share in the prestige of the legal discipline, if it positioned itself as above the fray of ideology – something that could be done only by adopting a clear positivist focus. The positivist focus also allowed jurists more generally to share in the prestige of the 'natural sciences' that were very much focused on classifying and systematizing observable phenomena.

In such a political and social context, *constitutional law* lagged behind other disciplines. There was no practice it could latch on to. To the extent that a constitutional text made reference to rights at all, these were not generally susceptible to judicial enforcement but merely directives to the legislator (mainly of symbolic significance, if at all). Perhaps the core issue of *International Law* in the increasingly positivist climate in the 19th century was how it could exist at all given the lack of an international sovereign, though a less conceptually driven positivism soon found its basis in the fact that states did in fact engage in Treaty making and had use for the kind of expertise that lawyerly exegesis can provide.

This was the time of triumph, however, for private law. The study of law at the continental European faculties was primarily the study of private law with freedom of contract, property and torts at its core. Private law was the domain of legal reasoning properly so called – whether it took the form of the common law splicing precedent or debates concerning codification. Private law provided for a sphere in which private individuals governed themselves – with the common law and the codes functioning as something akin to the constitution of an autonomous civil society. With the move from status to contract, here, at least the revolutionary ideals could find their firm foundation in the work of legal scholars.

More generally, great significance was attached to the distinction between (1) law (grounded in authoritative pronouncements ultimately traceable to a sovereign) and politics (assertion of will), (2) private law (reason, best left to legal experts) and public law (result of political choice enacted by the relevant authority) and (3) national law (grounded in a constitution through which people govern themselves) and international law (a code of conduct for a world of sovereign states in the limited domain of foreign affairs grounded in state consent). In conjunction with a constitutional ideal of parliamentarianism (often compromised by a constitutional status for monarchs), these distinctions and preoccupations are the characteristics of what I call *Classical Legal Liberalism.* Classical Legal Liberalism, then, describes a particular constellation of ideas that spelled out how the abstract principles of Political Liberalism were translated into a concrete institutional order and basic legal categories. Among private lawyers, in particular, a great many of these ideas still exert influence in Europe even today.

3.2. 1918–1992: Totalitarianism vs. Liberal-Democratic Constitutionalism

In World War I the *ancien régime* had committed political suicide. At this point, however, different anti-liberal forces that Hannah Arendt was the first to group together and call 'totalitarian' were on the rise and overthrew many liberal democracies in Europe. Fascism and Communism were the greatest challenges to Political Liberalism during this period and tore Europe apart in what has been called a European civil war, with German Nazism playing the most devastating role. Political Liberalism was chastised once again, this time by those speaking in the name of the two strongest political forces of the time: nationalism and socialism. Political Liberalism was now scolded as the ideological superstructure of the bourgeoisie, a Jewish invention grounded in a psychology of deracinated nomads, not compatible with the honor and glory of the nation. Whereas fascism was discredited after the destruction and atrocities of World War II, dictatorships lingered on in parts of Southern Europe until the 1970s. Communism was a force that, in Western Europe after World War Two was either non-existent (UK), weak and prohibited (West Germany), or parliamentarily tamed (as in France and Italy). However, it remained the reigning ideology and political practice in Eastern Europe until 1989 – in part enforced on the Eastern European Peoples by the Soviet Union as exemplified by the Soviet intervention in Hungary in 1956 and in Czechoslovakia in 1968.

The confrontation with the social, economic and political challenges that brought forward the ferocious political energies that made fascism and communism possible also changed dominant ideas about the institutionalization of the ideals of human right, democracy and the rule of law. Political Liberalism – when it ultimately prevailed – no longer resembled Classical Legal Liberalism. Both nationalism and socialism left deep traces in the legal imagination and found their imprint in a constellation of ideas that I will refer to as Liberal-Democratic Constitutionalism.

The most important politically salient transformation of this time period is the radical expansion of state regulation by the legislature, a massive expansion of the administrative capacities of the executive branches (the rise of the administrative state), used primarily to manage the economy and redistribute wealth (the social welfare state). Besides the remarkable expansion of administrative capacities and institutions, the perhaps most interesting institutional change for legal historians is the advent of constitutional courts and the rise of judicially enforceable constitutional rights. In the following, I will restrict myself to a brief account of how the understanding of rights changed the dominant understanding of Political Liberalism and helped undermine many of the basic categories of Classical Legal Liberalism.

After World War One, the idea that property rights and freedom of contract were the pillars for an apolitical social sphere that was free from regulatory intervention – subject to many early challenges, but exhibiting great staying power – became obsolete. Instead, the classical liberal state was transformed into what Carl Schmitt – describing political practices in the pre-Fascist late Weimar republic – called a total state. A total state was a state in which a 'motorized legislator', propelled by various interest groups, enacted antitrust law, labor law, public health law, *etc.*, to address economic and social concerns. This shattered the idea of the autonomy of private law as the self-constitution of an apolitical civil society. It also undermined the idea of a nightwatchman state in favor of a state whose task was to help ensure the social welfare of its citizens.

As a corollary of the radical expansion of public policies generally and the regulatory authority of the executive branch (and not just the experience of fascism from 1933–1945), the idea of the protection of rights would take on a radically different form after World War Two. In Germany – with a constitutional tradition perhaps as influential in the 20th century as its private law tradition had been in the 19th – the dangers of the total state, it seemed, could only be tamed by what might be called a *total constitution*. This is a constitution that incorporates a comprehensive system of constitutional rights. In German constitutional law, the scope of constitutional rights is as expansive as it can be. It includes a general right to liberty and a general right to equality. A great many politically salient issues would become the subject matter of constitutional disputes resolved ultimately by a constitutional court. Judicially enforceable rights, then, were no longer the rights guaranteed by private law or the whim of the ordinary legislator as a matter of public law. Instead a comprehensive system of rights would enable any individual adversely affected by actions of public authorities to seek a legal remedy by means of a constitutional complaint that her constitutional rights have been violated.

Besides bringing a new judicial actor into play that had the authority to set aside acts by parliament – a constitutional court as first conceived by Kelsen and institutionalized in Austria in 1920 – this also had far-reaching implications for the understanding of two core distinctions central to Classical Legal Liberalism. The first concerns the relationship between law and morality. Rights contained in national constitutional rights catalogues in Continental Europe are widely understood as abstract principles. When courts are enforcing rights they are not perceived by citizens to enforce the terms of a bargain between powerful groups who originally negotiated them. Nor are rights generally well understood as specific guarantees that respond to and seek to avoid the repetition of specific historical experiences (though of course there are specific guarantees of that nature, too). Instead, constitutional rights in Continental Europe are widely believed to be the codification of rights that all people can make a claim to in virtue of their humanity or in virtue of being a citizen in a democratic polity.

Instead of a clear divide between law and political morality, constitutional adjudication brought general practical reasoning (political morality or simply politics) to the heart of adjudication. Not surprisingly, perhaps the most influential legal theorists reflecting on the jurisprudential significance of this practice, Ronald Dworkin[36] and Robert Alexy,[37] defend a conception of law that establishes a deep connection between law and political morality. Both derive their conclusions by focusing on the practice of adjudication of rights. Both radicalize the positions adopted by early post-World War Two legal thinkers – Lon Fuller[38] and Gustav Radbruch[39] being perhaps the most prominent among them – who sought to establish a weak link between law and political morality. This is a clean break with the positivism that characterized mainstream scholarship and the selfunderstanding of legal practitioners in the world of Classical Legal Liberalism.

This *normative turn in jurisprudence* challenged and became the main competitor to the 'high positivism' exemplified by Hans Kelsen[40] and H.L.A.

---

36 Ronald Dworkin, *Taking Rights Seriously* (Cambridge, MA: Harvard University Press, 1977), *Law's Empire.*

37 Robert Alexy, *Theorie der Juristischen Argumentation* (Frankfurt am Main: Suhrkamp, 1978) (English: *Theory of Legal Argumentation* [Oxford: Clarendon Press, 1989]), *Theorie der Grundrechte* (Frankfurt am Main: Suhrkamp, 1986) (English: *A Theory of Constitutional Rights* [Oxford: OUP, 2002]).

38 Lon Fuller, *The Morality of Law* (New Haven and London: Yale University Press, 1963).

39 Gustav Radbruch, "Gesetzliches Unrecht und Übergesetzliches Recht," *Süddeutsche Juristenzeitung* (1945): 105–108.

40 Hans Kelsen, *Reine Rechtslehre* (2nd ed., Vienna: Deuticke, 1960, 1st ed., Berlin: Duncker & Humbolt, 1928).

Hart,[41] which followed or survived the jurisprudential burst of creativity exemplified, for example, by the Weimar debates about method (*Methodenstreit*)[42] or Scandinavian Realism[43] in the first half of the century. Both the practice of constitutional rights enforcement and the normative turn in jurisprudence were supported by a public climate in which ideological conflict was constrained by the political liberal vocabulary that was used to make claims. Not only was fascism dead as an ideological movement and political force, subtle continuities in the interstices of legal practice notwithstanding.[44] Communism, too, by the early seventies, had lost its appeal in many western countries. Intellectuals no longer lionized the USSR after its intervention in Prague in 1968 and the publication of Solzhenitsyn's novel on the '*Gulag Archepelago*', which was awarded the Nobel Prize in 1970. Furthermore, there was a general sense that the economic model of central planning was unlikely to be superior to a market economy if the latter was socially tamed and heavily regulated (the Third Way as it was understood then).

Furthermore, the death of all competitor ideologies was hastened by the fact that as the communists marched into a Prague where reformist students celebrated a new culture of freedom in the Spring of 1968 only to be crushed by Soviet tanks, in liberal democracies constitutional courts frequently protected the liberties of demonstrators and 'deviants'. With the successful reformist channeling and blunting of the student movements by the early seventies, support for courts authorized to strike down public legislation if it infringed individuals interests without support by good reasons was strong. But public reason did not just flourish in the reasoning of constitutional courts. More generally, the last three decades of the 20th century were conducive to an intellectual environment in which philosophers and political theorists rediscovered the 18th century tradition of practical reason.[45] In ad-

---

41 Herbert L.A. Hart, *The Concept of Law* (Oxford: Clarendon, 1960).

42 See the useful compilation of materials contained in: *Weimar: A Jurisprudence of Crisis*, eds. Arthur Jacobsen and Bernard Schlink (Berkeley: University of California Press, 2000).

43 See, for example, Alf Ross, *Towards a Realistic Jurisprudence in Law* (Copenhagen: Einar Munksgaard, 1946).

44 51 See *Darker Legacies of Law in Europe*, eds. Christian Joerges and Navraj S. Ghaleigh (Oxford: Hart Publishing, 2003).

45 The normative turn in jurisprudence was supported by the rehabilitation of practical reason and political philosophy following the hugely influential publishing of John Rawls, *A Theory of Justice* (Cambridge, MA: Harvard University Press, 1971) and a slew of major monographs on political philosophy ranging from Robert Nozick, *Anarchy State and Utopia* (New York: Basic Books, 1974) to Jürgen Habermas,

dition to political and constitutional theories about rights in the 1970 and 1980s, deliberative democracy begins to replace Schumpeterian Democracy and other theories of Parliamentarianism as the most prominent paradigm for thinking about democracy by the early 1990s.

The second implication of the expansive conception of rights described above concerns the relationship between private and public law. Whereas the turn to what Schmitt called the total state had revealed private law to be as much a subject of political decision-making as public law, now constitutional rights – through doctrines such a '*mittelbare Drittwirkung*' or 'horizontal effect' – were increasingly understood to be applicable as a standard for assessing not only public law, but also the legislation and interpretation of private law. Not only have both public and private law been subject to political intervention since the first part of the 20th century. In the second part, private law norms and their interpretation by civil courts have both been subjected to constitutional rights scrutiny by a constitutional court whose work is the focus of constitutional lawyers.

More generally, the 20th Century saw private law replaced by public law – and constitutional law more specifically – as the master discipline in law. The great legal debates of the 19th Century that resonated beyond the halls of the law faculties are the struggles surrounding the major codes, worked out to a large extent by scholars and ultimately adopted by parliaments. The greatest focus of legal attention in the 20th Century has been the constitution as a legal document, the constitutional judiciary as an institution and the struggle for an understanding of constitutional rights and their relationship to democracy as a theoretical challenge. Together with the rise of the administrative welfare state, these changes mark the transformation from Classical Legal Liberalism to what could be called Liberal-Democracy Constitutionalism.

These transformations and preoccupations, in conjunction with the dark shadow of the Cold War, helped to perpetuate and to further strengthen the traditional nationalist and statist understanding of the world of law. Notwithstanding some deep theoretical debates among international lawyers in the first decades of the 20th century, the growth of International Law did nothing to shake belief in the basic nature of the distinction between national and international law.[46] Nor did International Law become a required subject

Faktizitaet und Geltung (Frankfurt am Main: Suhrkamp, 1992). The dominant strand of this philosophizing, perhaps exemplified by Rawls and Habermas, is strongly influenced by Kant.

46 Characteristically neither in the general jurisprudendial account provided by Ronald Dworkin or Robert Alexy addresses International law, unlike their positivist predecessors Hans Kelsen and Herbert L.A. Hart, that devote special chapters to

of study, the way that Constitutional Law became a required subject of study in most places by the 1980s. International Law did develop and shed its ontological anxieties, as the ILO, the League of Nations to the UN, the establishment of the World Bank, the IMF and the GATT, as well as important human rights Treaties (such as the ECHR and the ICCPR) provided legally trained professionals texts and decisions to engage. International Law flourished, but it flourished as a specialized discipline. It was still animated by an *ethos* to fulfil International Law's bright future.[47] Clearly, the European Communities provided a remarkable supranational framework for the legal integration of EC Members after WWII. But it was not widely perceived as a politically relevant actor during most of this time. From the early seventies until the mid eighties, those who discussed the EC most likely would discuss what was then called the problem of *Eurosclerosis.* Even if the European Court of Justice (ECJ) had staked its claim that EU Law is the supreme law of the land in the early sixties, this was something of interest and enthusiasm for the International lawyers that specialized in EC Law. Even though the subtle and deep transformation of Europe[48] – the process of constitutionalization of European Law – had already occurred by the late eighties, it was something the wider public would wake up to only later. It occurred only when the Treaty of Maastricht threatened to take away people's national money and give them European citizenship in return.

3.3. Post 1992: Bread and Circus vs. Constitutionalism Beyond the State

With the fall of the Berlin Wall and the end of the Cold War, it seems that all the major ideological competitors to Political Liberalism and the master discourse of human rights, democracy and the rule of law have exhausted themselves. We are all Political Liberals now. Fundamentalist Islam, though a political challenge as a matter of domestic and foreign policy, and a security issue as far as it is linked to terrorism, is unlikely to become a politically potent force across Europe to seriously challenge Political Liberalism. Nor is it

---

International Law. Notably both Kelsen and Hart's jurisprudence are not especially grounded in constitutional law – they were writing before the adjudication of rights had become an important phenomenon in Europe. In addition Kelsen, at least, formed his major ideas during the inter-war period, in which International Law flourished. Not surprisingly his account of International Law is the least sceptical.

47 See David Kennedy, "Tom Franck and the Manhattan School," 35 *N.Y.U. J. INT'L L. & POL.* 397 (2002).

48 The authoritative account of this process remains Joseph H.H. Weiler, "The Transformation of Europe," 100 *YALE L.J.* 2403 (1991).

likely that a new nationalism or a new Christian religious fundamentalism will be able to threaten the basic commitments of Political Liberalism in Europe. But the political liberal tradition does face a serious threat. By perfectly tracing Hegelian dialectics, it is becoming apparent that the absence of a real enemy has unleashed intellectual and political forces that suggest that the days of grand political narratives, including the narratives surrounding human rights, democracy and the rule of law, are over. There are two mutually supportive trends that undermine the public salience of the liberal political tradition and hinder the development of a meaningful identity which is focused on constitutional patriotism.

First, if, as is frequently claimed in Europe, the contemporary constellation is a post-statist, post-national, post sovereign one, is it not only fitting that the basic ideas of the political liberal tradition, developed to tame and guide the exercise of public authority within the framework of the state, have also run their course? Is it possible for a post-statist world to exist, that is not also postmodern? Are there not an irreducible plurality of communities, identities and spaces for political and legal intervention? Should not the pretensions of grand narratives – even the grand narratives involving human rights, democracy and the rule of law – give way to contextual, local engagement that is appropriately sensitive to difference? Grand narratives and the master vocabulary they insist on are bad, because they tend to do violence to the colorful variety of legitimate claims that the social, political and legal world should be designed to respond to.

Second, this critical discourse emphasizing the local and contextual nature of all legal conflict, as well as pluralism and diversity more generally, dovetails nicely with economistic and utilitarian neo-liberal ideologies, in which there are only preferences and institutions – preferably markets – that need to be designed to maximize their realization. Here, the Marxist prediction that a *bourgeois* society will commodify all relationships and subject everything to market rules seems remarkably on point. The legal profession, certainly, is today conceived and regulated merely as a provider of services. Rather than guardians of public reason or the lawyer statesmen, the shrewd and appropriately specialized corporate lawyer is becoming the guiding ideal underlying legal education. On the other hand, the public sphere is increasingly trivialized as it is governed by economic imperatives that make it increasingly unsuitable as a medium for serious political deliberations.

From the Treaty of Maastricht to the Constitutional Treaty, the language of constitutionalism – citizenship, right, democracy, constitution – has been fully appropriated by the European Union. Yet, there is a temptation to see this as an unsuccessful cover up, a somewhat helpless attempt to downplay the fact that European electoral politics plays practically no role on the European level. The relationship between European citizens and their polity is not defined by the idea of citizens as a *zoon politicon, but the double image of a rationalist homo oecomonicus (bread!) and a post-modern homo ludens (circus!).* The European Union functions as a straightjacket for national political processes, while at the same time failing to give European citizens the capacity to hold European decision-makers collectively electorally accountable – there is no government that can be voted out of office.

What European citizens gain they gain as a breadwinner and consumer. The great challenge posed by the European Union both in its present and its future form is *to reconceive the political liberal tradition without the statist framework that originally served as its frame of reference.* The question is what the guarantee of human rights, democracy and the rule of law will amount to and what concrete legal and political form it will take in Europe at the beginning of the 21st century.

With European integration and globalization, electorally accountable institutions have been the great losers, whereas the executive branch, courts and transnational bureaucracies have been the great winners. European constitutionalism as a form of constitutionalism beyond the state raises a number of basic questions about the adequate institutional embodiment of political liberal ideals in transnational legal and political practices. Is the language of that tradition really little more than 'pathos and patina' to an economistic consumer society? Grappling with these questions is relevant not only for struggles over Europe's legal and political form. They raise many issues that mirror and foreshadow debates about the basic concepts and concerns relevant to assess and guide the development of global institutional practices. Any successful account of constitutionalism beyond the state then, is likely to embrace markets as a central institution within the overall constitutional framework and will emphasize the normative significance of pluralism, be it along the dimension of identities or political and legal practices. A great many other things, however, remain unclear.

At this point the historical account must end as the stage is cleared for the jurisprudential, legal and political debates that have accompanied European Union Law ever since it was catapulted from the niche of specialists into the glaring limelight of public scrutiny in the context of the ratifications of the Treaty of Maastricht in 1992. But it is already possible to identify what will be, in the perspective taken here, the four core conceptual and institutional *challenges* of European constitutionalism – and of constitutionalism beyond the state more generally. Only once these challenges have been met and a new account has gained widespread acceptance is it possible to describe the substantive terms of a new settlement. For now it must suffice to articulate the challenges.

First, the issue of *constitutional supremacy* is likely to be debated with new intensity in the context of the Constitutional Treaty. The Constitutional Treaty includes a clause that established the primacy of EU Law, but does not require ratification by a European constituant power, but makes do with the ratification according to national constitutional requirements. Furthermore, it contains a clause that seems to authorize states to protect their respective national constitutional and political identities. Is this sufficient to settle the supremacy issue? Can there be a supreme constitution without a constitutive act of 'We the People'? What exactly is required for a legal text to successfully claim that it is the supreme law of the land? Is it even desirable for the supremacy issue to be settled? Could it be more desirable to give up the idea of a legal world constituted by a hierarchy of norms with a supreme rule grounding the whole practice? Answering these questions is likely to require deep rethinking of the basic categories which the liberal tradition has traditionally used as a frame of reference.

The second issue is the issue of *democracy* and the much discussed 'democratic deficit' in the European Union. The central question is: how is it possible to remain faithful to democratic values in the context of supranational decisionmaking? What can be done about the sad state of affairs in the European Union as far as electoral decision-making is concerned? The core issue is that decision making on the level of the European Union cannot convincingly be attributed to any specific actor that could then be held accountable in elections for the result. Yet, the requirement to have electorally accountable institutions at the heart of the political process is exactly the minimal consensus on what democracy has been about both in the period of Classical Legal Liberalism and the era of constitutional democracy. But does it make sense to insist on such a requirement for the European Union or transnational legislation more generally?

Is a genuine European democracy even possible, given the current underdevelopment of a European public sphere and a lack of social cohesion on the European level? Or is the very absence of electorally accountable institutions at the heart of the European political process the reason why a robust European public sphere has not yet developed? Can the necessary social cohesion be generated by the right kind of institutional practices? Or is the establishment of meaningful electoral politics on the European level important only if and to the extent the European Union will become a more central actor in the areas of taxation, social welfare and security – issues of sufficient political salience to mobilize large constituencies?

This connects the discussion of democracy to the third core challenge. It relates to competencies and could be called the *subsidiarity challenge*. The idea of subsidiarity is in the process of taking the place that the term 'sovereignty' has traditionally occupied in order to defend national communities against undue infringements of their capacity to govern themselves. The basic idea is simple. For a whole host of reasons – including greater sensibility to local preferences, enhanced participation and respect for national identities – *prima facie*, decisions should be made on the level of Member States rather than the EU. Only when there are specific reasons of sufficient weight in specific circumstances – relating to such things as externalities, race to the bottom concerns, interest group politics or the expression of common values – should measures be taken by the EU rather than Member States.

The problem is that there is no consensus on what exactly the political implications of a commitment to subsidiarity are. What should the role of the Union be concerning redistributive politics, taxation and security, for example? Here the Constitutional Treaty does include some interesting procedural innovations involving national parliaments. But it remains an open question how the principle should or will be operationalized and interpreted by EU institutions, including the ECJ.

Finally, there is what could be called the *human rights challenge*. The relatively simple arrangement by which national constitutions establishes a set or even a system of basic rights to be enforced by a constitutional judiciary is substituted by something significantly more complicated in contemporary European practice. Basic Rights catalogues can now be found on the national level, the level of the European Union, the European Convention of Human Rights, as well as general International Human Rights Treaties (most prominently the ICCPR) and specialized human rights agreements. How should the interrelationship between all these guarantees be institutionally managed? To what extent should national courts take into account any or all of this in their adjudication of national constitutional rights norms? To what extent should discretion be accorded to national institutions in determining the protections afforded to their citizens (the ECHR uses the term 'margin of appreciation' in this respect[49]), to what extent should the guarantees of the European Union's Charter be applicable to Member States at all, rather than just to EU institutions?[50] What does it mean for the understanding of human rights on the European level that, both with regard to their

---

[49] See Handyside v. U.K., *European Human Rights Record* 1 (7 December 1976): 737.

[50] For example, would the ERT line of jurisprudence still be law of the land after the ratification of the Constitutional Charter, Art. II-51 notwithstanding?

sources[51] and their interpretation,[52] the ECJ has to take into account the determinations made by a diverse set of institutional actors? What, if any, conception of rights can make sense of such a convoluted practice?

4. Conclusion

This article is a defence and a further development of the idea of a thick constitutional patriotism and enlists a particular conception of legal history in its service.

Thick constitutional patriotism is an attractive conception of European identity for at least three reasons. First, it is a public identity which is rooted in an open, confident but *self-reflective universalism*. It does not need to identify an 'Other' to exclude as a means of self-stabilization. Second, it is not an identity tied slavishly to the European Union and its institutions but to European constitutional practice seen as a whole, as it developed over time. Its *commitment is to constitutionalism and the ideals that animate it, not to a particular constitution*. Such a focus has several advantages. It allows for more critical distance to the actual institutional practices on the European level. A European constitutional patriot can be for or against the Constitutional Treaty, for example, depending on the extent to which he understands it as a fitting embodiment of constitutional ideals. It also provides constitutional patriotism with a grounding that is deeper then an exclusive focus on the institutions of the European Union could provide. And it means that a European identity is not in conflict with, but enriches and deepens the understanding of various nationally focused identities, as well sharpening the awareness for Europe's common specificity. Third, a European identity focused on constitutional patriotism remains *open to contestation and difference*. The idea of constitutional patriotism merely provides a basic focal point for a plurality of identities that can challenge, complement and enrich one another. The ideas of human rights, democracy and the rule of law remain contested, both on the level of

---

51 The Constitutional Treaty mentions the Charter of Fundamental Rights as well as the traditional formula first used by the ECJ "Fundamental rights as guaranteed by the ECHR, and as they result from the constitutional traditions common to the Member States as general principles of the Union's law", while opening up the prospect accession to the ECHR in addition to all of this, see Art. II-7.

52 Art. II-52.3 prescribes that rights corresponding to rights in the ECHR shall have the same meaning as scope as defined therein, and Art. II-52.4 states that 'insofar as this Charter recognizes fundamental rights as they result from the constitutional tradition common to the Member States, those rights shall be interpreted in harmony with those traditions.'

abstract ideas and the concrete institutional and practical implications to be derived from them. It is the very fact that political and legal conflicts, when they get serious, are contested using the vocabulary of the tradition of constitutionalism that makes it a unique focal point for a common identity.

To some extent, the actual development of such identities depends on and focuses on the availability of rich historical narratives that can help foster and sustain it. The bare bone structure of one such a narrative, more narrowly focused on legal history, served to provide an illustration of the kind of phenomena that would come into view. The conception of legal history it exemplifies exhibits three core features. First, and most obviously, it takes a *European* rather than a national frame of reference. Even national historiography does well to contextualize its narrative and situate it in a European context. Second, the *structure of the narrative is provided by the focus on the legal and intellectual struggles connected to* Political Liberalism: The tradition of *human rights, democracy and the rule of law* and its implications for the design of legal institutions and the basic categories of law. Third, it *places the evolution of the basic institutions and categories of the law in its social and political context.*

It analyzes the basic institutions and legal categories in light of the normative ideals that underpin them and the social and political forces that sustain them. In this sense, the subject matter of its inquiry is not understood in positivist terms. The specifics even of this bare bone outline can and should be subject to dispute. The core point of this article would be successfully made, if it became clear that much can be gained by adopting a conception of European legal history illustrated here.

Without doubt, the development of thick constitutional patriotism in Europe depends on more than the *availability* of rich historical narratives that can sustain it. To some extent, it depends on a *proactive politics of memory* that members of civil society as well as public institutions at the national and European level support. There are a number of ways that the EU is already engaging in such politics. Why should the European Commission not, for example, provide funding for courses taught on European legal history at law faculties? But even if the politics of memory matters, it would amount to little more than shallow brand management if not supported by a political practice which connects memory to joint political action. It is the political process at the European level that has to provide citizens with an opportunity and an incentive to engage meaningfully with these ideals and narratives in the course of an ongoing political practice. Much would have to be said in this respect about current political practices, the constitution-giving process and the institutional reforms included in the Constitutional Treaty, but this is not the place to do it.

III. Forgiveness and Law

Svend Erik Larsen
(Aarhus University)

Forgiveness as a Challenge to the Law: A Literary Perspective

1. Forgiveness is Not a Feel-Good Attitude

Quite a few people take forgiveness to be a feel-good attitude, something mainly aiming at forgetting injustice or a way of exhibiting one's individual capacity to be a good human being, *really* good, by showing an ability to forgive certain deviations from collectively accepted norms. This widespread conception sparks two contrasting conceptions of forgiveness. One of them states that forgiveness is yet another example of how a firm position dissolves when we just turn the other cheek and don't stand up to the challenges and conflicts of life. The opposite conception holds that forgiveness, both on an individual and a collective level, is a powerful human resource that enables us to go on with life in spite of some injustice inflicted upon us and prepares us to face the messiness of human life.

In literature the two contrasting conceptions not only determine individual approaches to forgiveness, but frame the entire cultural and normative space in which individual characters interact and where both positions are defended simultaneously by different characters, narrators or institutions and their representatives. In this way literature exposes the normative complexity we have to confront in our lives whereas the political or judicial debate in a narrow sense only offers a too simple dichotomy. From Antigone's clash with Kreon in Sophocles' *Antigone* (fourth century BCE) via Prince Genji's conflict with the Japanese court in Murasaki Shikibu's *Genji Monogatari* (c. 1000) and Portia's cunning victory over Shylock in William Shakespeare's *The Merchant of Venice* (1593) to Rian Malan's South African auto-biography *My Traitor's Heart* (1991) literature explores the limits and contradictions involved in normative regulations of human life.[1]

---

[1] Sophocles, *Antigone* [fourth century BCE] in *The Theban Plays* (London: Penguin, 1973), 126–162; Murasaki Shikibu, *The Tale of Genji* (New York: Alfred Knopf, 1976); William Shakespeare, *The Merchant of Venice* [1593] (London: Routledge, 1989); Rian Malan, *My Traitor's Heart* (London: Vintage, 1991).

Here, and in many other texts across cultural and historical borders, forgiveness is a topic which opens a space both of reconciliation and of normative conflicts and thus outlines a zone that can be regulated only by a complex combination of formal or informal laws. The exercise of formal laws always have a triple task with different foundations: 1) to perform in accordance with a set of formally institutionalized rules based on jurisprudence; 2) to achieve an informal acceptance among people based on a sense of justice; and 3) to envision possible changes of the law or of legal practice based on political decisions. However, this triangular complexity in its entirety tends to be suppressed when the political debate emphasizes one of them, or when the need to reach a final verdict in the court room makes us focus on one of the other dimensions. My paper departs from the assumption that forgiveness embraces all three dimensions in a dynamical interaction without pushing any of them aside. Forgiveness is a complex social process:

1) *Remembrance:* Forgiveness is not about forgetting conflicts, but about remembering them, often a painful process of remembrance. First and foremost, forgiveness confirms that some injustice has happened. Without the permanent remembrance of this initial recognition of normative transgression, there is no forgiveness.

2) *Reiteration:* Forgiveness is not, like a verdict after the last appeal or a vote in parliament on a new legislation, an act that once and for all settles a case. Instead, it fosters a continuous process of a fragile and reiterated confirmation that a delicate balance of norms and values is possible without reaching complete reconciliation and without recurring to formal laws. Forgiveness invites to a negotiation of normative tensions which cannot be solved by a political or legal decision, but will continue to have a significant individual or collective presence in spite of such decisions.

3) *Limits of norms:* Forgiveness occurs as an individual act, but shows the limits of collective norms, legal justice included. Laws, formalized or not, are not able to cover all conflicts of social life. To take but one example, the ban on smoking in many countries gave rise to a heated discussion of the limit between private and public regulation of human interaction. Other conflicts, like genocide, are of a magnitude that no legal system can comprise in their entirety, but only provide with a scary visibility by targeting the main perpetrators in the vain hope that such atrocities therefore will never be repeated.[2]

---

[2] See, Hannah Arendt, *Eichmann in Jerusalem. A Report on the Banality of Evil* [1963] (London: Penguin, 1992); Tzvetan Todorov, "Les limites de la justice" in *La signa-*

In this framework forgiveness is a courageous way of constantly reminding us that there is a grey zone between formal law and the norms of collective human life and reminding us in such a way that our actions in this ambiguous space become an individual moral responsibility. This responsibility is never exhausted by one major gesture of forgiveness, but must transform itself into a fragile daily need to reconfirm the act of forgiveness. Forgiveness that cannot be or need not be repeated is not forgiveness, just a trivial excuse or an insincere lip service. This view of forgiveness is not a formal or universal definition, but a rather recent historical construction in Western culture. Forgiveness is not an ideal or metaphysical phenomenon, as in a religious perspective, but a concrete, historical act, shaped within and by changing cultural contexts to the extent that these contexts allow for forgiveness at all.

Literature and law meet in the grey zone of collective norm but coming from opposite sides of the normative spectrum: From the point of view of law the question is how much of this space can be and ought to be regulated by formal legislation to avoid conflicts arising from the individual arbitrariness when people take the law into their own hands. With self-defense as a tricky borderline case our laws forbid people to practice self-help – in contrast to other past and contemporary legal systems – but they require that people take forgiveness in their own hands to fill the gap between experienced injustice and formal justice. In some cultures self-help is condoned, in others it has to be brought to court – or forgiven.

From the point of view of literature as a reflection on the conditions of human life, the question related to the grey zone is different: How do unsolvable conflicts affect our lives, our self-understanding as humans and members of a community? Why are they there at all? What are the consequences of the paradoxes embedded in the contrast between what can be regulated by law and what cannot, but nevertheless has to be dealt with for life to go on? How are conflicts shaped between irreconcilable legal systems located in the same cultural space as for instance in the global multicultural

---

ture humaine. Essais 1983–2008 (Paris: Le Seuil, 2009), 231–250. See also, Hannah Arendt, *The Human Condition* (Chicago: Chicago University Press, 1958); Jacques Derrida, *Cosmopolitanism and Forgiveness* (London: Routledge, 2001); Richard Holloway, *On Forgiveness. How Can We Forgive the Unforgivable?* (Edinburgh: Canongate, 2004); Svend Erik Larsen, "Forgiving and Forgetting" in *Filologia, Memória e Esquecimento*, eds. Fernanda Mota Alves et al. (Lisbon: Ediçoes Húmus, 2010), 29–49; Paul Ricœur, *La mémoire, l'historie, l'oubli* (Paris: Le Seuil 2000); H. M. Wallace, J. J. Exline and R. F. Baumeister, "Interpersonal consequences of forgiveness: Does forgiveness deter or encourage repeat of offenses," *Journal of Experimental Social Psychology* 44 (2008): 452–460.

societies of the twenty-first century? Literature feeds on the paradoxes the legal system cannot solve, but has to be reminded of as part of its *raison d'être*.

Conflicts between legal systems not only include those between a Western legal system and systems originating elsewhere, like sharia or orthodox Judaism. But also within the Western tradition itself we have conflicting legal agents: martial law versus civic law as made visible in Guantánamo, a legal void that generates more revenge than reconciliation around the world. In the Roman Catholic countries we witness influences from the informal remnants of canon law, a formal system in the days of the inquisition, but now reduced to informal moral guidelines. It underpins the institution of confession, which is based on a cultural and specific conception of forgiveness. But the recent discussion of the way the Catholic Church around the world has handled cases of pedophilia committed by servants of the church has also shown that canon law still works as a shield against investigations and complaints based on civic law. At the same time, the request for forgiveness uttered by many victims of child abuse is stronger than their wish for a verdict.

Thus in the normative grey zone kept open by the possibility and the necessity of forgiveness as part of human life, law and literature intersect, each of them in need of the other to cover the complex reality of cultural norms. Literature is reminded that even in its most individual forms of expression it reflects the change of collective norms; on the other hand, even as a perfect formal system, the practice of law is inextricably linked to the conditions of messy individual lives that constantly transgress it, and to historical changes of the societies that have defined them. Law and literature both reflects complex and basic human interactions, and the formality of law and the informality of forgiveness both take part in this interaction.

2. Other Cultures, Other Times

However, forgiveness is not without formality, but its formal ramification is sensitive to cultural context and historical changes and often embedded in normative behavior less articulated than various types of formal laws, also when such laws are subject to change through cultural history. The particularity of a formal law can often be understood by an intrinsic interpretation of the texts that underpin it. Such an approach will not reveal the workings of forgiveness. Most often, the formal skeleton of forgiveness only becomes visible in concrete situations where contrasting contemporary cultural contexts or historical differences over time exposes the possibility and limits of forgiveness as such or the constraints of its particular manifestations. But in spite of such differences three features are always activated by forgiveness:

forgiveness is a demanding and at times provocative process; it questions the mutual possibilities and shortcomings of law and of forgiveness; and it has the power to change the daily lives of people.

A few examples from outside Europe and from previous periods in European culture will clarify my point. The case of the non-Japanese Asian women, Koreans in particular, who have been abused as prostitutes during WW2 by Japanese soldiers, has been disseminated around the world on various occasions. In spite of great media attention they cannot receive an official apology from Japan, not even recognition of the facts of their hardship. We are in a culture where forgiveness is not a positive value, but a strong and almost tabooed negative and almost suicidal attitude. Here, the grey zone of law and forgiveness was and still is shaped by a culture of honor and shame, as is also the case in large parts of the Muslim world and was the case in European culture until late eighteenth century with pockets still existing as in certain regions and in various brotherhoods and clubs, more or less militant organizations or some immigrant communities inside modern European.[3]

In a similar contemporary cross-cultural context the global media circulated in 2007 a story which may appear paradoxical to most Europeans. A group of Korean hostages, NGOs on a humanitarian mission, returned after six weeks from the Taliban after negotiations between their government and the rebels. But they did not jubilate in the airport and was not welcomed home as we have seen in Western countries on similar occasions. Heads low they asked for forgiveness from the public in a well prepared collective statement because they had let themselves be captured, although innocently, and by doing so they made their country lose face in the international limelight by being forced to negotiate with the capturers against the code of honor, also shared by the hostages and their families. On a humanitarian mission or not, they appeared as the guilty ones, not the terrorists.

The grey zone where law and forgiveness mingle is basically formed by cultural history beyond law and forgiveness as such. In a globalized world such conflicting conceptions of law and forgiveness are determined by local cultures, traditions and religious beliefs which, however, cannot be absorbed completely by any of them. If law and forgiveness are placed on a level above the cultural determinants – as for example in International Criminal Court (ICC) and its specific courts as those in session at the moment on the former Yugoslavia and on Rwanda – the exercise of both will have difficulties in

---

[3] J. G. Peristiany ed., *Honor and Shame. The Values of Mediterranean Society* (London: Weidenfeld and Nicolson, 1965); William Ian Miller, *Humiliation. And Other Essays on Honor, Social Discomfort, and Violence* (Ithaca: Cornell University Press, 1993).

being accepted. The ICC is not recognized worldwide. This very complexity of the universal and the local, of the formal law and informal normative codes embodied in an act of forgiveness has no shared platform, but when such clashes are captured in the fictitious world of literature exposing the paradoxes involved in their unavoidable coexistence in today's globalized cultures such culturally constitutive normative tensions are integrated in our culture.

This zone also nurtures more or less extreme myths on unredeemable violations of law and morality, particular when they take place in other cultures than one's own. With a retired and escaped military person from North Korea as the only source, Al-Jazeera reports in July 2009 that in the 1960s, and perhaps even still, handicapped children and other disadvantaged people have been used by the authorities to test chemical and biological weapons. "Si vous naissiez avec un handicap physique ou mental, le gouvernement pense que le meilleur moyen d'apporter votre contribution à la sociéte est de server de cobaye pour des essays d'armes biologiques et chimiques."[4] We don't know if there is more truth to this statement than to the Nazis' claim that Jews were eating Christian children for supper. In both cases very old European xenophobic myths from at least the Middle Ages are reenacted, demonizing foreigners as implied in unforgivable acts beyond any legal and moral standards.

Such acts were actually more than myths up till European modernity and had a clear position in formal, legal systems. So, beyond its cross-cultural significance in the world of today, this recent example of alleged barbarism on the part of foreigners also opens for a cross-historical view on the relation between forgiveness and formal law in European cultural history. The so-called *corpus vilis* – the evil body or the body embodying evilness – was sentenced to death, and often a very painful death after cruel torture, either because it was placed outside the law or because the destruction of the sinful body better prepared the soul for God's forgiveness. But in the early days of medical experiments from the early seventeenth century convicts might instead serve as material for experiments, at times even *in vivo*, or sell their bodies to medicine before execution to secure some money for their families.[5] They were all condemned for acts which bordered on what in earlier days was formally taken to be unforgivable, that is to say, acts beyond human law and beyond any human capacity to forgive, such as bestiality, offense of God or of the king, any kind

---

[4] *Libération*, July 25–26 2009.

[5] Lynn Hunt, *Inventing Human Rights* (New York: Norton, 2007), Ch. 2; Grégoire Chamayou, *Les corps vils. Expérimenter sur les êtres humains aux XVIIIe et XIXe siècles* (Paris: La Découverte, 2008).

of heresy or suicide. Also handicapped bodies were taken to be omens of some unforgivable acts often with the devil involved.

As long as God was there to take over in such cases, the unforgivable and the remedies against it were unambiguously located in systems of formal law resting on a stable divine foundation, and a perfect balance could always be reestablished in society after unforgiveable transgressions of the law, often through a process of spectacularly public and rapacious cruelty. When God disappeared as the basis of the law this foundation was replaced by universal human principles both on the level of the individual and the state, vaguely foreseeing also a kind of international court of justice to regulate conflicts between states. This happened first of all in Immanuel Kant's writings in the late eighteenth century, but although Kant and his contemporaries had the idea that also this foundation like the preceding divine one transcended history, based as it was on presumably irrefutable philosophical analyses, the matter of fact is that both the foundation of the law and the legislation itself became part of human culture and thus subject to historical change on new but not yet clearly established formal conditions with no absolute monarch or the church to play the leading role. Montesquieu made the first draft in 1748 in his *De l'esprit des lois* leading to various types of democratic parliaments as they have become established in parts of the world in an still ongoing process up to the present day and also beyond.

As pointed out by Lynn Hunt in *Inventing Human Rights* (2007), both the philosophical scrutiny of the universal principles and their political manifestations in the Human Rights declarations presupposed a purely anthropologically based empathy between humans across time and space. Although the shared empathy embracing all of mankind in the beginning was charged with a universalism as dogmatic as any metaphysical foundation, this assumption nevertheless paved the way for a purely historical contextualization of both formal legal systems and informal normative structures. Hence, the location of the unforgivable in a formal legal system on religious grounds had to be abandoned and was left to more volatile informal moral norms, to psychology and to the individual or collective sense of justice. The limit between the forgivable and the unforgivable, between informal and formal laws became a matter of constant debate, reformulation and therefore also the subject of modern literature and imaginary writing envisioning new standards for human life. Earlier, literature dealt with the unspeakable consequences of human expeditions into the domain of the unforgiveable. Now, the focus became the permanent negotiations of the definition, status and location of what could be considered unforgiveable on human grounds, and therefore also the changing status and effects of forgiveness.

This important historical shift was propelled by European secularization in the eighteenth and nineteenth centuries.[6] With the notion of universal Human Rights the freedom to practice legally all kinds of cruelty on the *corpus vilis* could not be upheld any longer. Simply by being human the individual body, whomever it belonged to, had the right not to suffer. The collective culture of pain was transformed into a psychological dimension of private life, celebrated or condemned, for example as sado-masochism.[7] The legal institution now became responsible for punishing without bodily suffering, and also became itself subject of forgiveness if it could not live up to the standards – the construction of the guillotine, the swift and painless killer-machine, exemplifies this concern. In medicine during the nineteenth century the obligation not to produce pain through experiments on volunteers, still often prisoners, was first a moral obligation, only later formalized as a legal requirement toward the end of the century and only much later extended to animals.

The center of forgiveness, also inside our culture, now moves from God to a 180 % opposite position in an interaction with new orientations of the legal system. This movement makes forgiveness an obligation for an individual subject or a collective subject, as for example an institution or a state, as we take it for granted in today's Western thinking, although more often than not this principle is difficult to carry out. But this is a recent, local development, mainly in Western culture, and not a development with universal or metaphysical status. As the case of the Korean hostages and the Asian comfort women showed, is also becomes a matter of cultural context who are the subjects to forgive and to be forgiven, and what can be forgiven and what cannot. With forgiveness as a case in point it becomes clear that the grey zone of conflict between the changing positions of formal and informal laws acquires a global dimension.

3. Typologies of Forgiveness

What emerges across the seven cases is that forgiveness is not a universal, monolithic or metaphysical phenomenon, but a culturally embedded, diversified and historical act, each case also showing a great variety of aspects of forgiveness. A typology will have to take these factors into account. I will do so by considering forgiveness in relation to 1) its medium of expression, 2) its levels of unfolding, 3) its goals and 4) its historical dynamics, still focusing on the interaction between law and literature.[8]

---

[6] Grégoire Chamayou, *Les corps vils* (Paris: La Découverte, 2008).

[7] David Morris, *The Culture of Pain* (Berkeley: California UP, 1991); Susan Sontag, *Regarding the Pain of Others* (London: Penguin, 2003).

[8] Charles L. Griswold: *Forgiveness. A Philosophical Exploration.*

1. Medium: It is evident that literature is predominantly verbal, since J. L. Austin's *How to Do Things With Words* (1962)[9] understood as a set of performative speech acts. Performative speech acts have the capacity to establish a real event that materializes in language without at the same time presenting a truth claim. If the utterer has a formalized or collectively acknowledged authority in relation to particular speech acts, then a truth claim, or other claims beyond discussion, can be part of the performance. This is what happens when a judge utters a verdict and sentences somebody to jail or to death, or when the court decides an acquittal. In contrast, in literature and as part of the very nature of its performative acts, authority and truth are always questioned. But both law and literature live by speech acts.[10]

The same goes for forgiveness whether you give it or ask for it. It has to be uttered, maybe indirectly. But as J. L. Austin has pointed out: The utterance 'I forgive' may just state the occurrence of the act itself. But based on this fact alone we cannot decide wether my speech act is serious or not. There is not always a formal authority behind the utterance that guarantees that I really mean it. That is why repetition is part of the unfolding of forgiveness, unlike a verdict but like the continuous questioning of the truth value of literature.

Therefore, forgiveness, literature and law are similar in the sense that they are based on performative speech acts. Literature and forgiveness are similar in the sense that they produce a continuous process, while law and forgiveness are similar in the sense that they require a decision on their sincerity or authority. Furthermore, law and forgiveness has the same aim: the prevention of revenge.

2. Levels of unfolding: Forgiveness, or an utterance of non-forgiveness for that matter, unfolds on various levels such as:

a) Individual level:
- self-forgiveness
- informal forgiveness of another individual
- semi-formal forgiveness of another individual, for example in the presence of a witness with a formal status
- formal forgiveness of another individual

---

9 John L. Austin, *How to Do Things With Words* [1962] (Oxford: Clarendon, 1970).

10 Anders Gullestad, Patrizia Lombardo and Lars Sætre eds., *Exploring Textual Action* (Aarhus: Aarhus University Press, 2010).

Such instances are of a predominantly psychological nature and a frequent topic in at least European literature, particularly from 1800 and onwards, and some are bordering on legal issues – like self-forgiveness among resistance members who have killed collaborators by order, an act which is necessarily legitimized by the law, or the semi-formal encounters with perpetrators or the more formal acts of forgiveness as staged in the South African *Truth and Reconciliation Committee,* conceived and chaired by Desmond Tutu 1993–1997.[11]

b) Social level:
- forgiveness directed from individuals to groups
- forgiveness directed from groups to individuals
- forgiveness directed from groups to groups

Here the cultural and historical differences intersect at a point where formal law and informal traditions are hard to sort out: individuals to groups as in case of Korean hostages referred to above, and groups to groups as when leaders of nations, companies etc. makes excuses to entire communities as the then newly elected Australian prime minister Kevin Rudd did to the aboriginal community. A particular instance of a relation of forgiveness between groups and individuals, although a failed one, is from the early 1950s. At that time the Danish government created a legal framework that allowed for the removal of bright Inuit kids age 5–8 to Denmark for education with the intention of returning them to Greenland as role models in a new Greenland. The well-intended project was no success. Some children returned later, now without language and family, and some stayed in Denmark also on alienating conditions. "It would help," says Carla now close to 70, "if the authorities asked for forgiveness. Then my family in Greenland would better understand."[12] The Danish government has never apologized.

c) Religious level:
- forgiveness directed from the divine center to humans
- forgiveness directed from man to the divine center

11 Michael Battle, *Reconciliation. The ubuntu Theology of Desmond Tutu* (Cleveland: The Pilgrim Press, 1997); Desmond Tutu, *No Future Without Forgiveness* (London: Rider, 1999); Pumla Gobodo-Madikizela, *A Human Being Died That Night.* (Boston: Houghton Mifflin, 2004); Thomas Brudholm, *Resentment's Virtue. Jean Améry and the Refusal to Forgive.* (Philadelphia: Temple UP Richard, 2009); Richard Dowden, *Africa. Altered States, Ordinary Miracles* (London: Portobello Books, 2009), 305.

12 *Politiken*, August 9 2009, cf. in a more general perspective: Janna Thompson, *Taking Responsibility for the Past. Reparation and Historical Justice* (Cambridge: Polity Press, 2002).

The first is at center stage in any legal system based on religion, in pre-seventeenth century Europe, in Islam as well as in orthodox Judaism. Religion marked the limit of the unforgivable, and forgiveness only belonged to God. The legal system did never take forgiveness into account, only God or the King, his worldly representative, and because of the religious foundation also ethical norms and other everyday norms of human interaction left no space for serious acts of forgiveness, only trivial excuses. To a large extent honor and shame were the nodal points of cultural value systems defining acts of forgiveness as the equivalent of loss of social status, and where they continue to occupy that position they still exclude forgiveness as a viable option.

In such contexts forgiveness was a defining feature of the hierarchical relation between the divine and the divine representatives in contrast to mankind. In Islam and in Judaism forgiveness confirmed the contract between humans and God. In *Leviticus* Ch 5 the case is clear: Man repents with offerings, also when he is ignorant of his sin, and God will forgive. A similar view is found in for example Sura 3 or Sura 8 in the *Qur'an* – obey Allah, behave well and you will receive forgiveness; if you sin and repent you will be forgiven, the forgiveness mostly meaning happiness in the afterlife, maybe through martyrdom.

Christianity introduces a new and revolutionary idea, most clearly articulated in St Matthews Ch 23, v 34: "Father, forgive them; for they know not what they do." Here forgiveness is unilateral, not based on a mutual contract as in the *Qur'an* and the Jewish Bible and also not presupposing repentance: you don't ask for forgiveness; you receive it just by being human, not by any intended or unintended acts presumed to be good. Here, and in contrast to other religions, forgiveness is no longer just the opposite of revenge, but simply belongs to another and more elevated category of acts.

Even more controversial is Jesus' argument in St Mark Ch 2, v 5–12 with the scribers in Capernaum concerning the lame man. Jesus forgives him, and the scribers find it blasphemous: forgiveness is God's prerogative. But Jesus claims that it is just as easy for the Son of man to forgive the palsy as to say, take your bed and go. Which then happens. An imaginary way of saying that forgiveness as an human act can make an unpredictable and miraculous change on earth, not only in heaven, – that is, if we go against the formal law of the scribers that only states what is right or wrong. Forgiveness opens our imagination of a shared human life toward the unimaginable: a speech act may produce change in human life.

This is the foundational idea of Desmond Tutu's reconciliation project, based on the African tradition of *ubuntu*, basically meaning hospitality, that is, willingness to open the door to everybody who knocks at it and is in need of shelter. This tradition, also known from other cultures, is here first taken in a wider sense and united with the Christian doctrine of the power of forgiveness before it is translated into an unorthodox court room practice: if the perpetrator describes his wrong-doings, and the victim shows up to testify, then the perpetrator will not be persecuted if he asks forgiveness and receives it. The success of the *Truth Reconciliation Committee* is both celebrated and criticized.

The second possibility, forgiveness from man to God, was almost a blasphemous idea. Job of the Jewish Bible or the story of Abraham on his way to kill Isaac on God's command may exemplify the complexity of the possibility.[13] The opponents to the Theodice in the midst eighteenth century after the earthquake of Lisbon turned the tables once and for all: if this was the work of God, it was unforgivable, that is from a universal human point of view.[14]

In the first case, God to man, the status of forgiveness marks an important difference between various legal systems based on religions, between civic law and canon law within the same society and between secular legal system and religious legal systems. All of this has a pressing importance in today's globalized, multicultural world. Here, a discussion of the different aspects and roles of forgiveness may be an opening for an intercultural legal study in relation to difficulties of establishing international law. Literature is a privileged place for the articulation of such differences in their complex coexistence.

The second case, man to God, is not an option in cultures with an undisputed divine center, but nevertheless imaginable in its literature, e.g. in the Greek stories on *hybris* and resilient personalities like Prometheus rebelling against God, or later in stories from the European Middle Ages on the emergence of the figure of the Devil as the fallen angel, Mephistopheles or Lucifer, impersonating the unthinkable rebellion against divine justice and its unquestioned right to define the unforgivable evil, placed beyond both law and forgiveness but inside literature.

3. Goals: Forgiveness may aim at
 - healing and therapy, collectively or individually
 - forgetting an injustice
 - remembering an injustice to overcome it
 - referring humans to the divine sphere
 - referring humans to individual responsibility

---

13 Troels Nørager, *Taking Leave of Abraham* (Aarhus: Aarhus University Press, 2008).

14 Svend Erik Larsen, "The Lisbon Earthquake and the Scientific Turn in Kant's Philosophy," *European Review* 14.3 (2006): 359–367.

These goals are not just a cluster of alternatives. Rather they refer to different historical contexts which now and then co-exist or co-existed in mutual misunderstanding, Tutu's reconciliation being one of them and the both traumatic and post-traumatic situation following the fall of the apartheid regime. No legal system can embrace this heterogeneity, but literature feeds on it as can be observed in South African literature since the 1970s and in literature developed in similar cultural contexts around the world.

4. *Historical dynamics:* When the system of law changed in Europe from a system defined by religion to a secular system based on democracy and human rights for each individual independent of class and social position, this process ran parallel to the development in literature of genres with multiple narrators and points of view as those of prose fiction, the novel in particular, or the creation of individualized genres as modern lyric, letters, confessions, autobiographies, essays etc.

The shift to secular laws also occurred concomitantly with the changing status of forgiveness from either being irrelevant to God and to humans, as for example in Antique religion or in Buddhism, Shinto tor Hinduism, or as being exclusively the business of God. From now on, forgiveness became an issue for humans only as an individual responsibility in the relationship to all of mankind – everyone is your equal as a human being – and in that capacity forgiveness for the first time began to develop as a positive element in the cultural value system. This shift produced an individual sense of guilt related to the insufficient capacity to forgive. The denial of offering or receiving forgiveness then became an almost inhuman gesture in need of thorough argumentation. In contrast, in cultures relying on honor and shame and thereby on a basic non-equality as the foundation of human existence as such, forgiveness was and still is a negative or excluded option, threatening the basic social hierarchies.

This historical development in Europe corresponds today to a co-existence of legal systems on partly irreconcilable backgrounds, a recurring topic in today's literature with a global perspective – migrant literatures, exile literatures, postcolonial literatures etc.

4. Literature and Forgiveness: Analytical Examples

The two following sets of analytical examples contain texts new and old, European and non-European, both sets related to a borderline case of forgiveness; the first on the individual basis, the second on a collective basis; the first related to resistance toward forgiveness, the second to a clash of cultural contexts for forgiveness.

4.1. Molière: Don Juan (1665) and Améry: Jenseits von Schuld und Sühne (1966)[15]

Don Juan is the icon of seduction. Indefatigable and never satisfied, he conquers every skirt he can possibly come across, noble girls or peasant girls, married women or virgins, alone or in couples. The more he conquers, the more he is bored – he changes constantly his rhetorical strategy, appearance and behavior to achieve a new trophy. Of course, as a ruthless nobleman he breaks every decent code of conduct characteristic of a responsible bourgeois or supported by the church of the seventeenth century, also when it comes to money borrowing, being disrespectful to his father, stabbing the governor to death, and cheating and lying whenever it suits his volatile self. However, in his own eyes his conduct is constant and persistent, always guided by the hunt for satisfaction on his own conditions. Therefore, in his own eyes he is also a man of honor no matter how much he is dishonored by his behavior in the eyes of others. "Non, non je ne suis point changé, et mes sentiments sont toujours les mêmes." (*Don Juan*, 5.2). And the law cannot get to him: he is a nobleman, above such rules, formal or not.

Molière meticulously renders an extreme case: no basic legal or informal rules are left unbroken, whether the mundane or the divine. Sganarelle, his servant, is terrified by being bound to such a master. But Don Juan himself has no fear – he has only done what he has to do according to his passionate nature, and what may be expected from a nobleman. Face to face with the statue of the governor he has murdered, he invites him to dinner, and the statue nods his head in affirmation to the joy of Juan and the terror of Sganarelle.

Upon his arrival the statue asks Juan if he repents which Sganarelle, supported by a female ghost, urges him to do to get salvation. Sganarelle attempts to embrace both divine and earthly justice in an act that unifies repentance on Don Juan's part with the forgiveness from God. But Juan refuses to take part (*Don Juan*, 5.1): "Non, non, il ne sera pas dit, quoi qu'il arrive, que je sois capable de me repentir." He gives deliberately his hand to the statue and burns in hell. His resistance to repentance is necessary to keep both his individual and social identity; otherwise he would have admitted that he has not been constantly the same man all the way through and that he had abandoned his sovereignty to rule his own life.

---

15 Jean-Baptiste Molière, *Dom Juan ou le Festin de Pierre* [1666] in *Œuvres complètes* 2 (Paris: Flammarion, 1965), 353–408; Jean Améry, *Jenseits von Schuld und Sühne. Bewältigungsversuche eines Überwältigten* [1966] (Stuttgart: Klett-Kotta, 1977).

Here, two approaches to forgiveness collide – one medieval related to a notion of law and forgiveness based on religion and the code of honor, the other to modern individualism where forgiveness is a matter of individual choice, but still with the code of honor and shame bridging between the two positions, and with the supernatural elements indicating that we are in a world of imagination, but still a possible world because Don Juan makes it *his* world by his refusal of repentance. To give or to receive forgiveness is part of the cultural universe he lives in, but not part of *his* life.

Jean Améry is the pen name for Hans Mayer, an Austrian born Jewish author and later a Belgian citizen who after participation in the resistance was taken by Gestapo, tortured and sent to the concentration camps. In his writings, *Jenseits von Schuld und Sühne* (1966) among others, he describes how torture first of all annihilates the personality and at the same time the confidence in the surrounding world – everything has lost its boundaries for ever. To be true to this experience is an essential part of his identity as an individual and as a Jew and therefore not to be forgotten on any conditions. One cannot forgive the tormenters and forget without giving up one's identity, as also Don Juan knew when it came to ask for forgiveness. At the end suicide could be one logical consequence – literal annihilation. Like many other survivors Améry killed himself in 1978.

But the philosophy of non-forgiveness is strong and goes beyond all revenge, justice or Nurnberg trial. Both revenge and forgiveness are impossible positions, close as they are to the idea of reestablishing a kind of balance in life, also because this experience outlines "die Grenze sprachlichen Mitteilungsvermögen" (*Jenseits,* 63). Placed on this boundary, every word he utters is his own and a means to re-conquer his life. This fight for a life of his own would be annihilated, and he himself as well, if he forgave. It is important for him to keep up his "Ressentiments" as he names one of the chapters of the book. Here he states that he is repelled by "Die in dieser Stunde bereits von Vergebens- und Versöhnungspathos vibrierenden Juden" (*Jenseits,* 106) and "Das Verbrechen verursacht Unruhe in der Gesellschaft; sobald aber das öffentliche Bewusstsein die Erinnerung an das Verbrechen verliert, verschwindet auch die Unruhe" (*Jenseits,* 115). Forgiveness means for him to cave in to the appeal to get over it, "fertigmachen", let time pass and life go on, and make people forget not the Third Reich in itself, but the existence of the barbaric in culture that confronts us every day, but which no law and no forgiveness can do away with, but which necessitates both: "Nun denn, ausgetragen könnte dadurch werden, dass in einem Lager das Ressentiment bestehen bleibt, und, hierdurch geweckt, im anderen das Selbstmisstrauen." (*Jenseits,* 124) Desmond Tutu's *ubuntu* is a foreign world to Améry.

4.2. Rahimi: Terre et cendres (1999) and The Saga of Gisli the Outlaw (c. 1270)[16]

In Atiq Rahimis short novel from Afghanistan *Terre et cendres* we are also in a universe split between two standards for law and for forgiveness based on honor and shame, but it is a contemporary world, showing the complexity of the problems already addressed by Molière. The novel deals with a non-individualistic culture in the literary manner of modern European novels with a subtle use of narrators: a grandfather, Dastaguir, is talking to himself. Gradually we see that the problem of self-forgiveness is at the center. It is now contextualized by an old culture based on honor and shame confronted with the globalized world, which now penetrates into the traditional world of the grandfather, but outside his comprehension.

In the aftermath of the Russian occupation in the late 1970s Dastaguir is travelling from his village with his grandchild to see his son, the boy's father, who works in the mines far away. Two events involving a necessary but impossible forgiveness are central: because of Russian bombings in 1979 the village is burnt down, his daughter in law is killed, burned to death while fleeing stark naked from the women's bath. At that moment her father in law saw her naked – unwillingly – but he saw her. This is unforgivable. The old man, like Job, finds God unjust, terrified by his own accusations: "la vérité est que Dieu ne se soucie guère de toi [...] Hélas, Dieu a abandonné ses creatures. [...] Tu blasphemes! Malheur aux tentations de Satan!" (39). He fights with himself how to tell his son. He never does.

The other event dates back from before the son left: with a spade Dastaguir's son has beaten the neighbor's son up convinced that he might have been flirting with his wife. He goes to prison and Dastaguir is proud that the son thus made visible that he defended the honor of the family. Forgiveness is not touched upon at all, that would have made his deed invisible. But now the old man himself is in dire need of forgiveness because of the shameful view of his daughter in law. But he can get it neither from his son, nor from Allah. He is left completely alone. Moreover, the mine owner – a multinational company – has not told the father that the son knew about the destruction of the family and the village. They hold that it would have been waste of time and money to let him go home and mourn as he should according to the code of honor.

And thus the son, too, has inflicted dishonor on his father without having any possibility of avoiding it. Moreover, the son also had a casualty which

---

[16] Atiq Rahimi, Terre et cendres (Paris: P.O.L., 1999); The Saga of Gisli the Outlaw [c. 1270], http://www.sagadb.org/gisla_saga_surssonar.en (October 24, 2010).

was not communicated to his folks back home. So, Dastaguir is dishonored once more by not being able to visit his son as he should have done. Yet another forgiveness is needed, but cannot be given. Everything is simply a result of the fact that the world is not governed by the code of honor anymore, without at the same time offering forgiveness as an acceptable option. The management of the mine is completely lawful and the old man is treated with dignity and politeness. But forgiveness is impossible or, if given, does not count. It would just be lip service. Here no law, no forgiveness neither from God nor man can compensate a complete dissolution of a cultural value system, a break-down which basically is the effect of the encounter between two cultures, the village and the mine, and two historical periods, a religious and a secular, reflecting the reality in a globalized world. Dastaguir is left with self-forgiveness, as in a modern individualized and secular world. But for him this is a non-existing option.

If the grandfather in this sense is a displaced medieval person, Gisli Sursson is a true one. His sister is married to Thorgrim, and he is himself a blood-brother by oath to Vestein. They are not on friendly terms in the family, and it is believed but never proven that Thorgrim kills Vestein in his bed. According to the law, built on a code of honor and the right to revenge inside certain informal but crystal clear rules Gisle can also kill one from the murderer's family. The law in Iceland was, as is known also in Dastaguir's world, a law that tells you what your rights are and issue a verdict, but as there is no police to execute the verdict, you are on your own if you want to get things right. This self-help is strictly regulated by the code of honor telling everybody unambiguously how to proceed.

But as both Thorgrim and Vestein are Gisli's kinsmen he cannot rely on the code of honor. Whatever he does, the law will be against him. If he does not kill Thorgrim, he will lose his honor; if he does kill him, he has killed his own kin and will be outlawed. That is however what he does, keeping his honor but also now being an outlaw who can be chased down by anyone. But those who try but cannot get to him are dishonored, and as he manages to survive until he dies in open battle he keeps his honor, also in his and his family's afterlife.

Here is no room what so ever for forgiveness, as was also the case when the Afghan son went to prison for having revenged himself on the neighbor's son. In Iceland and most of Europe this structure is changed first with the arrival of Christianity, and then with secularization. The old ways are long forgotten in Europe, until they now reach us again in the world of globalized migration of peoples and their cultures and with laws and norm for human interaction with or without forgiveness that travel with them. We just have to look into literature from our own cultural history to learn about our heritage with regard to laws, norms and forgiveness, and into contemporary literature to understand the complexity of the limit between formal law and informal norm as exposed through the issue of forgiveness.

5. Epilogue

I began with a reference to modern feel-good attitudes, and will end in the same vein with a standard model for trivial passionate crime fiction – based on a real story as it is called in the television program. Father and son is in conflict, the father a prototypical alpha-male, the son both resisting him and looking up to him, unable to find a room of his own. The father's new young wife is in love with the son who has his own affair running and rejects her passes. She wants revenge and lies to her husband about the relationship with his son. The father furiously takes a contract on his son. The son is killed and the wife's scheming behavior detected. She kills herself and the father is struck with horror and remorse when everything is revealed.

Well, this may sound like an American B-movie, but it is a condensed version of Euripides *Hippolytus* (fourth century BC). Here, everyone has lost his or her honor in the strict sense – Hippolytus has innocently attracted his stepmother, but nevertheless he did so; she, Phaedra, is simply a shameful case in her lack of self-control, and Theseus is exposed as blind in his alpha-male self-sufficiency. Now he cannot kill anyone anymore to relieve himself. His equals are gone, and in a culture of *hybris* it does not count to kill a bunch of subordinates. And forgiveness is not an issue. Maybe the whole affair may be a case for the law, but the legal system is in a dead end because two equal gods, Aphrodite and Artemis, are fighting about the case, and therefore, unlike other tragedies, an Athenian court cannot sort things out in the end, guided by Athene, Zeus or Apollo.

At this point of no solution comes the surprising ending which like Jesus in St Mark transcends it own context by an act of forgiveness, more powerful than the formal law.[17] The deadly wounded Hyppolitus is brought on stage and, inspired by Artemis, his last act is to forgive his father, set him free of guilt: "I forgive [λύω = set free] my father at thy [Artemis'] suit" – without Theseus having asked and without Hyppolitus respecting the humiliation it also contains toward Theseus, but finally showing his superiority over his father by playing an absolute impossible and unimaginable card and win in

[17] Euripides, *Ion, Hyppolitus, Medea, Alcestis* [fourth century BCE] (London: Heinemann, 1946), 274–275/v. 1441, v. 1448–1450.

such a way that it, in a still continuing series of rewritings, remediations and reinterpretations of the Phaedra story in Western culture, has made us remember the limits of law and the power of forgiveness in the grey zone of everyday life for centuries to come. The forgiveness has to be repeated. Theseus does not seem to believe it: "*Theseus:* Wilt leave me – and my conscience murder-stained?" / *Hypp.:* No, no! I do absolve [ἐλευθεσῶ = set free] thee of my death." That's what forgiveness can do: set free.

Hans Petter Graver
(University of Oslo)

Measure for Measure: On Law and Forgiveness

In Shakespeare's play "Measure for measure", Claudio faces execution for sexual immorality. His sister, Isabelle, appeals to the lord Angelo for his mercy. Angelo refuses to pardon Claudio, but is willing to barter Claudio's life for his sister's virginity. There is no doubt that Claudio is guilty of fornication – his lover Juliette is pregnant. There is on the other hand, no doubt that his sentence is unjust. The law has not been enforced for many years. Angelo, however, does not heed this. "The law hath not been dead, though it hath slept", he says. An example must be set, lest the law loses its power: "We must not make a scarecrow of the law, Setting it up to fear the birds of prey, And let it keep one shape, till custom make it Their perch and not their terror."

The story points to many issues regarding the relation between law and forgiveness. What is their relation – is forgiveness a way of tempering law's harshness? Law, or at least justice, has elements of "measure for measure" – the punishment should stand in relation to the crime, the price of a good in relation to its value. But what about forgiveness? Is mercy paid for an instance of forgiving, or does forgiveness require a different rationality? Many would perhaps say that law is a matter of justice, but forgiveness a matter of love, and that the rationalities of justice and love are fundamentally different.

Claudio is guilty of the crime he is convicted for. Surely, one cannot be forgiven for something one is not guilty of. But guilt presupposes conviction from a legal point of view. The right to be regarded as innocent until convicted in a court of law is even a basic human right. Does forgiveness then presuppose a conviction – or else, what kind is then the act of forgiving that takes the place of a legal conviction? And finally, forgiving is an act of recognizing the person, of bringing him back into society despite his wrongs. To what extent does this presuppose that punishment is served and that damages are paid? And how do we determine that such conditions are met, if not by the rationality of justice – measure for measure? But if love thus is bound by justice, where is the place for love as love and forgiveness as an independent measure of love?

In this article I will investigate some of these questions. I will look at the scope of mercy in law, the limits it sets to it and also the differences between mercy that may be granted by the law and forgiveness outside of the range of law. We shall see that there is scope for mercy in law in the form of equity, and that this mercy needs to take into account the person behind an act and not only the issue of whether an act or a set of circumstances fall within a legal rule. There is, however, as we shall see, good reasons to hold that equity differs from forgiveness in important respects, both as to the type of rationality it represents and as to who is in a position to grant mercy or to forgive.

ANGELO
Condemn the fault and not the actor of it?

Forgiveness and law are on different planes. Law is a matter of applying general rules to a set of facts. The rules are abstract, and set out conditions for their application, as well as the consequences. The legal issue is even in modern times basically as set out by Quintilian in his Institutio Oratoria: "By the accuser nothing more is to be kept in view than that he must prove that something was done; that a particular thing was done; that it was done wrongfully; and that he brings his action according to law."[1]

Forgiveness on the other hand, is a matter of treating a person, not an act or a set of circumstances. It is the person that is forgiven, not the criminal act committed by this person. Where law is a demand of justice, forgiveness is a demand of love, a person-to-person relationship. The perfect love of God, writes Werner G. Jeanrond, "which is present in the human being, loves what is sinful, bad foolish, and weak in order to make it just, good, wise and strong.[2]

Law is about passing judgment. A person is treated as an abstract category, based on the existence or non-existence of a set of facts necessary to apply a legal rule: has an act been committed, a promise made of events taken place for which the person is legally responsible. Forgiveness is about love and suspending judgment. This does not mean accepting everything that others do, but it does mean taking the view that their mistakes and sins do not tell us the whole truth about them. Tariq Ramadan says: "To judge is human, and to judge is to love. Suspending judgment is a better way of loving … and to love, in spite of judgment, is truly to love."[3]

Justice is proportional – distributional and retributional. Forgiveness is limitless. "There is no limit to the pardon, no moderation, no 'how much'".[4]

---

1 Quintilian, *Institutio Oratoria Book 3* chapter 6.85.
2 Werner G. Jeanrond, *A Theology of Love* (London: t&t Clark, 2010), 97–98.
3 Tariq Ramadan, *The Quest for Meaning* (Kindle edition, 2010) 3,441
4 Jacques Derrida, The Century and the Pardon, *le Monde des Debats No. 9* (December 1999) English translation http://fixion.sytes.net/pardonEng.htm

Law has ends, there are most often purposes or intents behind legal rules. But each time forgiveness is in the service of an end, "even if it were noble and spiritual (...) each time that it tends to establish a normality, (...) then pardon is not pure, nor its concept"[5] Law and forgiveness can be seen as opposites, law with its symmetry and harshness, forgiveness with its mildness and compassion.[6]

Clear as these starting points may be, in practice it is impossible to distinguish between treatment of the person and treatment of the act. In law, there must always be someone responsible for the deeds and acts that are committed. Legal duties, rights and obligations are always relations between subjects of the law, and these subjects are more often than not human beings. Concluding that a law is broken will therefore always entail that someone is held responsible. If forgiving entails that this person is pardoned from bearing the burden that the law sets out as the legal consequences of a certain event, this will have the effect that the law is not applied in the case. If the legal rule states that murder is punished by life imprisonment, and the murderer is forgiven by pardon, this instance of murder is not punished by life imprisonment. How then can law's demand for justice and love's demand for forgiveness be reconciled?

ISABELLA

I do think that you might pardon him,
And neither heaven nor man grieve at the mercy

The temptation to mitigate the harsh impact of the law in circumstances where the situation calls for sympathy for the person affected is the background to the old saying that "hard cases make bad law"[7] In such circumstances there is an inevitable and often strong temptation to offer a strained interpretation of the law to avoid the hard effect on the individual case.

The question was brought before an English court in the famous case of R v Dudley and Stevens from 1884. Two sailors were convicted and sentenced to death for killing a third member of their crew in order to survive on drinking his blood after a shipwreck. The sentence was accompanied by a recommendation for mercy. The death sentence was subsequently com-

---

5 Derrida l.c.

6 Martha C. Nussbaum, "Equity and Mercy," *Philosophy & Public affairs* 22.2 (1993): 83–125

7 Neil MacCormick, *Rhetoric and the Rule of Law* (Oxford: OUP, 2005), 49.

muted to life imprisonment, and the seamen were released after six months in prison.[8]

Lord Coleridge, C.J. stated in his opinion in the case that legally it could be no excuse for the crime of murder that the offenders killed to save themselves from thirst and starvation. He pointed out that "If therefore, (...) necessity of hunger does not justify larceny, what (could be) said to the doctrine that it justified murder?"

He added

> It must not be supposed that in refusing to admit temptation to be an excuse for crime it is forgotten how terrible the temptation was; how awful the suffering; how hard in such trials to keep the judgment straight and the conduct pure. We are often compelled to set up standards we cannot reach ourselves, and to lay down rules which we could not ourselves satisfy. But a man has no right to declare temptation to be an excuse, though he might himself have yielded to it, nor allow compassion for the criminal to change or weaken in any manner the legal definition of the crime. It is therefore our duty to declare that the prisoners' act in this case was wilful murder, that the facts as stated in the verdict are no legal justification of the homicide; and to say that in our unanimous opinion the prisoners are upon this special verdict guilty, of murder, ...

whereupon the Court proceeded to pass sentence of death upon the accused.

Why could not the Court take into account the special facts of the case, and the mitigating circumstances? In the words of Lord Coleridge:

> It is not suggested that in this particular case the deeds were devilish, but it is quite plain that such a principle once admitted might be made the legal cloak for unbridled passion and atrocious crime. There is no safe path for judges to tread but to ascertain the law to the best of their ability and to declare it according to their judgment; and if in any case the law appears to be too severe on individuals, to leave it to the Sovereign to exercise that prerogative of mercy which the Constitution has intrusted to the hands fittest to dispense it.

ANGELO

It is the law, not I condemn your brother

A legal cloak for unbridled passion and atrocious crime. Socrates warned about passions replacing the law, and he declined to ask his jury for pity or forgiveness.

> But, setting aside the question of public opinion, there seems to be something wrong in asking a favour of a judge, and thus procuring an acquittal, instead of informing and convincing him. For his duty is, not to make a present of justice, but to give judgment; and he has sworn that he will judge according to the laws, and

8 http://en.wikipedia.org/wiki/R_v_Dudley_and_Stephens 2 March 2010.

> not according to his own good pleasure; and we ought not to encourage you, nor should you allow yourselves to be encouraged, in this habit of perjury – there can be no piety in that.[9]

Cicero, however, disagreed with Socrates on this point, and said that he was "condemned solely for the offence of inexperience in oratory"[10] To what extent oratory and appeal to pity should rule the law is an issue of great controversy. But law is not law, and there is a distinction since classical times between the words of the law and the intent of law. Aristotle points out in his *Rhetoric* that *equity* has a place in this divide, where he states:

> Equity must be applied to forgivable actions; and it must make us distinguish between criminal acts on the one hand, and errors of judgement, or misfortunes, on the other. (A "misfortune" is an act, not due to moral badness, that has unexpected results: an "error of judgement" is an act, also not due to moral badness, that has results that might have been expected: a "criminal act" has results that might have been expected, but is due to moral badness, for that is the source of all actions inspired by our appetites.)[11]

He continues:

> Equity bids us be merciful to the weakness of human nature; to think less about the laws than about the man who framed them, and less about what he said than about what he meant; not to consider the actions of the accused so much as his intentions, nor this or that detail so much as the whole story; to ask not what a man is now but what he has always or usually been. It bids us remember benefits rather than injuries, and benefits received rather than benefits conferred; to be patient when we are wronged; to settle a dispute by negotiation and not by force; to prefer arbitration to litigation – for an arbitrator goes by the equity of a case, a judge by the strict law, and arbitration was invented with the express purpose of securing full power for equity.

So Aristotle seems not to fear the introduction of forgiveness into the legal assessment. Yet he is not quite clear on whether he is thinking about *interpreting* the law or making an *exception* to the law. He speaks about thinking about the man who framed the laws, and what he meant, and in the paragraph preceding the two I have cited here, he refers to "the defects of a community's written code of law" and "the sort of justice which goes beyond the written law". The existence of this sort of justice is, says Aristotle, "not intended, where they (the legislator) have noticed no defect in the law; intended, where they find themselves unable to define things exactly."

---

9 From Socrates' defense speech, Plato, *Apology Also known as "The Death of Socrates"* Translated by Benjamin Jowett (Project Gutenberg 2008, http://www.gutenberg.org/files/1656/1656-h/1656-h.htm)

10 Cicero, *De Oratore*, book I 233.

11 Aristotle, *Rhetoric* book I chapter 13 (17–19).

Thus Aristotle is still within the legal issue. He distinguishes between crimes and errors, and points to negotiation and arbitration as alternatives to law. The question he addresses is not to disapply the law, but to determine its scope – it is not of pardon, but of acquittal. But he does speak of mercy. Since this is in a context within the law, it gives us a cause to distinguish between equity as mercy within the law, and forgiveness as mercy outside the law.[12] Law is tempered in both instances. But in the former case it leads to acquittal or milder consequences, in the second to pardon.

Hannah Arendt has pointed out that the notion that sins can be forgiven was unknown to pre-Christian, Greek philosophy.[13] This explains maybe the ambiguity of Aristotle's text in the way he speaks both of interpreting the law, of equity and of mercy – taking into account the weakness of human nature and remembering benefits rather than wrongs. Aristotle himself did not have the conceptual framework to distinguish between equity and forgiveness, but his text points to the two paths that pity may take, and that it also has its place in law.

In modern legal systems, having regard to the person, his situation and his intents is a self-evident part of legal reasoning along with taking into account the "justice that goes beyond the written law". We see this not only in the sentencing part of criminal law, but also in civil legal matters, for example in the institutions of consumer bankruptcy and "*social force majeur*" where factors such as illness, unemployment and divorce may be taken into account when determining contractual obligations. Main parts of the public law of the welfare state grant economic and social rights on the basis of assessments of individual needs. Equity fills thus a prominent place in law, but this is not the same as forgiveness.

ISABELLA
Yet show some pity

We have seen the tensions and contradictions between law and forgiveness, but are they not also mutually interdependent? If there is no crime, is there anything to forgive? And how do we know that there is something to forgive, if we do not let the law determine that a crime has been committed? What if we let forgiveness take the place of law and forgive without legal proceedings establishing guilt?

---

12 See to this point Martha C. Nussbaum, *Equity and Mercy*, 96–97.
13 Hannah Arendt, *Responsibility and Judgment* (New York: Schocken books, 2003), 89.

In a legal context there is an important distinction between the finding of guilt and the sentencing. More generally, we can distinguish between the establishing of whether the conditions to apply a legal rule are met and the drawing of legal consequences from this fact. All legal rules can be formulated or reformulated as conditionals: if p, then x. This structure of legal rules also structures argumentation in law and separates the themes of argument into questions of fact, questions of categorizing these facts according to relevant legal rules and finally questions of determining and applying the legal consequences to the established facts according to the applicable rules. These are the three issues Quintilian refers to, when he states

> Beginning first of all with the defendant, by far the strongest mode of defense is if the charge which is made can be denied; the next, if an act of the kind charged against the accused can be said not to have been done; the third, and most honorable, if what is done is proved to have been justly done.[14]

When divided in this way, we see that pity has no place in the first topic; the question of whether a certain act has been committed or not by the accused, or the question of whether a certain set of events have taken place or not. One cannot meet the defendant's denial of the charge with forgiveness. Forgiving a person implies an accusation against that person that he or she has committed an act or is responsible for a certain set of events. As Vetlesen points out, victims often ask how they can forgive as long as the perpetrators show no sign of regret and assume no responsibility.[15] Forgiveness without legal or other proceedings establishing guilt is therefore dependant on either that the involved persons agree on the issue of guilt, or that reconciliation is deemed as important as to override considerations of justice and due process. Confession and asking for forgiveness renders legal process superfluous or irrelevant, the need for reconciliation may render it inexpedient.

For instance, the establishment The South African Truth and Reconciliation Commission rested on the basis that the conflict during the apartheid period "resulted in violence and human rights abuses from all sides. No section of society escaped these abuses".[16] A purpose of the commission was "to enable South Africans to come to terms with their past on a morally accepted basis and to advance the cause of reconciliation". More specifically, the elements of the Promotion of National Unity and Reconciliation Amendment Act 87 of 1995 are set out as following:

---

[14] Quintilian, *Institutio Oratoria* Book 3 chapter 6.83.

[15] Arne Johan Vetlesen, *Evil and Human Agency Understanding Collective Evil* (Cambridge: CUP, 2005) Kindle edition location 4,187.

[16] http://www.justice.gov.za/trc/ October 27, 2010.

- To provide for the investigation and the establishment of as complete a picture as possible of the nature, causes and extent of gross violations of human rights committed during the period from 1 March 1960 to the cut-off date contemplated in the Constitution, within or outside the Republic, emanating from the conflicts of the past, and the fate or whereabouts of the victims of such violations;
- the granting of amnesty to persons who make full disclosure of all the relevant facts relating to acts associated with a political objective committed in the course of the conflicts of the past during the said period;
- affording victims an opportunity to relate the violations they suffered;
- the taking of measures aimed at the granting of reparation to, and the rehabilitation and the restoration of the human and civil dignity of, victims of violations of human rights;
- reporting to the Nation about such violations and victims;
- the making of recommendations aimed at the prevention of the commission of gross violations of human rights;

The general aims of the act were thus much broader than the aims of legal proceedings, which have as their themes the establishment of guilt and meting out of punishment. Punishment is not even among the elements, whereas amnesty, on the other hand is. This does not in itself entail that gross injustices are forgiven. Such arrangements are more driven by the interests of the state to come to terms with the past than by a desire to forgive. One could also, with Vetlesen, say that demanding public acts of forgiveness is a category mistake that infringes on the privacy of the victims since forgiveness remains a difficult and acutely personal issue.[17] Public institutions cannot forgive. Politicians can give amnesties and mediators reconcile, but neither have the mandate nor the power to forgive. However, reconciliation does share one central trait of forgiving, namely the re-integration of the sinner into society so that the sinner and his victims can take up normal social relations.

ANGELO

I show it most of all when I show justice;
For then I pity those I do not know

So we see that all issues are not brought to justice, even where there is evidence of a crime having been committed. Due process requires that it is so when we want to hold a person responsible – also in the sense of forgiving

---

[17] Vetlesen, *Evil and Human Agency* l.c.

him. But what about the perpetrator who admits and repents? He can be forgiven, but does not justice and even forgiving demand that he is brought to justice and submits to the law? Does not justice demand that criminals are brought to justice, that transgressions of rights are defended, that violations are prosecuted? Are truth commissions and amnesties contrary to the demands of justice?

Rudolf von Ihering, in his famous essay "The Struggle for Law", held that it is a duty of the state and of every citizen to uphold their legal rights, and to uphold their legal positions. "The maintenance of law and order by the state is nothing but a continual struggle against the lawlessness which violates them", he wrote.[18] He also maintained that everyone has a duty to defend their rights, and anyone refraining from performing this duty acts not only against his own interests, but against the interests of all.

> The existence of all the principles of public law depends on the fidelity of public officials in the performance of their duties; that of the principles of private law, on the power of the motives which induce the person whose rights have been violated to defend them: his interest and his sentiment of legal right. If these motives do not come into play, if the feeling of legal right is blunted and weak, and interests not powerful enough to overcome the disinclination to entering into a controversy and the indisposition to go to law, the consequence is that the principle of law involved finds no application."[19]

I think most will agree with von Ihering in that justice requires that crimes are not overlooked or forgotten. A survivor of Auschwitz observed when asked about forgiveness, "it can happen that when a man forgives, he feels guilty because he no longer feels the hatred which he ought to feel: he sees forgiveness as a kind of betrayal of those tortured and exterminated, somehow failing to keep faith."[20]

It is a basic requirement of the rule of law that the officials of the law uphold it. Even forgiveness requires this, because forgiveness requires repentance, and repentance first of all requires not forgetting what one has done. To say that love demands leniency is mistaken. A person, who out of pity is not brought to trail "has received neither justice, nor love, but injustice, covered by sentimentality."[21] In cases where crimes are not addressed, they can be neither brought to justice nor forgiven.

---

18 Rudolph von Jhering, *The Struggle for Law.* Translated from the Fifth German Edition by John J. Lalor. Second Edition, with an Introduction by Albert Kocourek. (Chicago: Callaghan and Company, 1915), 6.

19 Rudolph von Jhering, *The Struggle for Law,*72.

20 Engelking, sited from Arne Johan Vetlesen, *Evil and Human Agency* location 4,221.

21 Paul Tillich, *Love, Power and Justice* (Oxford: OUP, 1960), 15.

It could therefore be said that if society and the state allows violations and crimes to be forgotten, it deprives the victim of the possibility to forgive, and the violator the chance to be forgiven. Hannah Arendt makes this point about the Nazi crimes against Jews and humanity, crimes society was unable either to punish or forgive. It was a past that grew worse over time "partly because the Germans for such a long time refused to prosecute even the murderers among themselves", and partly because of "the inability of civilized court-room procedures to come to terms with it in juridical form."[22]

But once the duty to prosecute and defense of rights is grounded on the collective interest, collective interests may override the duty to pursue illegalities and injustices as the case of truth and reconciliation committees show. But even though such procedures lead to that violations are not prosecuted, the procedures must be seen as alternatives to justice, and not as instances of forgiveness.

Justice, however, does not require that all crimes are prosecuted. Many legal systems distinguish between felonies and misdemeanors – crimes where prosecution is decided by the state and lesser crimes where prosecution only occurs after request from the offended. At this point, it is not up to the state or the collective to forgive. So if felonies are not prosecuted, the justification must lie in some way in the public good – in the need for reconciliation, in that other measures are more effective in rehabilitating the offender so he does not commit crimes again or in other such public considerations.

In real life we know that many crimes are not prosecuted out of lack of resources. When we hear that the police have dropped a case for economic reasons we are offended, and have reason to state that justice has not been served. This does not entail, however, that the offenders are forgiven. They have in a way been deprived of an opportunity of being forgiven.

This is different in the case of the offended not pressing for prosecution. We understand him if he finds his interests better served in not pressing charges, we forgive him if he abstains from weakness and we do not condemn him for his act of forgiveness without giving the offender his due process of law. The obligation posed on the citizens by Ihering is far too harsh for the modern view of law and responsibility.

ISABELLA

O, it is excellent to have a giant's strength;
but it is tyrannous to use it like a giant

22 Hannah Arendt, *Responsibility and Judgment*, 55–56.

The second issue is deciding on the interpretation and application of a legal rule to the specific facts. That is deciding "if an act *of the kind charged* against the accused can be said not to have been done". This is a matter of categorization which has to be decided by legal means. It is here the temptation to mitigate the harsh impact of the law in circumstances where the situation calls for sympathy for the person affected may result in "bad law". A basic requirement of law is universality, and universality breaks down if the application of a rule takes to great an account of the particularities of the case. If each case is decided by its merits, law breaks down.

As Aristotle shows us, mercy and regard to excuses nevertheless have their place here in the form of equity, but not in the form of forgiveness. Equity demands that the spirit of the law is taken into account, and that it is not brought to bear on instances it is not intended for, and that the judgment that it presupposes is exercised in a just manner. But equity is still within the rationality of justice and not a disregard for the law, properly interpreted and applied. Both legality and equity are in this way integrated into the operation of the law.[23]

This is also the point made by Lord Coleridge in R v Dudley and Stevens. To kill out of hunger is not the kind of self-defence envisaged by the law, even if there are many mitigating circumstances in the case. Equity requires us to take the situation and the intent into account, in the form of the subjective consciousness and the right to self-defence, and the excuse of necessity. In the case of the ship-wreck, there is no doubt that the intent of the surviving sailors was to kill. It is their suffering, and their struggle to preserve their own life, that may be brought into the case as mitigating circumstances.

But as Lord Coleridge points out; there is a difference between acting out of necessity and yielding to a temptation. "It must not be supposed that in refusing to admit temptation to be an excuse for crime it is forgotten how terrible the temptation was; how awful the suffering; how hard in such trials to keep the judgment straight and the conduct pure", Lord Coleridge states, "but a man has no right to declare temptation to be an excuse, though he might himself have yielded to it, nor allow compassion for the criminal to change or weaken in any manner the legal definition of the crime."

It is the same point Hannah Arendt makes when she referring to Mary McCarthy points out that there is a difference between forcing and tempting, and that "if somebody points a gun at you and says, 'kill your friend or I will

---

[23] John Tasioulas, "The Paradox of Equity," *Cambridge Law Journal* 55.3 (1996): 456–69.

kill you', he is tempting you, that is all".[24] While such a temptation may be a legal excuse, Arendt says, it is never a moral excuse. So we may forgive a person who was unable to resist a temptation, but not excuse him, and the judgment of his act must be based on the legal categorization of the act, and not on the individual and mitigating circumstances.

So we see that equity and forgiveness differ in the important respect that equity is bound by justice and the demands of the rule of law, whereas forgiveness is unbound by this. Law in this way sets limits to mercy where love is limitless in its mercy and reconciliation. This limit to mercy is important to uphold, even against the demands of love. It is tyrannical rulers who say "since I love you and you love me, I don't need to get justice from you or you from me, for love eliminates the need for justice."[25] Love and justice are therefore not in conflict, even though love may demand a leniency that the law may not give.

ISABELLA

Go to your bosom; Knock there, and ask your heart what it doth know

The third issue, when the facts and the crime are established, is the issue of legal consequences that should follow from application of the applicable rule. In criminal cases the sentencing, in torts the compensation, in contracts the restitution. But what is just punishment, what is adequate compensation and what constitutes restitution? In many cases the law opens for discretion and judgment, taking also into account if "what is done is proved to have been justly done".

There is, of course, room for equity in the application of a rule in the same way as in determining whether it is applicable. But, in contrast to forgiveness, it is even here the case that equity follows the logic of justice, not of love. The scope for substantive justice is often wider when deciding upon the legal consequences of a situation than when deciding upon which rule is applicable. But reasoning about substantive justice is still justice, and must take into account factors such as legality, the purpose of the law, the general applicability of the result and so on.

There is, however, one aspect of equity that is similar to forgiveness. This is the fact that they are both asymmetrical; it is always only the question of absolving the violator, never to aggregate the consequences of the violation, no matter how exceptional and hideous it may be. This is self-evident in the

---

24 Hannah Arendt, *Responsibility and Judgment*, 18.

25 Paul Tillich, *Love, Power and Justice*, 82.

case of forgiving. But since equity follows the logic of justice, one would expect the logic to go both ways; mitigating the consequences where there are mitigating circumstances and aggregating the consequences where there are aggravating circumstances. To a certain extent this is also the case – at least in sentencing in criminal cases. But the sentence may never surpass the limit set by the law, and equity does not give reason to extend the scope of a criminal prohibition. The reason for this asymmetry in equity is found in its integration in law, and in its co-operation with the principle of legality.[26]

On the other hand, are there not crimes so hideous that they cannot be forgiven; is there not a certain measure of symmetry also in forgiving? Is there a difference between those transgressions we are confronted with daily and with which we know how to come to terms or get rid of either through punishment or forgiveness, and those offences where all we can say "this should never have happened"? This distinction, Hannah Arendt points out, "is similar to the distinction of Jesus of Nazareth between the transgressions I am supposed to forgive "seven times a day" and those offences where "it were better for him that a millstone were hanged about his neck and he cast into the sea."[27] Derrida on his side claims that it is only the unpardonable that in truth can be pardoned, and that Arendt's position stems from a confusion of accepting the wrong and forgiving the wrongdoer.

So law limits the claim to mercy and the scope of love's forgiveness. But one may also with to the German-American theologian and Christian existentialist philosopher Paul Tillich say that love transcends justice and adds to its power.[28] Where pity and mercy in law must be limited by justice's demand for proportionality, love may demand going beyond what is proportional.

Every being has a claim to being reaccepted into the unity to which it belongs. Proportional justice demands retribution, love demands forgiving, that is accepting he who is unjust as just. This is fulfillment of justice, says Tillich, because it is "the only way of reuniting those who are estranged by guilt."[29] "Nothing seems to contradict more the idea of justice than this doctrine", and yet, "nothing less than this is the fulfillment of justice". As the case of R v Dudley and Stevens shows, the temporal ordering of the events is of importance. It is not incoherent of the judge to pass sentence and at the same time issue a recommendation for pardon. There is no contradiction be-

---

26 John Tasioulas, *The Paradox of Equity*.
27 Hannah Arendt, *Responsibility and Judgment*, 73–74.
28 Paul Tillich, *Love, Power and Justice*, 13.
29 Paul Tillich, *Love, Power and Justice*, 86.

tween law and forgiveness if law comes first, and forgiveness thereafter. It can even be argued that this sequence is demanded by both justice and love.

Law may also pardon. A legal pardon can be distinguished from forgiveness in that pardon is an execution of public power, of the sovereign prerogative of mercy.[30] Pardon must also be distinguished from equity, either in interpreting the rules or in the meting out of the consequences of a violation of the rules. A pardon is an executive decision to reduce or remove a lawfully imposed punishment. This distinction is very clear in the story of R v Dudley and Stevens where the court imposed the death penalty and the Queen issued a pardon which lead to the release of the two shipmates. Pardon may be based on considerations of mercy and equity, but is also based on expedience. A pardon presupposes that enforcement of the sentence is unnecessary to uphold the force of the law. Apart from that, it is difficult to envisage rules for the exercise of pardon. In the United States, an Appeals court has even gone so far as to state that the dispenser of clemency "need give no reasons for granting it, or for denying it … The governor may agonize over every petition; he may glance at one or all such petitions and toss them away."[31] Nevertheless, pardon is wrongly implemented if it is used to restore the legitimacy of a verdict which is unjust or inequitable. Dreyfuss was wrongly pardoned instead of acquitted when the upholding of his sentence became untenable.

ISABELLA
My brother did love Juliet,
And you tell me that he shall die for it.
ANGELO
He shall not, Isabel, if you give me love.

These two lines of the conversation between Isabella and Angelo in "Measure for measure" show the complex relations between love and justice. Love, or at least the manifestations of love, may constitute a breach of obligations. Fornication may be prohibited by law, forgiving a crime instead of prosecuting and punishment may be contrary to justice. On the other hand, love may redeem the offender. In some instances it may lead to his pardon, in all instances it should lead to forgiveness, to reunite the lawbreaker and society. On the personal plane forgiveness cannot be demanded, only given, and reunites those estranged by guilt and offence.

---

30 Austin Sarrat and Nasser Hussain eds., *Forgiveness, Mercy and Clemency* (Stanford: Stanford University Press, 2007), Introduction, 3.

31 Austin Sarrat and Nasser Hussain eds., *Forgiveness, Mercy and Clemency*, 6

Taken into the context of the play, the two lines acquire a more sinister tone. The love Angelo speaks of is Isabella's virginity, and the price he will pay is her brothers' life. Angelo speaks not the language of love, but the language of justice; measure for measure. Yet he is not just, but unjust. To determine this, we need the yardstick of justice – love says nothing about the proposition of Angelo. Yet love says everything about the crime of Isabella's brother, who sought his lover's bed of out of love, not lust, and was therefore the most just.

IV. Justice, Culture and Copyright

Mia Rendix
(University of Copenhagen)

Copyright as Moral Strategy of Reclaiming the Past: The Return of the Icelandic Sagas

From Legal Property Ownership to Moral Claims

Justice has been a constant philosophical issue in legal theory from Socrates and up until today. Today the term is being widely used and discussed in the areas of copyright, intellectual property rights and cultural heritage. Justice has moved from being an objective, unchanging legal term to a subjective, often paradoxical and ambiguous concept surrounded and defended by complex rhetoric and discourses of morality and identity. This article investigates the move from the legal sphere of copyright to the ideological claims of cultural heritage from a moral perspective and discourse in a specific case: the year-long battle between Iceland and Denmark regarding the return of the Icelandic sagas. I will examine the two countries' rhetoric and implementation of rhetorical and literary devices and will attempt to uncover the complex transformation of the oppositional discourses of the two countries. Iceland and Denmark represent two very different visions of moral rights and the relation of such rights to ideas of justice, copyright and cultural heritage.

In the heated discussions of the legal or moral ownership of art objects and their relationship to a nation's cultural heritage and history, legal studies have been involved with different versions of justice. Since UNESCO first used the term "cultural property" in 1954, the term has undergone significant changes not only in the anthropological, but also in the literary and cultural context. Former colonial states have now achieved formal state sovereignty. This has resulted in a higher level of self-consciousness and self-esteem on the part of such states, which in turn has led to a quest for identity and origins through the pursuit of what they consider to be their rightful cultural property. The case of the Icelandic manuscripts is one case in point; other cultural heritage claims have been raised by ethnic minorities (Australian aboriginals, the Samic people or Native Americans) who do not have national sovereignty or legal ownership to back up their claims. Instead, these minorities focus on the moral ownership of certain cultural heritage objects. Suddenly, legal and objectively defined arguments are being trumped by morally, ideologically and emotionally charged arguments that are almost impossible to reject or challenge without being accused of cultural imperialism and aesthetic, Western ethnocentrism or even fascism. In 2008, James Cuno, the director of The Art Institute of Chicago and author of the highly debated book *Who owns Antiquity?*, wrote that,

> The idea of cultural property has become a political trump card. At a conference in Athens in March, organized in part by a UNESCO intergovernmental committee, the concept expanded even further: Certain categories of cultural property are irrevocably identified by reference to the cultural context in which they were created (unique and exceptional artworks and monuments, ritual objects, national symbols, ancestral remains, dismembered pieces of outstanding works of art). It is their original context that gives them their authenticity and unique value.[1]

This change in the meaning of "cultural property" has had quite an effect on the development of museums, just as it has changed the nature of international commerce. It furthermore seems to have changed traditional notions of national property and ownership, in opposition to universalist visions of the Cultural Commons and *Bildung* in the Enlightenment sense of the word. At the moment, a transatlantic diplomatic crisis between Europe and the United States is building up. The Google-digitization project involving Harvard University's archives has prompted strong reactions from the old world that does not view the digitization and open-access-idea as progressive and democratic. Instead, France and Germany argue that the rights of the authors, artists and publishers have been violated and that the Europeans should remain not only cautious, but also legally and ideologically opposed to the whole process.

But how to solve this basic opposition and antagonism – between the national/essentialistic claim of cultural property/identity and the global/universal case for open-access as a democratic vision intended to preserve a common world heritage? The problems and challenges of cultural heritage are commonly divided between former colonial rulers and their colonies turned states. The legal case is often presented together with emotional and moral arguments to win back a lost patrimony. In addition, the debates and policy-making have been split between the legal tradition of Anglo-American "property laws" and the European "*droit moral*" when dealing with the challenging and complex *ménage a trois* of cultural heritage, copyright and general intellectual property-related issues. The return of the Icelandic sagas provides an interesting case study of the reconciliation of cultural heritage,

---

[1] James Cuno in "Connections Antiquities, the World Is Your Homeland" by Edward Rothsteinin, *New York Times*, May 27th 2008 – available at http://www.williams.edu/go/native/rothstein-cuno.htm.

copyright and general intellectual property-related issues in the current climate.

A Model Case and an Example to Follow?

In 1971 Denmark officially returned the majority of the sagas to Iceland. Archeologists, historians, anthropologists, politicians, and Icelandic citizens have since canonized the case as a model for the world to follow regarding the return of cultural heritage. This is how Jeanette Greenfield, who is a legal expert on cultural heritage issues, describes the return of the sagas, for example:

> The case of the Icelandic manuscripts is the outstanding example of a major state-to-state return of cultural property. It was an unusually civilized and rational act in the face of all the common legal, political and historic arguments against return.[2]

During the nineteenth and twentieth centuries, Icelandic intellectuals and politicians revitalized the sagas as crucial symbols of Icelandic mythology and identity by repeatedly referring to:

> [the] image of a glorious past to boost the confidence of the nation they wanted to 'awaken', at the same time as it helped them to garner sympathy for their cause abroad. To them the achievements in the past indicated what the nation could become in the future, in both cultural and economic terms, once it had freed itself from a foreign yoke.[3]

In his foreword to Greenfield's book, the Icelandic historian and cultural researcher Magnus Magnusson rather touchingly articulates the value of the manuscripts to the Icelanders. He relates how, on April 21 1971, as the Danish Minister of Education Helge Larsen handed over the two greatest sagas *Flateyjarbok* (= *Book of Flat-Island*) and *Codex Reginus* (= *The King's Volume*) to his Icelandic counterpart and a cheering crowd of 15,000 ecstatic Icelanders, streets in Iceland were empty, flags were flying, and the whole thing was presented as the biggest cultural happening in Iceland – ever:

---

2 Jeanette Greenfield, *The Return of Cultural Treasures* (Cambridge: CUP, 1996), 5.

3 Gudmundur Halfdanarson, "Interpreting the Nordic Past: Icelandic Medieval Manuscripts and the Construction of a Modern Nation", in *The Uses of the Middle Ages in Modern European States*, eds. Robert J. W. Evans and Guy Marchal (Houndmills, Basingstoke, Hampshire: Palgrave Macmillan 2010), 3. The article was published in late December 2010, but Halfdarnarson generously agreed to let me read and quote from his draft before publishing it. The referred page numbers are from this draft.

> The significance of these saga manuscripts to the people of Iceland would be impossible to exaggerate. They have been the root and the stock of Icelandic culture, the life-blood of the nation, the oldest living literature in Europe, enshrining the origins of Icelandic society (...) Indeed, when the Icelanders took up the struggle for freedom and independence from Denmark in the nineteenth century, the saga literature was both their inspiration and their justification.[4]

Magnusson's fond memories are both descriptive and normative of the specific Icelandic case and of other eyewitnesses' depictions of various homecoming ceremonies in honor of the long-awaited return of their cultural property. Professor Greenfield's view of the sagas' homecoming is representative of the more scholarly views on the case of the Icelandic sagas. Other scholars, from Iceland, Denmark and around the world, agree that the return was a success without precedent – legally, politically, and ideologically.

However, what is distinctive about the canonization of the case is the repeated use of a legal perspective concerning what was essentially a non-legal case. Usually, the claims of cultural heritage are legally structured and articulated, but in the case of the sagas there was no legal case – instead, Iceland formulated a convincing moral claim to which Denmark responded. Because of the missing legal argument I find it difficult to categorize the Icelandic case as a model case for most cultural heritage claims. Instead of a legal interpretation I propose a perspective on the case which is more humanities driven in its focus on the moral structure and discourse that became the chosen legitimate and official discourse as well as a huge motivating factor for the Icelandic case. What I find interesting is applying a rhetorical and literary perspective on the moral claims that can be read as pure textual discourse with internal dissonances and ideological schisms. Contradictions are revealed in the arguments of the ownership and politics of cultural heritage by both Iceland and Denmark. Thus, it is crucial to take a second look at the case and it is my main argument that both the Icelandic and the Danish rhetoric include fundamentally different notions of what I refer to as "moral justice" and "aesthetic justice".

Cultural Heritage Claims as a Question of Moral Justice

In both the Icelandic and Danish discourse and context, a significant vocabulary and rhetoric of positive, even at times romantic and glorifying words surrounding the word "justice" has been utilized. Etymologically, the word refers to objectivity. Quoting *The Oxford Dictionary,* "justice" is defined

[4] Greenfield, *The Return of Cultural Treasures*, 4.

as: 1) just behavior or treatment, 2) the quality of being just or 3) the administration of law or some other authority according to the principles of just behavior and treatment. To do oneself justice; to perform as well as one is able; to do someone/thing justice; to treat or represent someone or something with due fairness. But the objectivity inherent in the term is challenged when moral valorizations and thus subjectivity is the chosen discourse and result.

When considering the case in relation to expressions of moral justice, the Icelandic case is extraordinary because both Iceland and Denmark had to abandon legal terminologies and legal procedures: Iceland had no absolute legal or judicial right to claim the manuscripts.[5] Before his death, the great Icelandic scholar Arne Magnussen wrote his will, wherein he donated the sagas to the Arnamagnaean Institute in Copenhagen. So any removal would be an obstruction of the basic law of private ownership. In wanting the sagas back to Iceland, Icelanders claimed what essentially amounted to the illegal expropriation of private property, and Iceland accordingly (and appropriately – at least in a legal sense) never took any official legal action against the Danish state during the long-lasting claim.

Instead, Icelanders conducted a rhetorical as well as ideological campaign via newspapers, television, diplomatic letters etc., using terms such as "natural justice", "moral obligation" and "moral responsibility" to obtain everything that was "by, for and on Iceland".[6] Icelanders claimed their "moral right."[7] Supplementary observations show that the Icelandic rhetoric insistently expressed the use of the imperative, demanding "should" instead of the futuristic "could" in the formulation of Icelanders' right to have the sagas returned. Both professionally and personally, Sigorour Nordal, the Icelandic professor and official representative of the Icelandic government, represented a moderate and diplomatic point of view. Yet, he took the Icelandic claim a step further by characterizing it as an expression of a truly global humanity – implicitly indicating that if one were opposed to the sagas' return to Iceland, one could not be included in the category of universally acknowledged humanists, democrats, philanthropists etc. Thus, there seemed to be an inherent undercurrent of an essentialistic opposition between good and evil created by both the Icelandic people and several Danish supporters. Echoes of American appeasement and glasnost politics come to mind when

---

5 Greenfield, *The Return of Cultural Treasures*, 20.

6 Sigrún Davisdóttir, *Håndskriftsagens saga* (Odense: Southern University Press, 1999), 268. Original Danish quote: "af, for og på Island." My translation.

7 Davisdóttir, *Håndskriftsagens saga*, 151.

reading the Danish legal philosopher and lawyer Jørgen Jørgensen Koch's description of the Icelandic claim as "the intended appeasement, atonement and mutual good-will".[8]

It is indeed ironic that the Icelanders explicitly and collectively started out by arguing their premise as a dedicated version of Immanuel Kant's theory of justice based on Kant's rational philosophy on freedom, human dignity and universal human rights – only in order to end up advocating an individual, regional and national demand for property. This latter way of arguing would lean towards Aristotle's virtue-based approach to the philosophy of justice as that which people morally deserve. The Kantian-inspired syllogism made by the Icelanders seemed to be the deductive argument that in claiming the sagas back, they acted rationally and autonomously and thus proved their human dignity and universal moral rights – the Icelanders had the right motive and were doing the right thing for the right reason.

Along the way, Iceland progressed from objective legal terminology to subjective morals and identity politics. This rhetorical transformation was needed and it was indeed both a basic expression of the Icelandic feelings and a clever strategy. The shift in argumentation transcended any of the legal perspectives and instead created a mythological and literarily inspired narrative based on Icelandic folklore, culture and regional myths: how the sagas expressed the core of Iceland, the genesis and essence of how Iceland was created and developed as a society with its own laws, infra-structure and identity. Nordal was very aware of how best to appeal to Danish feelings – of "how much it was possible to emotionally move the Danish people".[9] By adopting Aristotle's dictum of fulfilling the Greek tragedy by infusing the literary concept of pathos instead of the rhetorical device of logos or nomos, Icelandic diplomacy repeatedly referred to the "feelings of the people".[10] Therefore, Nordal and others created a highly emotional and almost religious discourse on Iceland's right to the sagas: "The manuscripts are like a part of us", stated Alexander Jóhannesson, rector of the University of Iceland in 1939; they are "like flesh of our flesh and blood of our blood".[11]

From a post-colonial and horizontally structured perspective, the return of the sagas was a democratic right. According to the Icelandic politicians

---

8 Davisdóttir, *Håndskriftsagens saga*, 268.

9 Davisdóttir, *Håndskriftsagens saga*, 133. The original Danish quote is: "hvor langt det var muligt at man kunne bevæge danskerne". My translation.

10 Davisdottir, *Håndskriftsagens saga*, 141. The original Danish quote is: "folkets følelser." My translation.

11 Halfdanarson, "Interpreting the Nordic Past: Icelandic Medieval Manuscripts and the Construction of a Modern Nation", 4.

and the Icelandic people, it was the fair and just claim of a once oppressed Icelandic people, who now stepped up to the dominating Danish master and demanded their rightful possessions and independence. A member of the Icelandic parliament, Alþingi, remarked:

> The Danes will understand our demands and rights when they pause to think, when they reflect on their own destiny, as all small nations must do at the present time. Every nation must attempt to defend itself and its independence, with all means available, and then it is impossible to refuse other nations their rights. (...) We expect full understanding and fairness from the Danish nation and the Danish authorities on this issue.[12]

But the Icelanders kept using paradoxical rhetoric. They referred to a post-modern world, constantly on the brink of atomization and alienation but spoke of themselves as a self-confident global "we" who, because of the "historical and ideological decentralization", were part of a larger democratic movement with a "common voice of justice and consanguinity". But if the careful reader recognizes the last quotation it is no coincidence: Iceland quotes the American Declaration of Independence from 1776, in which the American people legally, ideologically, and morally declared the United States to be fully liberated from the evil wrong-doings of their English commander. Obvious differences aside, it is a curious and interesting parallel that Iceland created. Thus, the immanent vision and constant expression of existential self-reliance and moral superiority, political autonomy and cultural-aesthetic exceptionalism may be found in the rhetoric of independence of both America and Iceland – both countries articulated the belief in creating and controlling their own course of history and identity in the name of democracy and human rights. It is no coincidence that Iceland and America cooperated closely during the 1950s and their relationship was described as "intimate".[13]

Legally speaking, Denmark had a splendid case: The state of Denmark owned the original saga texts which had been given as a private gift by Arne Magnusson, as we saw. Because of the right of private property, Iceland could not demand any legal actions and Denmark had no illegal actions to defend. But despite this overwhelmingly good case, the Danish State will-

---

12 Halfdanarson, "Interpreting the Nordic Past: Icelandic Medieval Manuscripts and the Construction of a Modern Nation", 5.

13 Davisdóttir, *Håndskriftsagens saga*, 198. The reason why Iceland had such strong connections to the USA was because of the Marshall-aid, which helped save and rebuild the Icelandic economy during the 1950s. For a more detailed look at the relationship between the two countries see: Þór Whitehead, *The Ally Who Came in from the Cold A Survey of Icelandic Foreign Policy 1946–1956* (Reykjavik: University of Iceland Press, 1998).

ingly engaged in the return of the saga manuscripts – an action not based, however, on the horizontally structured and democratic claim by the Icelanders. Officially, Denmark agreed to engage in a constructive dialogue even though several politicians, especially from the more conservative political parties, did not ecstatically endorse the Icelandic claim and fought all the way for the sagas to stay in Copenhagen. The critical hesitation from the Danish sceptics was based in part on academic arguments and scientific questions concerning how to preserve the sagas. But it was also based on a political fear that the return of the manuscripts might undermine a focused, collective co-operation of the Nordic countries in pursuit of the promotion of Scandinavian culture and literature as a part of an active and fruitful interaction between Europe and the United States.[14]

In addition to the Icelandic discourse, the Danish rhetoric and argumentation transcended the normal legal terminologies and phrases in defining the Danish response as "a gift from the Danish" people, a "result of the Danish will", and a pro-active "Danish initiative".[15] Ultimately, the Danes responded to the horizontal claim of the Icelanders of their rights with a vertically structured discourse. Denmark was the patient, loving and forgiving parent, who was not bothered too much by the insistent tantrums of the rebellious child and, with a sense of doing a parental charity, Denmark agreed to return the sagas to Iceland. This almost overbearing choice of rhetoric, discourse and diplomacy would perhaps be altered significantly if the parts were reversed and it was Denmark who claimed the entire works of Hans Christian Andersen back from Iceland. But whether the Danish response and political process towards the returning of the historic manuscripts were the result of pragmatic strategic thinking or sincere empathy of the Icelandic request, the former colonial state government also engaged in paradoxical communication, intentionally or not.

While the official rhetoric was vertically formalized, the semantic intention progressed into what I would call a progressive, global and horizontal concept of justice that was advocated by the American legal philosopher John Rawls in his influential *Political Liberalism* from 1993. Rawls wanted to respect the idea of reasonable pluralism,[16] which acknowledges the diversity in various people's moral and religious opinions and the resulting disagreements. Of course this attempt at liberal neutrality seems ambitious, even

---

[14] Þór Whitehead, *The Ally Who Came in from the Cold.*

[15] All three quotes from Halfdanarson, "Interpreting the Nordic Past: Icelandic Medieval Manuscripts and the Construction of a Modern Nation", 5.

[16] John Rawls, *Political Liberalism* (New York: Columbia University Press, 1993).

naive, in a heated struggle over the ownership of cultural heritage, but the Danes were nevertheless eager to present their case as justice for the common good. By suggesting a shared ownership, the Danish government in reality forced the Icelandic counterpart to refuse the proposal because of the nationalistic feelings of the Icelandic people. Thus, Denmark could 1) stigmatize Iceland as ungrateful and not willing to compromise and 2) represent itself as the progressive part in the case, who was only interested in a fair and justified return for the common-universal sake of the Icelandic people.

Having looked at the two colliding, paradoxical and transformational concepts of moral justice, it is interesting to consider the other aspect of the case: The aesthetic justice. Here, the Icelandic and Danish rhetoric and arguments are transformed back and reversed again and the two countries switch sides. The Icelandic saga dispute not only expressed the above-mentioned moral issues; the case also became symbolic of two fundamentally different notions of art and of the manuscripts as symbols of literary works or literary texts.

Cultural Heritage Claims as Universal or Local Literary Art

Hitherto, I have discussed the sagas as a crucible of the various and often controversial and notorious discussions of legal property and its fusion with morality and ideology. Now the perspective changes from a moral context to an aesthetic analysis of the two different perceptions on the part of Iceland and Denmark, respectively, as to whom the literary work of art belongs to. A central question is the different concept of an artist/Icelandic author and the intention of an art object/the sagas.

Through the universal premise of Kantian human rights, moral obligation and the Icelandic autonomy and dignity, the Icelandic scholars, historians and politicians transformed the rational argument into a discourse on national rights and claims within a postcolonial perspective: The Icelandic people expressed a fundamental right to their past, their history, culture and identity outside the legal sphere and the cultural heritage claim thus ended up being a question of morality. Understandable as the Icelandic case was, it was difficult for the Danish state to criticize, problematize or object at all to the claim from Iceland. If Denmark refused to return the sagas (on the basis of the obvious Danish rights of property), a diplomatic and political crisis would emerge and portray Denmark as an old colonial power that still would not accept the loss of its former colony. Because Iceland replaced the formal legal objectivity with a moral subjectivity it was impossible for the Danish state to do anything but welcome the initiative.

However, if we consider the Icelandic rhetoric concerning the actual sagas as literary and mythological narratives, it is notable how the parts were reversed once again. Icelanders talked of the sagas as having their natural origins in Iceland – the sagas "were conceived of and composed by people in this country, written in Iceland and preserved in Iceland for a longer or shorter period of time" and they were "to be returned to their proper home."[17] The global pronouncing of Iceland as a world-collective "we" as we saw in the above-mentioned analysis on the legal-moral claims, was replaced with an inclusive and regional articulation of one Icelandic voice directly from god: "Vox populi, Vox Dei"[18] was paralleled with the sagas' literary origins even though it was clear that a specific author of for instance the Eddic poetry could not be specified. Again, Iceland used the term "justice" when talking of the sagas as literary works: Iceland wanted to appeal to "the Danes' sense of justice"[19] and described their claim as based on local stories of unique Icelandic law and justice. As mentioned earlier, Iceland was consciously or unconsciously inspired by US independence and the Icelandic rhetoric is again miming the American jeremiads and their particular biblical language. Professor Olafur Lárusson has described them in this way:

> The land of the sagas has been our promised land, a beautiful and glorious land, to which we have looked for inspiration in times of need, and to which we have sought strength, courage, and hope. The sagas showed how Iceland was a long time ago, and we have believed that what the country once was, it could become again.[20]

The essentialist vision of the sagas was developed by Sigurour Nordal in his "Book Prose Theory" that opposed the "Free Prose Theory" – Nordal argued that the sagas were fiction written *by* Icelandic authors *for* Icelandic readers:

> The main objective of Sigurður Nordal and his Icelandic colleagues in this effort was to prove that the sagas and the other literary works preserved in the Icelandic manuscripts were, in fact, an *Icelandic* and only an Icelandic national heritage. The literature emerged in close interaction between individual authors and their audience, they maintained, and therefore these works emerged like cooperative projects, where the audience (the Icelandic nation) and the few outstanding Icelandic authors who had composed or compiled them worked together to create literary

---

17 Halfdanarson, "Interpreting the Nordic Past: Icelandic Medieval Manuscripts and the Construction of a Modern Nation", 6.

18 Davisdóttir, *Håndskriftsagens saga*, 145.

19 Halfdanarson, "Interpreting the Nordic Past: Icelandic Medieval Manuscripts and the Construction of a Modern Nation", 5.

20 Olafur Larússon, *Árbók Háskóla Íslands. Háskólaárið 1946–7* (Reykjavik, 1947), 92

> masterpieces. Icelandic culture had certainly developed from Nordic roots, and the Icelandic literati had worked with common Germanic and Scandinavian themes, but in their preserved form their literary works were shaped by Icelandic tastes and reflected Icelandic conditions – therefore they exemplified the Icelandic literary genius. For this reason the literature and the 'vehicles' which preserved them – the medieval manuscripts – belonged to no other nation than the Icelanders, and the only logical place for keeping them was the new centre for Nordic medieval studies, the University of Iceland.[21]

These statements clearly depict the Icelandic concept and particular vision of art. It is difficult not to categorize the insistence on "oneness" as a romantic idea of art – art as a sort of divine discourse from a, in this case Icelandic, deity-entity that refused to separate the authorial origin from authorial intention. Iceland repeats what Mircea Eliade has named "the myth of the eternal return" – how mankind ritually and repeatedly clings to a circular-cyclical mythical narrative:

> This eternal return reveals an ontology uncontaminated by time and becoming (…) Everything begins over and over again at its commencement every instant. The past is but a prefiguration of the future (…) nothing new happens in the world, for everything is but the repetition of the same primordial archetypes.[22]

Via the sagas the Icelandic people are able to narrate an authoritative and religious identity typology and modus that are stable, timeless, legitimate, holy and paradigmatic. The sagas represent and articulate a divine and ontological essence that allows no pain and suffering for the true believers. Ultimately, the sagas are able to purge and purify the Icelandic people from all their troubles, trials, tribulations and sins and reestablish the balanced relation between Iceland and the universe/cosmos:

> For us, the essential thing is that there is everywhere a conception of the end and the beginning of a temporal period based on the observation of biocosmic rhythms and forming part of a larger system – the system of periodic purifications (cf. Purges, fasting, confessions of sins, etc.) and of the periodic regeneration of life. (…) that a periodic regeneration of time presupposes, in more or less explicit

---

21 Halfdanarson, "Interpreting the Nordic Past: Icelandic Medieval Manuscripts and the Construction of a Modern Nation", 10. The "Book Prose Theory" was also a reaction against the Norwegian attempt to locate the Icelandic sagas' origin in Norway and reduce the manuscripts as vessels of Norwegian culture. The Norwegian historians Rudolf Keyser and Peter Andreas Munch were the pioneers and founded the "Norwegian Historical School". Keyser and Munch were influenced by the German romantics, especially Ficte's theories on cultural nationalism.

22 Mircea Eliade, *The Myth of the eternal Return, Or Cosmos and History* (Princeton: Princeton University Press, 1991), ix.

> form – and especially in the historical civilizations – a new Creation, that is, the repetition of the cosmogonic act.[23]

Also, this romantic idea of the sagas as a Work with a capital "W" and the example of exclusive authorship was not meant to be aimed at a fragmented, atomized and decentralized group of readers-audiences outside Iceland. The sagas of Njal and Edda were solely written and meant for Icelandic readers. Subsequently, the Icelandic state operated within an exclusive terminology of the text as a closed work of art with the primary intention as well as the unique access of the Icelanders. Only the Icelandic people were able to decipher and decode and understand the exceptional Icelandic mythology and identity as expressed by the sagas. Iceland, in the end, presented a subjective, conservative and regressive-nostalgic claim of their sagas as artistic works that did not correspond with their postcolonial and democratic claim of moral property.

To support this argument it is furthermore important to consider the Icelandic notion of art objects; their being and essence. In various interviews and during several national hearings the Icelandic officials, politicians and scholars focused on the essence of the sagas and the meaning of the Icelandic myths as being able to express "the greatness and the horrors of Icelandic history and soul" and "the beauty and excellence of the Icelandic people".[24] Here, the Icelandic rhetoric again adopts an Edmund Burke-analogue and conservative idea of art as being able to not only express beauty but also allows the perceivers (e.g. the Icelanders) of the art objects to experience a sublime essence of horror. But the overwhelming and frightening sublimity at the same time evokes a pleasure in seeing an overpowering or vast malignant object of great magnitude, one that could destroy the observer, according to the German philosopher Arthur Schopenhauer and his philosophy on the essence of an object, the unchangeable, the eternal stability. Reversely and according to the official Icelandic case, this potential destruction and following reconstruction was at the same time the premise for the "true understanding" of the Icelandic manuscripts, myths, folklore and rituals – a unique insight that the Danes or other countries' citizens did not have the chance to experience. As opposed to the rational-universal motive of the political-ideological plea for the sagas to return to Iceland, the aesthetical-artistic claim of Iceland adapts to a vertical and exclusively homogeneous concept of the sagas as objects of art.

---

[23] Eliade, *The Myth of the eternal Return,* 52.

[24] Halfdanarson, "Interpreting the Nordic Past: Icelandic Medieval Manuscripts and the Construction of a Modern Nation", 151.

Predictably, the Danish government responded to the case of Icelandic copyright with an oppositional rhetoric – not exactly confrontational but very different in its view on art objects, literature and authorship. Denmark now engaged in a horizontally structured rhetoric. Instead of claiming the vertical, overbearing and sometimes even slightly arrogant voice of the former colonial master, the majority of the Danish politicians and scholars involved in the case suddenly saw the sagas as articulating more universal themes than particular Icelandic ones. In other words: The sagas were not defined solely by the original authors and the manuscripts were certainly not restricted to Icelandic readers and their unique interpretation. The Danish vision of Denmark acting out as the (superior) generous giver in a charitable handing back the sagas (down) to (the subordinate) Iceland transformed into a preliminary objection: Even as the saga texts unfolded their narratives, characters and events in a typical Icelandic context and history, the themes were undoubtedly "common for all people" and the sagas were more to be considered as science than national folklore:

> In their view, significant collections of cultural artefacts, such as the Arnamagnæan Collection in Copenhagen, were coherent units which must be kept intact, because in time they become, irrespective of the origins of their individual parts, a 'cultural heritage' in themselves. This was the basic premise for the opinions of the directors of the Danish National Archives and the Royal Library mentioned before, as they were convinced that Denmark had strong claims to keep the manuscripts, in spite of their Icelandic origins. Through their meticulous scientific work since the seventeenth century and the publications and translations of the manuscripts into modern languages, members of Danish academia had set their mark on the medieval heritage, and thus transformed it into something it had not been before. According to this interpretation, the manuscripts were scientific objects rather than 'living' cultural artefacts.[25]

We note how the Danish rhetoric now advocated the literary objects as more than literary works of art – they were scientific texts, which not only widens the intentional audience. It also means an open, multilayered system of language, ideology and rhetorical patterns. The Icelandic epics, myths and local rituals of the sagas could teach mankind scientific and universal insight, philosophical realization and existential clarification. Denmark, then, promoted a transnational, open-access vision of art for the sake of general and global enlightenment and thus articulated – consciously or unconsciously – a horizontal, inclusive and heterogeneous vision of literature and literary intention as multi-layered. This decentralization of the literary text also

---

25 Halfdanarson, "Interpreting the Nordic Past: Icelandic Medieval Manuscripts and the Construction of a Modern Nation", 12.

showed itself in the thematization of the sublime, which Iceland represented. Denmark never talked of "essence", "unique insight" or "exceptional" in relation to the Icelandic sagas as art objects embodying a certain kind of imposing soul or being of the objects. Instead, the Danish rhetoric was limited to the neo-Kantian talk of art objects in general as expressing "boundlessness" and being "indefinite" (accessible and open to all) and shifted the focus from the texts/art objects to the readers/perceivers – or as the Danish government put it: "Readers of the world".[26]

Copyright and Cultural Heritage as Humanistic Epicenters of Rhetoric, Morality and Art

Professor Jeanette Greenfield repeatedly defines the case of the Icelandic sagas as "The extraordinary feat of return" and "an example and incentive for the rest of the world on how to resolve sensitive disputes." "This case serves as an international model for other cultural restitution cases", she writes.[27] But even though the dispute between Iceland and Denmark ended on a friendly note, this is certainly no guarantee that other restitution claims, which will be or are currently handled outside court, will end in rapturous applause – just think of the various demands within the past few years of the return of cultural heritage. I do not think that it is possible to apply the Iceland-Denmark-case to the ongoing heritage-claims around the world – simply because there was no legal case. Denmark agreed to give back the sagas and in return Iceland agreed to preserve the manuscripts in the best possible way and also to ensure that Denmark would have unrestricted access to the literary classics. Maybe the case can be a moral example to follow. Because the issue of copyrighting art and creativity is complex and difficult in practice, both in legal, political and cultural terms, the emotional arguments of the right to reclaim and possess original cultural objects in their original geographical context seem to have the majority of people's sympathy on both sides of the Atlantic. Ideologically, it seems fair that once stolen or colonized art (from Australian aboriginals for instance) and cultural objects should return to their owners – it certainly does from a local-national and emotional point of view. The postcolonial movement and quest for self-control and self-reliance has been necessary and important. Furthermore,

---

26 Sólrún Jensdottir, "Áform um l'ydveldisstofnun 1941 og 1942. Saga XVI 1978" in *Videnskab og håndskriftsag. Island – Danmark og håndskriftsagen*, ed. S. Haugstrup Jensen (Askov Forlag, 1957), 6.

27 Greenfield, *The Return of Cultural Treasures*, 40–41.

the issue of turning art objects into a commodity still provokes the widespread romantic idea of art as divine inspiration and thus sacred to the profane-capitalist powers that want to earn money on "our" art and culture.

However, this understandable but also nostalgic-regressive and often politically correct argument is being challenged by the global technology, web 2.0 and the world-wide discussions on digitization of a country's cultural heritage. Whether out of cultural necessity or plain economic interest, it is a fact that the web 2.0 and its global opening-up to access has challenged the national-regional insistence on exclusive rights. Even if a country or state wishes to limit the access or sharing of their cultural heritage, the web has made it possible and very easy to elude these legal or moral restrictions. Thus, it is noteworthy that all the legal claims of getting back one or several cultural objects always use the word "preservation" in their arguments.

But to preserve is not necessarily a limited skill or craft that cannot be fulfilled and unfolded outside the home country or state of the cultural objects. Sometimes the preservation of the artifacts can be handled by more advanced technology and thus be preserved in foreign countries – preservation is indeed not an entirely cultural or psychological ability. In the last ten years Google's agreement with Harvard and Oxford has proved fruitful (notwithstanding the controversial law suits from various author organizations) as has the European web initiative *Europeana*, which allows worldwide citizen access to European cultural treasures. Whether the digitized sagas, which presently are being prepared, will be associated with *Europeana* is yet to be seen, but the question is whether the global digitization wave step-by-step will minimize or enhance the local-regional-national-exceptional Icelandic claim of the sagas as Icelandic cultural heritage. Currently, Harvard's director of libraries, Professor Robert Darnton, is trying to launch a National American Digital Library. Darnton speaks of "a library without walls", a "new republic of letters"[28] – not only for Americans but for the rest of the world. People everywhere will be able to participate in a new digital enlightenment and hopefully gain pure "self-improvement"[29].

The other side of that coin is, of course, the ideological and democratic problems ensuing; that the colonial traumas of former colonized states and minorities risk being reissued and revitalized if the intellectual property

---

28 Robert Darnton, "A Library without Walls" in *The New York Review of Books*, 2010. See: http://www.nybooks.com/blogs/nyrblog/2010/oct/04/library-without-walls/[Accessed on January 5, 2011]

29 Robert Darnton, "Can we create a National digital Library?" in *The New York Review of Books*, 2010. See: http://www.nybooks.com/articles/archives/2010/oct/28/can-we-crea te-national-digital-library/ [Accessed on January 5, 2011]

rights – that ideally should protect their heritage – end up repeating past Western/American/ethnocentric suppression and formal power structures. Perhaps part of the solution may be a horizontal acknowledgement of the negative discussion on the "loss" that the minorities suffer when deprived of their original folklore artifacts/objects, culture and rituals – an acknowledgement which will subsequently be followed up with economic compensation based on positively formulated copyright privileges.

Fiona Macmillan
(School of Law, Birkbeck, University of London)

Rights, Culture, Property: In Search of a New Design for Intellectual Space

"Reshaping narrow law and art
Whose symbols are the millions slain [...]"[1]

1. Introduction

The twentieth century was, perhaps, one of the bloodiest and most violent in the rich course of violent and bloody human history. And this despite – or possibly because of – the growth of the "science" of law and rights at both the national and international levels. What answer has law to the millions slain, dispossessed, suppressed, repressed? "Human rights" is law's ever-present response to this litany of suffering. This is not to suggest that any major steps have been made with respect to the improved recognition or enforcement of some of the most basic rights generally recognised as falling within the "human rights" camp. But our recent lamentable history has given us a renewed respect for the *idea* of human rights – a beautiful idea, one for the true believer. In a wide range of literature, academic and activist, the true believers in the idea of human rights play out their argument by regarding the characterisation of something as a human right as a "trump card", that is, as the end to all arguments. As always, this is a technical, scientific, legal claim. But even in technical terms the argument is problematic: if everything that seems a good or fair or morally defensible thing automatically becomes a "human right" then every so-called human right is reduced to the symbolic and legal significance of the most banal, and the very idea of "human rights" as the unsurpassable moral high ground, the trumps of trumps, disappears. This is a particularly undesirable state of affairs in a world where it is already the case, at least in the context of international legal governance, that human rights are not a trump card.[2]

---

1 F. R. Scott, *Villanelle for Our Time*, with thanks to Leonard Cohen for setting it to music on *Dear Heather* (Columbia, 2004).

2 See Robert Howse, "Human Rights in the WTO: Whose Rights, What Humanity?" *European Journal of International Law* 13 (2002): 651–660; Fiona Macmil-

It may be the case, then, that there are rights or interests which are worthy of protection despite the fact that it seems overblown (and dangerous) to describe them as "human" rights. Intellectual property interests, for which the best attempts at justification are based on the argument that they confer advantages on society as a whole,[3] might be a good example of this type of legal interest or right. Some other possible candidates for non "human rights" rights are rights to culture, cultural identity, cultural self-determination, and cultural heritage. To argue that these types of rights are not human rights in the sense of trumping all other rights or interests is, however, problematic. For one thing, at least some types of rights to culture are recognised in a range of international human rights conventions.[4] For another, denying that rights to culture are human rights suggests an intellectual association with the refusal to recognise so-called "third generation" human rights[5] – a position that lacks both charm and humanity. The problem here might be the lumping together of all sorts of different rights under a common rubric, rather than distinguishing some third generation rights from others. But since this sounds a bit defensive it seems best, for the moment, to leave open the question of whether rights to culture, or some aspects of such rights, should be protected on the basis that they are human rights.

---

lan, "International Economic Law and Public International Law: Strangers in the Night," *International Trade Law and Regulation* 10 (2004): 115–124; Fiona Macmillan, "Looking Back to Look Forward: Is there a Future for Human Rights in the WTO?" *International Trade Law and Regulation* 11 (2005): 163–180; Fiona Macmillan, "The UNESCO Convention as a New Incentive to Protect Cultural Diversity," in *Protection of Cultural Diversity from a European and International Perspective*, eds. Hildegaard Schneider and Peter van den Bossche (Antwerp: Maastricht Series in Human Rights, 2008), 163–192; Anne Orford, "Beyond Harmonization: Trade, Human Rights and the Economy of Sacrifice," *Leiden Journal of International Law* 18 (2005): 179–213.

3 See, e.g., Neil Weinstock Netanel, "Copyright and a Democratic Civil Society," *Yale Law Journal* 106 (1996): 283–388; Jeremy Waldron, "From Authors to Copiers: Individual Rights & Social Values in Intellectual Property," *Chicago-Kent Law Review* 69 (1993): 841–888; William van Caenegem, "Copyright, Communication & New Technologies," *Federal Law Review* 23 (1995): 322–347.

4 For reasons sketched out in the next section of this chapter, I do not accept that the same argument can be made for intellectual property rights on the basis of the Universal Declaration of Human Rights, Art 27.2 and the UN Covenant on Economic, Social and Cultural Rights, Art 15.1(c).

5 Meaning economic, social and cultural rights as laid out in the UN Protocol on Economic, Social and Cultural Rights.

In order to investigate the connection between human rights, rights to culture and intellectual property rights, this chapter focuses on three issues. First, the chapter considers the nature of the rights to culture and the extent of the protection of cultural rights in international legal instruments. Secondly, the chapter considers whether there should be a right to culture and/or cultural self-determination. Thirdly, assuming that legal regimes should recognise some concept of a right to culture or cultural self-determination, the chapter turns to an examination of the nature of that right. This part of the chapter concerns itself, in particular, with the question of the relationship between cultural property and intellectual property. It is not premised on the idea that the mere fact that there may be good, if different, reasons for protecting both cultural property and intellectual property – reasons possibly falling short of a justifiable claim to the status of "human rights" – suggests the necessity of a connection in legal form between cultural property and intellectual property.

2. Is There a "Right to Culture"?

2.1. International Legal Instruments

There are a range of UNESCO Conventions that bear directly on the question of "the right to culture" (if there is one), encompassing interests in cultural property, cultural identity and cultural heritage. These Conventions are: the Convention on the Protection of Cultural Property in the Event of Armed Conflict of 1954, which came into force in 1956, and its two Protocols; the Convention on the Means of Prohibiting and Preventing the Illicit Import, Export and Transfer of Ownership of Cultural Property of 1970, which came into force in 1972; the World Heritage Convention of 1972, which came into force in 1975; the Convention on the Protection of Underwater Cultural Heritage of 2001, which came into force in 2009; the Convention for the Safeguarding of Intangible Cultural Heritage of 2003, which came into force in 2006; and the Convention on the Protection and Promotion of the Diversity of Cultural Expressions of 2005, which came into force in 2007. Of course, it may seem somewhat irregular to have mentioned the first four of these Conventions in the present context. This is, perhaps, because the persistent connection between some types of cultural rights and intellectual property rights has tended to suggest that what might be described as "tangible culture" is an entirely different order of things to more intangible forms. This distinction is problematic not least because what makes tangible items culturally important, at least within the legal regime envisaged by UNESCO, is the symbolic and thus intangible value accorded to them.[6] The final section of this chapter questions the tangible/intangible taxonomy, but I am nevertheless in thrall to it with the result that this section will have more to say about the last two of the UNESCO Conventions listed above. However, in the context of an examination of where human rights start and end in this disputed territory and what their significance to it might be, before focussing on the UNESCO Conventions it is necessary to consider their international legal background.

Prior to the entry into force of these Conventions, international legal obligations with respect to culture, cultural self-determination and cultural diversity could only be gleaned from the composite effect of a range of provisions found in the human rights covenants to the Charter of the United Nations. The provisions of these Covenants that may be argued to operate together in order to create a right to cultural self determination are Articles 1, 19, 27 of the Covenant on Civil and Political Rights (CCPR) and Art 15 of the Covenant on Economic Social and Cultural Rights (CESCR). When these provisions are analysed it can be seen that it is probably more appropriate to characterize their composite effect as creating, if anything, a right to cultural self-determination, which in turn suggests the valorisation of cultural diversity.

The general right to self determination is laid down in CCPR, Article 1.1, which provides:

> All peoples have the right of self-determination. By virtue of that right they freely determine their political status and freely pursue their economic, social and cultural development.

As can be seen, this right is conferred on "[p]eoples" rather than individuals and, obviously, it leaves open the somewhat delicate question of how such entities might be identified or defined. While "peoples" may, presumably, be constituted by the citizens and residents of a particular nation state, it is also clear from Article 1.3 that this is not the only method of constituting a "people".[7] On the other hand, it appears to be the case that ethnic, religious or linguistic groups are not necessarily "peoples" for the purpose of Ar-

---

6 See Janet Blake, "On Defining Cultural Heritage," *International and Comparative Law Quarterly* 49 (2000): 61–85, 73ff.

7 CCPR, Art 1.3 provides: The States Parties to the present Covenant, including those having responsibility for the administration of Non-Self-Governing and Trust Territories, shall promote the realization of the right of self-determination, and shall respect that right, in conformity with the provisions of the Charter of the United Nations.

ticle 1.1 since Article 27 confers a range of somewhat more limited rights on such groups:

> In those States in which ethnic, religious or linguistic minorities exist, persons belonging to such minorities shall not be denied the right, in community with the other members of their group, to enjoy their own culture, to profess and practice their religion, or to use their own language.

The individual rights that contribute to this composite right of cultural self-determination are laid out in CCPR, Article 19:

1. Everyone shall have the right to hold opinions without interference.
2. Everyone shall have the right to freedom of expression; this right shall include freedom to seek, receive and impart information and ideas of all kinds, regardless of frontiers, either orally, in writing or in print, in the form of art, or through any other media of his choice.

These are complemented by CESCR, Article 15:

1. The States Parties to the present Covenant recognize the right of everyone:
   (a) To take part in cultural life;
   (b) To enjoy the benefits of scientific progress and its applications;
   (c) To benefit from the protection of the moral and material interests resulting from any scientific, literary or artistic production of which he is the author.
2. The steps to be taken by the States Parties to the present Covenant to achieve the full realization of this right shall include those necessary for the conservation, the development and the diffusion of science and culture.
3. The States Parties to the present Covenant undertake to respect the freedom indispensable for scientific research and creative activity.
4. The States Parties to the present Covenant recognize the benefits to be derived from the encouragement and development of international contacts and co-operation in the scientific and cultural fields.

As is not infrequently the case with provisions of this sort in international instruments, the exact ambit of the provisions in CCPR and CESCR are far from clear. One example of this is the right in Article 15.1(a) "[t]o take part in cultural life", which is obviously of some significance in the context of a right to cultural self-determination. However, Article 27 of CCPR and Article 15.1(c) of CESCR have attracted particular debate. This is because it is frequently argued that these provisions support the characterisation of intellectual property rights as human rights. Article 27 of CCPR is said to ground the grant of intellectual property rights to protect traditional and Indigenous cultural expressions and knowledge. Article 15.1(c) of CESCR is said to ground intellectual property rights, in general, on a human rights basis. A similar argument is frequently made with respect to the precursor of Article 15.1(c), Article 27.2 of the Universal Declaration of Human Rights

(UDHR). This is not surprising since CESCR, Article 15.1, is clearly based upon Article 27 of the UDHR, which provides:

1. Everyone has the right to freely participate in the cultural life of the community, to enjoy the arts and to share in scientific advancement and its benefits.
2. Everyone has the right to the protection of the moral and material interests resulting from any scientific, literary or artistic production of which he is the author.

It is evident that none of Article 27.2 of the UDHR, Article 15.1(c) of CESCR or Article 27 of CCPR necessarily mandate intellectual property protection in the form in which it currently prevails. It is also clear that whatever means are chosen to implement the rights contained in these Articles, those rights must be balanced against the other rights laid down in Articles 27 of the UDHR, Article 15 of the CESCR, and in the Covenants as a whole.

The relationship between these provisions and the bulk of the UNESCO Conventions listed at the beginning of this section is, admittedly, a little obscure. However, all the UNESCO Conventions, with the exception of the Convention on the Means of Prohibiting and Preventing the Illicit Import, Export and Transfer of Ownership of Cultural Property,[8] make a justificatory appeal to some variation on the "common heritage of humanity" (or "mankind", as humanity was previously known), while at the same time becoming ensnared in the obvious problem that the right to have one's cultural property, heritage, identity, protected is national, sub-national, regional, tribal or some other anthropological variation on a group comprising less than humanity as a whole.[9] This particular dilemma is eerily reminiscent of the pervasive problem of human rights, for which the rhetorical universal concept of the "human" stripped of all other affiliations seems in constant conflict with the diverse reality of humanity.

The clearest relationship between the human rights conventions and the UNESCO Conventions can be seen in relation to the Convention for the

---

[8] Although, the UNIDROIT Convention on Stolen or Illegally Exported Cultural Objects of 1995, which seeks to operationalize the 1970 UNESCO Convention (see UNESCO Information Note, *UNESCO and UNIDROIT: Cooperation in the Fight Against Illicit Traffic in Cultural Property*, UNESCO Doc CLT-2005/Conf/803/2, Paris 2005, and Lyndel Prott, "UNESCO and UNIDROIT: A Partnership against Trafficking in Cultural Objects," *Uniform Law Review* 59 (1996): 59–71), refers to "the heritage of all peoples." It may also be relevant to note in this context that the UNESCO Convention itself makes reference to "universally recognized moral principles."

[9] See also Blake, "On Defining Cultural Heritage," 69–71; Ana Filipa Vrdoljak, *International Law, Museums and the Return of Cultural Objects* (Cambridge: CUP, 2008).

Safeguarding of Intangible Cultural Heritage and the Convention on the Protection and Promotion of the Diversity of Cultural Expressions. Both Conventions appear to give some structure to the rights in the pre-existing human rights instruments. It is also evident from the Preambles and operative provisions of both Conventions that they firmly lodge themselves within the human rights camp, even if neither goes so far as to create a new human right. (The temptation to comment on the fact that both Conventions were concluded earlier this century when human rights rhetoric was, as now, highly fashionable in international legal circles is too hard to resist.). The Convention for the Safeguarding of Intangible Cultural Heritage states in the second paragraph of its Preamble that it is "*Referring* to existing human rights instruments" and then cites in particular, those instruments considered above. The Convention on the Protection and Promotion of the Diversity of Cultural Expressions pushes the human rights envelope considerably further than its older sibling,[10] which is perhaps a consequence of the escalating obsession with the language of human rights. So far as the Preamble is concerned, amongst an enormous list of other things, it declares itself to be, in the words of the first five paragraphs:

> *Affirming* that cultural diversity is a defining characteristic of humanity,
> *Conscious* that cultural diversity forms a common heritage of humanity and should be cherished and preserved for the benefit of all,
> *Being aware* that cultural diversity creates a rich and varied world, which increases the range of choices and nurtures human capacities and values, and therefore is a mainspring for sustainable development for communities, peoples, and nations,
> *Recalling* that cultural diversity, flourishing within a framework of democracy, tolerance, social justice and mutual respect between peoples and cultures, is indispensable for peace and security at the local, national and international levels,
> *Celebrating*, the importance of cultural diversity for the full realization of human rights and fundamental freedoms proclaimed in the Universal Declaration of Human Rights and in other universally recognized instruments [...]

The location of the Convention within the stable of human rights instruments, which is suggested in the Preamble is reinforced by a number of the operative provisions of this Convention. Two such provisions are of particular note in this respect. One is the first of the Convention's so-called guiding principles in Article 2.1, which provides:

---

[10] For an assessment of the relationship between this UNESCO Convention and existing international human rights obligations, see Christoph Beat Graber, "The New UNESCO Convention on Cultural Diversity: A Counterbalance to the WTO?" *Journal of International Economic Law* 9 (2006): 553–574, 560–563.

> Cultural diversity can be protected and promoted only if human rights and fundamental freedoms, such as freedom of expression, information and communication, as well as the ability of individuals to choose cultural expressions, are guaranteed. No one may invoke the provisions of this Convention in order to infringe human rights and fundamental freedoms as enshrined in the Universal Declaration of Human Rights or guaranteed by international law, or to limit the scope thereof.

The other relevant article, however, provides the clearest invocation of the authority and relevance of the pre-existing human rights instruments. This is Article 5.1, which is concerned with the obligations of the parties to the Convention:

> The Parties, in conformity with the Charter of the United Nations, the principles of international law and universally recognized human rights instruments, reaffirm their sovereign right to formulate and implement their cultural policies and to adopt measures to protect and promote the diversity of cultural expressions and to strengthen international cooperation to achieve the purposes of this Convention.

Both the Convention for the Safeguarding of Intangible Cultural Heritage and the Convention on the Protection and Promotion of the Diversity of Cultural Expressions are notably light with respect to positive obligations imposed on state signatories. The former mandates the creation of lists without much more, while the latter is even less demanding. It may be a coincidence that these two UNESCO Conventions, which are so high on human rights-speak, are so low on real obligations – but I doubt it.

2.2. Relationship Between the UNESCO Conventions, Intellectual Property Rights, and the World Trade Organization Agreements

Neither UNESCO Convention has much to say about intellectual property rights. The Convention for the Safeguarding of Intangible Cultural Heritage mentions intellectual property rights in the context of providing, in its Article 3(b), that nothing in the Convention affects "the rights and obligations of States Parties deriving from any international instrument relating to intellectual property rights or to the use of biological and ecological resources to which they are parties". The only reference to intellectual property in the Convention on the Protection and Promotion of the Diversity of Cultural Expressions occurs in its Preamble, which recognises "the importance of intellectual property rights in sustaining those involved in cultural creativity". The Conventions do not suggest that these rights are critical to realizing their objectives, and only the Convention for the Safeguarding of Intangible Cultural Heritage appears to give any recognition to the potential of intellectual property rights to interfere with those objectives. The absence of much in the way of references to intellectual property rights as a mode for the realisation of Convention objectives is, at least, notable in relation to the Convention for the Safeguarding of Intangible Cultural Heritage. On the other hand, it seems particularly odd that the Convention on the Protection and Promotion of the Diversity of Cultural Expressions is so little concerned with the negative effects of intellectual property rights.[11] The original UNESCO Declaration,[12] upon which the Convention was based, included in its action plan the need to ensure the protection of copyright but "at the same time upholding a public right of access to culture, in accordance with Article 27 of the Universal Declaration of Human Rights".[13] The Declaration also drew a parallel in its Article 1 between biological diversity and cultural diversity. In the light of this, it is interesting to note that the framers Convention on Biological Diversity were far more anxious about the role of intellectual property in securing biological diversity. Its Article 16.5 provides:

> The Contracting Parties, recognizing that patents and other intellectual property rights may have an influence on the implementation of this Convention, shall co-operate in this regard subject to national legislation and international law in order to ensure that such rights are supportive of and do not run counter to its objectives.

By contrast, the UNESCO Convention seems to envisage no conflict. This would not matter in the least, but for the fact that the operation of the international copyright system has a negative impact on cultural diversity.

The threat that the international copyright system poses to cultural diversity and self-determination is a consequence of the process by which it commodifies and instrumentalises the cultural outputs with which it is con-

---

11 Although it would be unwise to ignore the potential negative effects of intellectual property rights on the protection of intangible cultural heritage: see, e.g., *European Communities – Protection of Trademarks and Geographical Indications for Agricultural Products and Foodstuffs*, WT/DS/290/R, 15/3/2005; see also Michael Blakeney, "Biotechnology, TRIPs and the Convention on Biological Diversity," *Bioscience Law Review* 4 (1998–1999): 144–50; Michael Blakeney, "Protection of Plant Varieties & Farmers' Rights," *European Intellectual Property Review* 24 (2002): 9–19; G. E. Evans and Michael Blakeney, "The Protection of Geographical Indications after Doha: Quo Vadis?" *Journal of International Economic Law* 9 (2006): 575–614, 582–586.

12 UNESCO Universal Declaration on Cultural Diversity, Adopted by the 31st Session of UNESCO's General Conference, Paris, 2 November 2001.

13 See note 12, Main Lines of an Action Plan for the Implementation of the Universal Declaration on Cultural Diversity, para 16.

cerned.[14] There are five interdependent aspects of copyright law that have been essential to this process.[15] The first and most basic tool of commodification is the alienability of the copyright interest. A second significant aspect of copyright law making it an important tool of trade and investment is its duration. The long period of copyright protection increases the asset value of individual copyright interests.[16] Thirdly, copyright's horizontal expansion means that it is progressively covering more and more types of cultural production. Fourthly, the strong commercial distribution rights,[17] especially those which give the copyright holder control over imports and rental rights, have put copyright owners in a particularly strong market position, especially in the global context. Finally, the power of the owners of copyright in relation to all those wishing to use copyright material has been bolstered by a contraction of some of the most significant user rights in relation to copyright works, in particular fair dealing/fair use and public interest rights.

Viewed in isolation from the market conditions that characterise the cultural industries, copyright's commodification of cultural output might appear, not only benign, but justified by both the need for creators to be remunerated in order to encourage them to create[18] and, in particular, the need for cultural works to be disseminated in order to reap the social benefits of

---

14 For an account of the overlaps between the concepts of culture with which the UNESCO Convention is concerned, and the subject matter of copyright law, see Macmillan, "The UNESCO Convention as a New Incentive to Protect Cultural Diversity."

15 For a fuller version of this argument see: Fiona Macmillan, "Copyright and Culture: A Perspective on Corporate Power," *Media and Arts Law Review* 10 (1998): 71–81; Fiona Macmillan, "Copyright and Corporate Power," in *Copyright and the Cultural Industries*, ed. Ruth Towse (Cheltenham: Edward Elgar, 2002), 99–118; Fiona Macmillan, "The Cruel ©: Copyright and Film," *European Intellectual Property Review* 24 (2002): 483–492.

16 See Ruth Towse, "Copyright, Risk and the Artist: An Economic Approach to Policy for Artists," *Cultural Policy* 6 (1999): 91–107.

17 See esp. the WTO TRIPs Agreement, Arts 11 and 14(4), which enshrine rental rights in relation to computer programmes, films and phonograms; WIPO Copyright Treaty 1996, Article 7; and WIPO Performances and Phonograms Treaty 1996, Articles 9 and 13.

18 See, however, Ruth Towse, *Creativity, Incentive and Reward: An Economic Analysis of Copyright and Culture in the Information Age* (Cheltenham: Edward Elgar, 2001), esp. chs. 6 and 8, in which it is argued that copyright generates little income for most creative artists. Nevertheless, Towse suggests that copyright is valuable to creative artists for reasons of status and control of their work.

their creation.[19] However, viewed in context the picture is somewhat different. Copyright law has contributed to, augmented, or created a range of market features that have resulted in a high degree of global concentration in the ownership of intellectual property in cultural goods and services. Five such market features, in particular, stand out.[20] First, is the internationally harmonised nature of the relevant intellectual property rights.[21] This dovetails nicely with the second dominant market feature, which is the multinational operation of the corporate actors who acquire these harmonised intellectual property rights while at the same time exploiting the boundaries of national law to partition and control markets. The third relevant feature of the market is the high degree of horizontal and vertical integration that characterises these corporations. Their horizontal integration gives them control over a range of different types of cultural products. Their vertical integration allows them to control distribution, thanks to the strong distribution rights conferred on them by copyright law.[22] The fourth feature is the progressive integration in the ownership of rights over content and the ownership of rights over content-carrying technology. Finally, there is the increasing tendency since the 1970s for acquisition and merger in the global market for cultural products and services.[23] Besides being driven by the regular desires (both corporate and individual) for capital accumulation,[24] this last feature has been produced by the movements towards horizontal and vertical integration, and integration of the ownership of rights over content and content-carrying technology.

---

19 For arguments about the importance of copyright in securing communication of works, see van Caenegem, "Copyright, Communication & New Technologies," and Netanel, "Copyright and a Democratic Civil Society."

20 For a fuller discussion, see Fiona Macmillan, "Public Interest and the Public Domain in an Era of Corporate Dominance," in *Intellectual Property Rights: Innovation, Governance and the Institutional Environment*, ed. Birgitte Andersen (Cheltenham: Edward Elgar, 2006), 46–69.

21 Through, e.g., Berne Convention for the Protection of Literary and Artistic Works of 1886, the TRIPs Agreement, Arts 9–14, the WIPO Copyright Treaty, and the WIPO Performances and Phonograms Treaty.

22 For a discussion of the way in which the film entertainment industry conforms to these features, see Macmillan, "The Cruel ©."

23 See Ronald V. Bettig, *Copyrighting Culture: The Political Economy of Intellectual Property* (Boulder: Westview Press, 1996), 37ff. See also Joost Smiers, "The Abolition of Copyrights: Better for Artists, Third World Countries and the Public Domain," in *Copyright and the Cultural Industries*, ed. Towse, 119–139.

24 Bettig, *Copyrighting Culture,* 37.

So far as cultural diversity and self-determination are concerned, the consequences of this copyright facilitated aggregation of private power over cultural goods and services on the global level are not happy ones. Through their control of markets for cultural products the multimedia corporations have acquired the power to act as a cultural filter, controlling to some extent what we can see, hear and read.[25] Closely associated with this is the tendency towards homogeneity in the character of available cultural products and services.[26] This tendency, and the commercial context in which it occurs, has been well summed up by the comment that a large proportion of the recorded music offered for retail sale has "about as much cultural diversity as a Macdonald's menu".[27] It makes good commercial sense in a globalized world to train taste along certain reliable routes, and the market for cultural goods and services is no different in this respect to any other.[28] Of course, there is a vast market for cultural goods and services and, as a consequence, the volume of production is immense. However, it would obviously be a serious mistake to confuse volume with diversity.

The vast corporate control over cultural goods and services also has a constricting effect on what has been described as the intellectual commons or the intellectual public domain.[29] The impact on the intellectual commons manifests itself in various ways.[30] For example, private control over a wide

---

25 See further Macmillan, "Public Interest and the Public Domain in an Era of Corporate Dominance,"; and, in relation to the film industry, see Macmillan, "The Cruel ©," 488–489. See also Ann Capling, "Gimme shelter!" *Arena Magazine* (February/March 1996): 21–24; Richard L. Abel, *Speech and Respect* (London: Stevens & Son/Sweet & Maxwell, 1994), 52; Richard L. Abel, "Public Freedom, Private Constraint," *Journal of Law and Society* 21/3 (1994): 374–382, esp 380.

26 See also Bettig, *Copyrighting Culture.*

27 Capling, "Gimme shelter!" 22.

28 See Theodore Levitt, "The Globalisation of Markets," *Harvard Business Review* 61 (1983): 92–102. Cf. John Gray, *False Dawn: The Delusions of Global Capitalism* (New York: The New Press, 1998), 57–58. However, Gray's view seems to be that diversity stimulates globalization, which must be distinguished from the idea that globalization might stimulate diversity.

29 This is a concept that has become, unsurprisingly, a central concern of intellectual property scholarship: see, e.g., *Intellectual Property: The Many Faces of the Public Domain*, eds. Charlotte Waelde and Hector L. MacQueen (Cheltenham: Edward Elgar, 2007).

30 See further Macmillan, "The Cruel ©"; Macmillan, "Public Interest and the Public Domain in an Era of Corporate Dominance,"; Fiona Macmillan "Commodification and Cultural Ownership," in *Copyright and Free Speech: Comparative and International Analyses*, eds. Jonathan Griffiths and Uma Suthersanen (Oxford: OUP, 2005), 35–65.

range of cultural goods and services has an adverse impact on freedom of speech. This is all the more concerning because control over speech by private entities is not constrained by the range of legal instruments that have been developed in Western democracies to ensure that public or governmental control over speech is minimised.[31] The ability to control speech, arguably objectionable in its own right,[32] facilitates a form of cultural domination by private interests. This may, for example, take the subtle form of control exercised over the way we construct images of our society and ourselves.[33] But this subtle form of control is reinforced by the industry's overt and aggressive assertion of control over the use of material assumed by most people to be in the intellectual commons and, thus, in the public domain. The irony is that the reason people assume such material to be in the commons is that the copyright owners have force-fed it to us as receivers of the mass culture disseminated by the mass media. The more powerful the copyright owner the more dominant the cultural image, but the more likely that the copyright owner will seek to protect the cultural power of the image through copyright enforcement. The result is that not only are individuals not able to use, develop or reflect upon dominant cultural images, they are also unable to challenge them by subverting them.[34] Coombe describes this corporate control of the commons as monological and, accordingly, destroying the dialogical relationship between the individual and society.[35] Some remnants of this dialogical relationship ought to be preserved by copyright's fair dealing/fair use

---

31 See further Fiona Macmillan Patfield, "Towards a Reconciliation of Copyright and Free Speech," in *Yearbook of Media Law and Entertainment Law*, ed. Eric M. Barendt (Oxford: Clarendon Press, 1996), 199–233; Macmillan, "Commodification and Cultural Ownership."

32 See, e.g., the discussion of the justifications for the free speech principle in Barendt, *Freedom of Speech*.

33 See further, e.g., Rosemary J. Coombe, *The Cultural Life of Intellectual Properties* (Durham/London: Duke University Press, 1998): 100–129, which demonstrates how even the creation of alternative identities on the basis of class, sexuality, gender and race is constrained and homogenised through the celebrity or star system.

34 See, e.g., *Walt Disney Prods v Air Pirates*, 581 F 2d 751 (9th Cir, 1978), *cert denied*, 439 US 1132 (1979). On this case, see Waldron, "From Authors to Copiers: Individual Rights & Social Values in Intellectual Property"; Macmillan, "Public Interest & the Public Domain in an Era of Corporate Dominance." See also Margaret Chon, "Postmodern 'Progress': Reconsidering the Copyright and Patent Power," *DePaul Law Review* 43 (1993); 97–146; Dorean Marguerite Koenig, "Joe Camel and the First Amendment: The Dark Side of Copyrighted and Trademark-Protected Icons," *Thomas M Cooley Law Review* 11 (1994): 803–838; Macmillan Patfield, "Towards a Reconciliation of Copyright and Free Speech."

35 Coombe, *The Cultural Life of Intellectual Properties*, 86.

right. It is, after all, this aspect of copyright law that appears to be intended to permit resistance and critique.[36] Yet the fair dealing defence is a weak tool for this purpose and becoming weaker.[37]

These constrictions of the intellectual commons (or public domain) affect its vibrancy and creative potential. They also tend to undermine the utilitarian/development justification for copyright, which is increasingly seen as the dominant justification for copyright protection, especially in jurisdictions reflecting the Anglo-American bias on these matters. As is well-known, the general idea underlying this justification is that the grant of copyright encourages investment in the production and dissemination of the cultural works, which is essential to the development process.[38] However, the consequences of copyright's commodification of cultural goods and services, as described above, seem to place some strain on this alleged relationship between copyright and development. This argument may be illustrated by reference to the World Commission on Development and Culture's concept of development as being about the enhancement of effective freedom of choice of individuals.[39] Some of the things that matter to this concept of development are "access to the world's stock of knowledge, … access to power, the right to participate in the cultural life of the community"[40] – all ideas that are reprised by UNESCO in one form or another in its subsequent Convention on the Protection and Promotion of the Diversity of Cultural Expressions. The edifice of private power that has been built upon copyright law has deprived us all to some extent of the benefits of this type of development. As Waldron comments, "[t]he private appropriation of the public realm of cul-

36 See Jane M. Gaines, *Contested Culture: The Image, the Voice and the Law* (Chapel Hill/ London: the University of North Carolina Press, 1991), 10.

37 See further Macmillan, "Public Interest & the Public Domain in an Era of Corporate Dominance."

38 For a good example of a statement of this rationale, see the Preface to World Intellectual Property Organization, *Guide to the Berne Convention for the Protection of Literary and Artistic Works*, Geneva 1978. For discussion of this rationale, see e.g. Waldron, "From Authors to Copiers: Individual Rights & Social Values in Intellectual Property," 850ff; Fiona Macmillan Patfield, "Legal Policy and the Limits of Literary Copyright," in *Textual Monopolies: Literary Copyright and the Public Domain*, eds. Patrick Parrinder, Warren L. Chernaik. and Warwick Gould (London: Office for Humanities Communications, 1997), 113–132.

39 World Commission on Culture and Development, *Our Creative Diversity*, Paris 1996, 2nd ed. For a detailed and persuasive account of this approach to development, see Amartya Sen, *Development as Freedom* (New York: Knopf, 1999).

40 World Commission on Culture and Development, *Our Creative Diversity*, Introduction. See further, Macmillan, "Copyright and Culture: A Perspective on Corporate Power"; Macmillan, "Copyright and Corporate Power."

tural artefacts restricts and controls the moves that can be made therein by the rest of us".[41]

None of these problems have been alleviated by the fact that the international copyright system has been embedded in the World Trade Organization as a result of its Agreement on Trade-Related Intellectual Property Rights (TRIPs Agreement).[42] In fact, there are good reasons for thinking that the TRIPs Agreement and the WTO agreements more generally have exacerbated these problems.[43] So far as the TRIPs Agreement is concerned, the reification of intellectual property rights as trade rights, capable of enforcement through a system of trade retaliation, seems emphasize certain aspects of the international copyright landscape at the expense of others. This perception is reinforced by two further factors. The first is that the TRIPs Agreement has shown itself to be a useful uniform basis upon which to negotiate bilateral investment treaties, which may strengthen the oligopolistic nature of the market for cultural goods and services.[44] Indeed, wrapped up in this observation, is the further suggestion that the TRIPs Agreement might be even better characterised as an investment agreement than as a trade agreement.[45] (Either way, its capacity to nourish cultural self-determination and diversity seems rather limited.) The second factor reinforcing the nature of the change in the international copyright landscape is that the interpretation and enforcement of international copyright law is now in the hands of trade law experts, who are not necessarily experts in intellectual property law or practice.

However, the problems that copyright law operating in accordance with the TRIPs Agreement might pose for the protection of cultural diversity or

---

41 Waldron, "From Authors to Copiers: Individual Rights & Social Values in Intellectual Property," 885.

42 TRIPs Agreement, Art 9.1, incorporates Berne Convention, Arts 1–21, except Article 6*bis* (moral rights) by reference. TRIPs Agreement, Arts 10–14 add some further obligations. In particular, Arts 11 and 14.4 broaden the exclusive rights of the copyright holder by the addition of rental rights in relation to computer programmes, films and phonograms. However, neither of these provisions are unique in international copyright law: see WIPO Copyright Treaty 1996, Art 7; and WIPO Performances and Phonograms Treaty 1996, Arts 9 and 13.

43 For a fuller version of this argument see Macmillan, "The UNESCO Convention as a New Incentive to Protect Cultural Diversity."

44 See Peter Drahos, "BITS and BIPs: Bilateralism in Intellectual Property," *Journal of World Intellectual Property* 4 (2002): 791–808.

45 Macmillan, "Looking Back to Look Forward: Is there a Future for Human Rights in the WTO?"

self-determination are only the beginning of the threat that the WTO agreements might pose to the protection of cultural rights. The reasons for this lie in the fact that, unlike the TRIPs Agreement, the other WTO multilateral agreements are dedicated to reducing national barriers to trade using three main tools, which are the reduction of tariffs, the reduction of non-tariff barriers, and "the elimination of discriminatory treatment in international trade relations".[46] The elimination of discriminatory treatment is effected through the principles of national treatment and most favoured nation (MFN) treatment.[47] Taken together these two principles provide that a WTO member state may not create a trade disadvantage *vis a vis* domestic goods and services for like goods or services coming from another WTO member state, nor may they discriminate between like goods and services coming into their jurisdiction from more than one other member state.[48] The WTO agreements laying down obligations pursuant to the principles of national treatment and MFN treatment are subject to a range of exceptions allowing governments to take steps that would amount to breaches of these principles in some cases involving pressing national priorities, but the exceptions are limited and narrowly drawn.

In terms of the picture painted above of cultural domination by private actors, a national government may wish to take steps at the national level to ameliorate the effects of the oligopolistic markets for cultural goods and services. For example, it may wish to attempt to prevent the swamping of local culture as the result of the homogenising effect of global media and entertainment oligopolies by providing for quotas, local content restrictions or subsidies for local cultural production.[49] All these sorts of devices run the risk of falling foul of WTO rules. The Agreement which has the capacity to be the particular culprit is the General Agreement on Trade in Services

---

46 See the Preamble to the Agreement Establishing the World Trade Organization, 15 April 1994.

47 In fact, both these principles make an appearance in the TRIPs Agreement, Arts 3 (MFN) and 4 (national treatment), but their significance in this context appears to be limited to the requirement that that national legal entities (human or artificial) are all to be regarded as being alike.

48 Consistently with the WTO's somewhat inconsistent approach, WTO law and practice embrace a number of derogations from these principles: e.g., the GATS permits measures that are inconsistent with MFN: see GATS, Art II; and the exceptions for customs unions in GATT, Art XXIV, & GATS, Art V, involve inconsistencies with both principles.

49 That is, some of the types of devices envisaged by the Convention on the Protection and Promotion of the Diversity of Cultural Expressions, Art 6.

(GATS).[50] Due to the somewhat unusual nature of the GATS as a bottom-up liberalising agreement, WTO members are only bound by the liberalising provisions of GATS if, and to the extent that, they have accepted obligations in the relevant sector.[51] There is not yet any general agreement or protocol on liberalisation of obligations in the audio-visual sector,[52] which is the sector in which the cultural effects of the copyright-induced oligopolies are most keenly experienced.[53] However, some WTO members have undertaken relevant obligations and there is considerable international political pressure for more liberalisation in this sector.[54] On the other hand, limited resistance in the form of, for example, the European Union's Audio-Visual Services Directive[55] provides some political counterweight. Similarly, at a more general level, China's invocation of the Convention on the Protection and Promotion of the Diversity of Cultural Expressions in the context of a WTO dispute with the US over Chinese import restrictions on publications, music and audio-visual products[56] might herald increasing inter-

---

[50] Although the WTO General Agreement on Trade and Tariffs (GATT) and the WTO Agreement on Subsidies and Countervailing Measures may also have a part to play. The difficulties posed by these agreements are comparable, if not identical, to those posed by the GATS. In relation to the GATT, it should be noted that it has, in Art IV, a special regime in relation to films permitting internal quantitative measures, however pressure has been applied by the US to force other WTO members to abandon Art IV regimes: see Michael Hahn, "A Clash of Cultures? The UNESCO *Diversity Convention* and International Trade Law," *Journal of International Economic Law* 9 (2002): 515–552, 522–523.

[51] GATS, Art VI and XVI. In relation to the process of progressive liberalization, see Art XIX.

[52] Cf the GATS Annexes on Air Transport Services, Financial Services, Negotiations on Maritime Transport Services, Telecommunications, and Negotiations on Basic Telecommunications.

[53] See, e.g., Graham Dunkley, *The Free Trade Adventure: The WTO, the Uruguay Round & Globalism – A Critique* (London and New York: Zed Books, 2001), 183–187; Macmillan, "The Cruel ©: Copyright and Film,"; Macmillan, "Public Interest and the Public Domain in an Era of Corporate Dominance,"; Bill Grantham, *"Some Big Bourgeois Brothel": Contexts for France's Culture Wars with Hollywood* (Luton: University of Luton Press, 2000).

[54] See further Graber, "The New UNESCO Convention on Cultural Diversity: A Counterbalance to the WTO?" 569–570; Dunkley, *The Free Trade Adventure: The WTO, the Uruguay Round & Globalism – A Critique*; Grantham, *"Some Big Bourgeois Brothel": Contexts for France's Culture Wars with Hollywood*; Hahn, "A Clash of Cultures? The UNESCO *Diversity Convention* and International Trade Law," 526.

[55] 2007/65/EC, modifying Directive 89/552/EEC.

[56] *China – Measures Affecting Trading Rights and Distribution Services for Certain Publications and Audiovisual Entertainment Products*, WT/DS363/AB/R, 21/12/2009.

national resistance, even though it did not convince the WTO Appellate Body.

In the context of a discussion of international instruments affecting the protection of cultural rights, the important thing about the WTO agreements, including the TRIPs Agreement, is not just that they have the capacity to adversely affect some cultural rights, but also that they famously contain no "cultural exception". This means that, as China found, there is almost no space in the WTO system for a consideration of cultural interests or rights.[57] The only clear exception to this absence of a cultural exception occurs in relation to some types of tangible cultural property under the provisions the General Agreement on Trade and Tariffs.[58] The question of the cultural exception in the WTO was, however, long debated[59] and it can hardly be a surprise that those countries who lost this debate strongly supported the conclusion of the Convention on the Protection and Promotion of the Diversity of Cultural Expressions.

3. Should There be a Right to Culture or Cultural Self-determination?

There are a variety of reasons that might militate in favour of the international legal protection of cultural rights. One of these might be their possible characterisation as human rights. However, it is not clear that such a characterisation, or lack of such a characterisation, is of much assistance in resolving the problem. Besides anything else, if intellectual property rights can also be said to be grounded in human rights[60] and they conflict with cultural property rights, only a stalemate can follow. In the end, to argue that only some aspects of a right to culture constitute human rights, properly defined, is interesting but does not resolve the question of which, if any cultural rights should be subject to legal protection. There may be reasons for protecting a range of cultural rights other than the fact that they are human rights. These might include the arguments that the safeguarding of cultural

---

[57] For a fuller version of this argument, see Macmillan, "The UNESCO Convention as a New Incentive to Protect Cultural Diversity."

[58] See WTO General Agreement on Trade and Tariffs (GATT), Art XX(f), which provides an exception for measures "imposed for the protection of national treasures of artistic, historic or archaeological value."

[59] For an account of the history of the debate in the WTO over the absence of a cultural exception, see Hahn, "A Clash of Cultures? The UNESCO *Diversity Convention* and International Trade Law"; Graber, "The New UNESCO Convention on Cultural Diversity: A Counterbalance to the WTO?" 554–555.

[60] An argument with which I disagree, but certainly not an uncommon one.

heritage, cultural diversity and cultural self-determination are, to borrow the language of the UNESCO Conventions, "a guarantee of sustainable development",[61] "of general interest to humanity",[62] and "a common heritage of humanity".[63] In light of these fairly good reasons for protecting cultural rights, perhaps it is unnecessary to do more damage to the symbolic and moral significance of the concept of human rights by attempting to load too much of the baggage of cultural rights (or intellectual property rights) onto its bandwagon.

In any case, as a tool of international lawmaking human rights have also been somewhat compromised. The international human rights instruments are, of course, part of the system of public international law that grew out of the Dumbarton Oaks negotiations. Growing up next to this system is the system of international economic law, inaugurated at Bretton Woods, but acquiring a new significance with the advent of the WTO in 1994. The point about these systems is that they are sealed in the sense that they contain no meaningful legal mechanisms for interacting with each other.[64] This has, of course, lead to a fragmentation of international law-making.[65] The fact that there is very little space in WTO law for the protection of human rights,[66] let alone cultural rights, is a reflection of this fragmentation. Consequently, the question of whether cultural rights are human rights is not germane in the context of a consideration of WTO law. This might not matter too much, but for the highly tenable proposition that with its strong enforcement procedures, the system of WTO law has become the pre-eminent international

---

61 Convention for the Safeguarding of Intangible Cultural Heritage, Preamble; and see also Convention on the Protection and Promotion of the Diversity of Cultural Expressions, Preamble.

62 Convention for the Safeguarding of Intangible Cultural Heritage, Art 19.2.

63 Convention on the Protection and Promotion of the Diversity of Cultural Expressions, Preamble.

64 See Macmillan, "International Economic Law and Public International Law: Strangers in the Night."

65 *Fragmentation of International Law: Difficulties arising from the Diversification and Expansion of International Law*, Report of the Study Group of the International Law Commission, 13 April 2006, UN Doc. A/CN.4/L.682, 1–256, and 18 July 2006, UN Doc. A/CN.4/L.702, 1–25.

66 An attempt might be made to argue that argue that the exception for "measures necessary to protect public morals," which appears in GATT, Art XX(a) and GATS, Art XIV(a), allows the penetration of human rights norms into the WTO. However, the argument is not strong: see Macmillan, "The UNESCO Convention as a New Incentive for the Protection of Cultural Diversity."

legal system:[67] a proposition that does not seem at odds with the outcome of the recent WTO dispute between China and the US.[68] In light of the failure of WTO law to give consistent protection to human rights or cultural rights, many would not regard its systemic pre-eminence as a comforting state of affairs.

It is not easy to know the best way to approach a solution to this problem. One possible approach is the alteration of WTO law so that its putative focus on open and efficient world markets takes due account of important countervailing interests such as human rights and cultural rights. However, despite arguments to the contrary,[69] one might wonder whether it is sensible or desirable to see the trade liberalisation agenda as incorporating the human rights agenda. Such an argument is, in Alston's words, "a form of epistemological misappropriation".[70] The WTO is not an appropriate body to oversee the protection of human rights, nor of rights relating to cultural diversity and self-determination.[71] This creates some difficulties in relation to suggestions that a link might be created by inserting a cultural exception into the WTO agreements,[72] or even the ingenious device of a procedural clause in the form of a WTO Ministerial Decision.[73] Another choice would be to pit the political power of human rights and cultural rights law and rhetoric against the WTO system. So far as human rights are concerned, this might be regarded

---

67 See further David Kennedy,"The International Style in Postwar Law and Policy: John Jackson and the Field of International Economic Law," *American University Journal of International Law and Policy* 10 (1995): 671–716; and Macmillan, "International Economic Law and Public International Law: Strangers in the Night."

68 See note 56.

69 See, e.g., Ernst-Ulrich Petersmann, "Time for a United Nations 'Global Compact' for Integrating Human Rights into the Law of Worldwide Organizations: Lessons from European Integration," *European Journal of International Law* 13 (2002): 621–650; Joel P. Trachtman, "Institutional Linkage: Transcending 'Trade and …'," *American Journal of International Law* 96 (2002): 77–93.

70 Philip Alston, "Resisting the Merger and Acquisition of Human Rights by Trade Law: A Reply to Petersmann," *European Journal of International Law* 13 (2002): 815–844, 826.

71 See further Macmillan, "International Economic Law and Public International Law: Strangers in the Night."

72 Even if this was politically viable in the current international climate, which seems unlikely given the opposition of the US to the conclusion of the UNESCO Convention: see, e.g., Graber, "The New UNESCO Convention on Cultural Diversity: A Counterbalance to the WTO?" 560; Hahn, "A Clash of Cultures? The UNESCO *Diversity Convention* and International Trade Law," 522–525.

73 See Graber, "The New UNESCO Convention on Cultural Diversity: A Counterbalance to the WTO?" 572–573.

as problematic. There are two reasons for this. One of these is concerned with the damage that has been done to the symbolic power of the concept of human rights by its overuse. The other depends on the very nature of human rights: the hollowed out concept of the human, stripped of race, religion, ethnic affiliation, the empty "human" essential to the universality of the human in human rights laws, seems a weak and meaningless abstraction to pit against the powerful concept of the global market delivering economic benefits to all.[74] Perhaps, however, there is still enough vitality in the more specific concept of cultural rights to offer at least a political counterbalance to the power of the WTO system. The UNESCO Conventions concluded this century might be thought to demonstrate this proposition. Nevertheless, the question of how we make cultural rights strong enough and specific enough to confer proper legal protection remains.

4. Cultural Rights and Intellectual Property Rights?

This brings us back to the question of the relationship between cultural property and intellectual property. There has been a remarkable persistence in claims to connect cultural rights and intellectual property rights. This is despite the fact, as this chapter has sought to demonstrate, that the system of intellectual property rights is in conflict with many of the rights that might be described as cultural rights. This section, which attempts to interrogate the relationship between intellectual property and cultural property, and between intellectual property rights and cultural rights, is based upon a claim that what is common to intellectual property and cultural property is that both make an appeal to the preservation or reservation of property rights in cultural artefacts in some form. In order to demonstrate this claim, I am using the concept of cultural property broadly to include both tangible and intangible cultural property.

Legally speaking, claims to cultural property are claims by a state or by a community (somehow defined) to certain property rights. As already noted, these rights are recognised in international legal instruments, in particular the various UNESCO Conventions already enumerated. Consequently, they are also present in various forms in national law. Where international law recognises these rights as belonging to community then it often identifies that community as global, or as humanity in general. Nevertheless, as is the nature of international law, these global rights and rights of humanity are to be

[74] See Orford, "Beyond Harmonization: Trade, Human Rights and the Economy of Sacrifice."

enforced through the agency of states. The protection of world heritage sites under the World Heritage Convention is an example of this. In this case, the type of property right asserted is generally a right of preservation and sometimes a right of access. National laws often make similar claims to artefacts falling within the general rubric of "heritage". In these cases a wide range of rights are asserted, from full state ownership, through rights of preservation exercised by the state, to rights vested in the state to control physical movement of artefacts. The last is often particularly important in state regimes relating to tangible cultural property. Pursuant to the UNESCO Convention on the Means of Prohibiting and Preventing the Illicit Import, Export and Transfer of Ownership of Cultural Property, states may, for example, attempt to prevent certain artefacts leaving their territories on the ground of their significance as "heritage".[75] Obviously, some of these types of rights do not map onto intangible cultural property. Nevertheless, whether cultural property is tangible or intangible the essential features of cultural property are: first, that it is "owned" in common or publicly, or if not owned publicly then subject to limitations on the usual rights that private ownership confers; secondly, that the ownership rights focus on preservation, access and the sharing of benefits associated with it; and thirdly, that the role of cultural property rights are to prevent or limit the privatisation of cultural property.

Claims to intellectual property are, of course, quite different since they focus on a private property right. Further, unlike cultural property, they are never claims to tangible property, but rather claims to intangible rights (albeit claims that often implicate tangible objects).[76] In general this means that although there maybe tangible objects that simultaneously attract claims for intellectual property rights and cultural property rights we are rarely in danger of confusing or eliding the two types of property claims. Things are otherwise, however, in the realm of intellectual or intangible space. Here, the dangers of confusing, eliding and overlapping cultural rights and intellectual property rights are considerable.

In the imaginations of intellectual property scholars, intellectual or intangible space tends to consist of two parts, the public domain and the private domain. Much has been made of the intellectual public domain.[77] It has been

---

[75] As already noted, one of the few species of cultural rights recognised by WTO law, see note 58.

[76] In fact the relationship between intellectual property and tangible objects is often problematic. The most obvious example of this relates to the intellectual property protection of works of visual art: see Fiona Macmillan, "Is Copyright Blind to the Visual?" *Visual Communication* 7 (2008): 97–118.

[77] See note 29.

reified, and then valorized, as the place where community and culture are protected from "property", meaning privately owned property, and where creativity consequently flourishes. Thus the relationship between the intellectual public domain and the intellectual private domain looks something like the relationship between raw materials and manufactured products. Since, at least theoretically, cultural property is publicly owned or subject to limitations on the right of ownership, it would seem to fall within the intellectual public domain. This suggests that the division between cultural property and intellectual property in intellectual space looks very much like the divisions between knowledge and innovation, idea and expression, and (most perplexingly) nature and culture – all being variations on the raw materials/manufactured products metaphor. Under these circumstances, the main role of cultural property rights must surely be to protect the public domain from the encroachments of the private domain, not to mimic those encroachments.

This would all sound beautifully convincing were it not for two issues. The first is the claim to some sort of hybrid space in the intellectual domain in which cultural property, owned on a communal basis, is protected through a property device that mimics, or is, private intellectual property. This is, of course, the basis for the claims for the protection of traditional cultural expressions and knowledge through intellectual property-like devices. These claims, being claims by a community forming less than the public as a whole, to cultural property in the form of intellectual property, strike right at the heart of the hidden or obscured relationship between intellectual property and cultural property. They are founded on the assertion that this cultural property can only be preserved through its transformation into private property. An examination of these claims casts some light on the second outstanding issue, which is the more general question of the appropriate role of cultural property rights in preserving and maintaining cultural property in the intangible realm. This issue is addressed in the final paragraphs of this chapter.

Turning first then to the question of the protection of traditional cultural expressions and knowledge. Intellectual property law has experienced considerable technical difficulties in re-shaping itself to protect communal interests in traditional cultural expressions and knowledge.[78] This is doubtless partly a reflection of the technical distinctions between cultural property and intellectual property. There has also been a marked lack of political will, both

---

[78] See, e.g., Michael Blakeney, "The Protection of Traditional Knowledge Under Intellectual Property Law," *European Intellectual Property Law Review* 22 (2000): 251–261.

at the national and international level,[79] which one might suspect is a consequence of the linkage between this agenda and a wider agenda concerned with political, social and cultural self-determination for Indigenous peoples. (The technical legal problems and the political reluctance are surely related. Suffice it to say that the seemingly endless capacity for reinvention that intellectual property has displayed in, for example, the context of the digital revolution seems to have been singularly lacking in the context of traditional cultural expressions and knowledge.) However, the present focus is less on the question of legal and political modalities and more on the danger of confusing the roles of cultural and intellectual property.

As already noted, claims to communal intellectual property rights in traditional cultural expressions and knowledge are, at least so far as they are concerned with preserving cultural property, premised on the argument that the best defence to the cultural threat posed by private intellectual property rights encroaching on those cultural rights is to turn those traditional cultural rights into private rights. This argument has an intrinsic appeal. Moreover, the post-colonial political context of these claims is not easy to ignore. However, if we recognise traditional cultural property as intellectual property, do we do some damage to the preservation of that property – that is, to the preservation of culture and heritage of a particular group or community? Blakeney has argued that treating traditional cultural property as intellectual property means corralling it into the shape of Western intellectual property law.[80] If the item of cultural property is a story, music, or an artwork then it has to be fitted into copyright law; designs and symbols must fit into the netherworld of the relationship between copyright, designs and trade marks; knowledge about local flora and fauna must be fitted somewhere into patent law, plants breeder's rights and geographical indications. This will mean that different levels of protection will apply to different types of traditional knowledge and culture. In short, as Fitzpatrick and Joyce argue, the end result is that occidental intellectual property law comes to constitute traditional, or non-Western, culture and heritage.[81] In so doing, it changes the

---

79 See Michael Blakeney, "Protecting Traditional Cultural Expressions: The International Dimension," in *New Directions in Copyright Law*, eds. Fiona Macmillan and Kathy Bowrey, volume 3 (Cheltenham: Edward Elgar, 2006), 3–14.

80 See Blakeney, "The Protection of Traditional Knowledge Under Intellectual Property Law."

81 Peter Fitzpatrick and Richard Joyce, "Copying Right: Cultural Property and the Limits of (Occidental) Law," in *New Directions in Copyright Law*, ed. Fiona Macmillan, volume 4 (Cheltenham: Edward Elgar, 2007), 171–192.

shape of that heritage in ways that are not necessarily the consequence of the reflexive cultural practice that constitutes so-called traditional cultural expressions and knowledge.[82] This seems to be inimical to the very purpose of protecting cultural property.

The brief examination of non-Western forms of cultural and/or intellectual property poses two questions: Do we leave cultural property, widely defined, in the intellectual public domain where it can be freely mined as raw material for intellectual property, but where it might not be adequately conserved or preserved as cultural property? Or, do we privatise it through intellectual property rights and progressively destroy its distinctive character as cultural property and heritage? These questions are, of course, part of a much larger problem about the preservation and conservation of intangible cultural property in the intellectual domain. It almost goes without saying that, in intellectual space, the problem of the relationship between cultural property and intellectual property is unresolved by law. Consequently, the question of preserving or conserving cultural property in intellectual space remains inadequately addressed. The suggestion that the best method of preservation and conservation of intangible cultural property is by its privatisation in the form of intellectual property does, however, seem naive. As this chapter has sought to argue, not only is intellectual property ill-equipped to protect cultural rights, it is clearly implicated in the constriction and possible destruction of some cultural rights.

We need to solve this problem by a much more complex articulation of the intellectual or intangible domain. Specifically, I think we need to start moving away from the simplified binary divide of the intellectual public domain and the intellectual private domain of intellectual property law. Or, at least, away from the notion that the intellectual public domain is some undifferentiated concept equating to the "commons" in Roman law.[83] Let us start, instead, to give some much more complex legal architecture to the public domain of intellectual space. A blueprint for such architecture might include:

---

82 As Fitzpatrick and Joyce argue in "Copying Right: Cultural Property and the Limits of (Occidental) Law," 171–173, so-called "traditional knowledge and culture" would never have survived if it had not been "dynamically generative and relational" and "capable of being utterly responsive, comprehensively self-transgressive."

83 See further Carol M. Rose, "Romans, Roads and Romantic Creators: Traditions of Public Property in the Information Age," *Law & Contemporary Problems* 66 (2003): 89–110.

- a notion of the difference between what is publicly owned in intellectual space and what is in the commons – that is, unowned – in intellectual space and thus ripe for appropriation;
- an associated recognition that some things can never be owned, at least privately, because of their cultural significance;
- development of the concept of group and communal rights, belonging to less than the public as a whole, bounded by property on the outside, but inside promoting freedom and space for creativity, innovation, invention, and cultural conservation.[84]

Failure to develop the same complex architecture in intellectual or intangible space as that which we have developed in tangible space for the preservation of heritage and cultural property, only invites constant encroachment by the type of private propertisation in intellectual space that undermines and destroys claims to cultural property in that space. The power of intellectual property rights in the context of the ascendant system of WTO law makes this an urgent political and legal project.

---

[84] On each of these points, see further Macmillan, "Altering the Contours of the Public Domain."

Helle Porsdam
(University of Copenhagen)

Epilogue
Cultural Heritage and Law: The Case of Cultural Looting

'Transnational studies' seem to be all the rage within both the humanities and the social sciences these days. A number of conferences are dedicated to this theme – in June 2011, the members of the German American Studies Association gathered in Regensburg to discuss "Transnational American Studies",[1] for example – just as various journals invite contributions that touch on it in some way. Take the journal *Diaspora: A Journal of Transnational Studies*, published by the University of Toronto Press, whose official webpage tells us that it is "dedicated to the multidisciplinary study of the history, culture, social structure, politics, and economics of both the traditional diasporas – Armenian, Greek, and Jewish – and the new transnational dispersions which in the past four decades have come to be identified as 'diasporas.' These encompass groups ranging from the African-, Chinese-, Indian-, and Mexican-American to the Ukrainian- and Haitian-Canadian, the Caribbean-British, the Antillean-French, and many others".[2]

This academic development reflects the way in which social movements and phenomena increasingly transcend national borders and mobilize constituencies around the globe on issues such as human rights, as well as the way in which NGOs and associations set common standards for professionals everywhere. The global economy is furthered by transnational patterns of consumption, moreover, and migration leads to the formation of social networks linking communities together in new and unexpected ways. There is a certain irony in the fact, therefore, that when it comes to cultural heritage – to the legacy of physical artifacts and intangible attributes of the people and groups involved here – the development seems to be going in the exact opposite direction: "The policies of most source nations and the international dialogue about cultural property still are heavily nation-oriented", as

---

1 Please see http://www-deas.uni-r.de/amerikanistik/dgfa_conference_2011/ for more information on this meeting.

2 Please see http://www.utpjournals.com/diaspora/diaspora.html – last visited on January 9, 2011.

John Henry Merriman puts it.[3] And not only are such policies nation-oriented; they are also calling into question the (transnational) principle of cultural artifacts as the legacy of all humankind – the idea that is expressed in the preamble of the Convention for the Protection of Cultural Property in the Event of Armed Conflict from 1954: "*Being convinced* that damage to cultural property belonging to any people whatsoever means damage to the cultural heritage of all mankind, since each people makes its contribution to the culture of the world".[4]

The international controversy over who owns culture is the topic of this final essay. In their contributions to this volume, Fiona Macmillan and Mia Rendix have already touched upon this. I will focus on a Danish case – the alleged looting by the Swedes in the seventeenth century of one of the first Danish laws, the Jutlantic Law from 1241. Most often, since the 1970s when restitution of cultural heritage started to become a very hot international political issue, the debate has concerned antiquities or the stolen treasures of the ancient world. As former colonies sought to stand on their own, they would reclaim their own history by asking to have the artifacts that tie them to it returned to their own care. Sharon Waxman describes the situation very well:

> Over the past two hundred years, antiquities and monuments have been ripped from the ground and shipped across the world, and many of these pieces now reside in the vast collections of the great museums of the West. Should they stay where they are – at the Louvre, the Metropolitan Museum of Art, the British Museum, and elsewhere – exhibited and preserved with care, accessible to avid crowds of visitors from around the world? Or should they return to their countries of origin, whose demands for restitution have grown ever more vociferous, a chorus of dissatisfaction from across the ancient world?[5]

The underlying issue concerns identity: "The battle over ancient treasures is, at its base, a conflict over identity, and over the right to reclaim the objects that are its tangible symbols".[6] My focus being on a Danish-Swedish cultural heritage quarrel, I obviously do not participate directly in this more postco-

---

3 John Henry Merryman, "The Nation and the Object," in *Whose Culture? The Promise of Museums and the Debate over Antiquities,* ed. James Cuno (Princeton: Princeton University Press, 2009), 183–203, 183.

4 Convention for the Protection of Cultural Property in the Event of Armed Conflict, available at http://www.icomos.org/hague/ – last visited on visited January 9, 2011.

5 Sharon Waxman, *Loot: The Battle over the Stolen Treasures of the Ancient World* (New York: Times Books, Henry Holt and Company, 2008), 2–3.

6 Waxman, *Loot,* 3.

lonial discussion. However, as members of the right-wing, nationalistic Danish party, the Danish People's Party, are currently doing their best to appropriate and (mis)use this postcolonial discourse in their attempt to make the Swedes give back to Denmark the Jutlantic Law – by means, for example, of referring to international declarations on cultural property – it is highly relevant to my story.

I shall therefore start by taking a look at the post-1970s battles over restitution – over who 'owns' antiquities and cultural heritage – before I move ahead with my analysis of the Danish-Swedish case with all its cultural political and legal aspects. I shall end by briefly touching on the issue of cultural looting and global security – on what happens when looting becomes a tool for organized criminal groups. Throughout, my intention is to point to a potential new area of study for people interested in law and humanities: the looting of cultural heritage. Like the other topics covered in this volume of essays, the looting of cultural heritage raises questions that directly involve both law and the humanities. From topics such as the right to property, ethical ownership, and the public responsibilities of museums, to threats to cultural artifacts from war, pillage, and development, and international cooperation to preserve collections in both the developed and the developing world – issues potentially dealt with here are right at the intersection of law and humanities.

1. Whose Culture Is It?[7]

"The great international collectors and curators, once celebrated for their perceptiveness and perseverance, are now regularly deplored as traffickers in, or receivers of, stolen goods", writes Kwame Anthony Appiah. "Our encyclopedic museums, once seen as redoubts of cultural appreciation, are now suspected strong-rooms of plunder and pillage".[8] This development is a very interesting one and any attempt to describe how and why it came about involves a number of issues with which we have concerned ourselves over the past few years in the humanities and social sciences.

Encyclopedic museums are a legacy of the Enlightenment. The idea was to have the whole world under one roof, thereby providing an intellectual

---

7 I have borrowed this sub-heading from Kwame Anthony Appiah's article "Whose Culture Is It?" in *Whose Culture?* ed. Cuno, 71–86. This article builds on Chapter 8 ("Whose Culture Is It, Anyway?") in Appiah's book *Cosmopolitanism: Ethics in a World of Strangers* (New York: W.W. Norton, 2006), 115–35.

8 Appiah, "Whose Culture Is It?" 71.

challenge to people who wanted to think differently about the world. The British Museum, created in 1753, is often mentioned as the encyclopedic museum *par excellence.* In 2003, to coincide with the opening of the Enlightenment Gallery in the newly restored King's Library at the British Museum, the British Museum Press published a beautiful book in order to explain the particular view of the Enlightenment embodied in the new gallery and its permanent display, entitled *Enlightenment: Discovering the World in the Eighteenth Century.* In his preface to this book, Neil MacGregor, Director of the British Museum, talks about the museum as "an astonishing place" – "the only place in the world where you can see the cultures of the globe gathered together under a single roof. Founded 250 years ago as an encyclopaedia of knowledge – the built equivalent of France's *Encyclopédie* – it has undergone many changes, but its founding ideals remain as valid today as in 1753: that every citizen should have free access to the sum of human understanding".[9]

In his contribution to James Cuno's recent volume on *Whose Culture?*, MacGregor elaborates on this idea of the world under one roof. The British Museum was established very specifically, he maintains "for everybody, for the whole world". In this view,

> the British Museum's collection was a means to knowledge, a path to a better understanding of the world, and a way of creating a new kind of citizen for the world. It is important to insist that the notion of 'citizen' in this case was never a national one. The museum was only called the British Museum because it was not the king's museum; it belonged in a very real sense to the people, to citizens.[10]

To the donor of the museum's founding collection, Sir Hans Sloane, the museum "was to be a civic space in which a discussion could take place and in which we could understand a little better the world and our place in it". When he first offered his collection to the British government, he made it clear that if things did not work out with his native country, he would turn to the Royal Academies of St. Petersburg, Paris, Berlin, and/or Madrid. He only had two conditions – "that the collection would always be together for study and that it would always be open, free to anybody to visit" – and whichever academy showed itself willing to meet these two conditions, would get the collection.[11] Had not the British proved themselves willing to go ahead and

---

9 Neil MacGregor, Preface to *Enlightenment: Discovering the World in the Eighteenth Century*, ed. Kim Sloan (London: British Museum Press, 2004), 6.

10 Neil MacGregor, "To Shape the Citizens of 'That Great City, the World'," in *Whose Culture?* ed. Cuno, 39–54, 39.

11 MacGregor, "To Shape the Citizens of 'That Great City, the World'," 40.

meet these conditions, that is, Sloane's famous collection might today very well have been on display in one of these other cities.

The underlying idea here was, and still is, the oneness of humanity – the world as irrevocably and irretrievably interconnected. Cultural artifacts are the common heritage of us all; they deserve as broad an audience as possible and are best displayed in a cross-cultural and comparative context. The ideal of the encyclopedic museum has nothing to do with national ownership, in other words. And precisely because this ideal was furthered by national wealth and imperial power in the past, "such wealth and powers", argues MacGregor, "is an inheritance that can – and should – very properly be put at the disposal of the whole world. And it is surely more important now than ever to insist that the world is one and that we who work in museums are doing something to shape the citizen of 'that great city, the world'".[12]

What MacGregor, Cuno and others see as the *promise* of the encyclopedic museum collections – "the museum as a repository of things and knowledge, dedicated to the museum's role as a force for understanding, tolerance, and the dissipation of ignorance and superstition about the world, where the artifacts of one culture can be seen next to those of other times and other cultures without prejudice"[13] – others see as their biggest problem, however. "Do only ignorant laypeople gaze on the colossal bust of Ramses II at the British Museum and ask themselves how it ended up there? Is it only the unschooled visitor who looks at the soaring columns from the Temple of Artemis at the Met and questions why it exists in this place?" asks Waxman in *Loot: The Battle over the Stolen Treasures of the Ancient World.*[14] It is the way in which most major museums in the world have obtained large parts of their collections that is at stake here. A fair number of the antiquities and cultural artifacts so proudly on display at museums such as the British Museum and the Metropolitan Museum of Art have been acquired in dubious ways – through looting, pillage or plunder. Such looting, moreover, is not just a feature of the sordid past of the imperialist West; international attempts by UNESCO and other international institutions to make such looting illegal notwithstanding, cultural artifacts are being looted on an ongoing basis to serve the lucrative private market in illicit artifacts.

It may well be, as Cuno writes, that "culture is poorly served by politics", but the issue of who owns culture and cultural heritage has become a hotly

---

12 MacGregor, "To Shape the Citizens of 'That Great City, the World'," 54.
13 James Cuno, Introduction to *Whose Culture?* ed. Cuno, 1–38, 28–29.
14 Waxman, *Loot*, 5.

contested political one today.[15] Roughly – and grossly simplified – those who seek to deconstruct the Enlightenment are also highly suspicious of the idea or principle behind the encyclopedic museum. As they see it, the encyclopedic museum is the cultural temple of the West – a temple which pays tribute to Western ways of thinking and is mostly interested in non-Western artifacts as objects that display various stages along the way toward sophisticated Western civilization. In her chapter on the British Museum, for example, Waxman only has contempt for what she terms MacGregor's "new philosophy for a multicultural age" – a philosophy which does not "dispel the fundamental problems attached to holding on to objects taken from their place of origin without permission. Especially if those places of origin want, indeed feel they need, those objects returned".[16] The British Museum still holds on to the Elgin Marbles, taken from Greece two centuries ago, just as the Egyptians have so far had no luck in claiming the return of the Rosetta Stone. These are just two of the most famous cases, of course; many other pieces are still housed in the British Museum about whose provenance not much is known.

When modern nation states today claim that the cultural patrimony represented by such pieces is a source of identity and esteem, is this an expression of "historic justice, the righting of ancient wrongs from the age of imperialism? Or is it a modern settling of scores by the frustrated leaders of less powerful nations?" Waxman asks.[17] Undermining, as it arguably does, the very purpose of cultural exchange and mutual understanding, the claim for restitution by once-colonized nations may be seen as a way to assert a moral imperative over their former colonizers. "A reaction to American political and military supremacy can be felt in the restitution battles, just as the vestiges of anger over European colonialism are evident in the conflict. Similarly, the responses of the Western nations have often betrayed an arrogance that has served to stoke the flames of resentment over trampled national dignity".[18] Still, as Waxman herself correctly points out, there are no easy answers here. At least not when it comes to whether or not the Elgin Marbles should go back to Greece; looting of the sort for which the Nazis were responsible is obviously quite another matter.

Context – historical, cultural, social and political – clearly matters. There has always been grave robbing, just as the victorious party during times of

---

[15] Cuno ed., *Whose Culture?* 27.
[16] Waxman, *Loot*, 211, 212.
[17] Waxman, *Loot*, 3.
[18] Waxman, *Loot*, 7.

war has always exerted its right to 'the spoils of war'. It is only in more recent times that such 'activities' have taken on negative connotations, and that the international community has attempted to criminalize them. As previously alluded to, moreover, the postcolonial turn in the humanities and the social sciences has offered a whole new theoretical framework for discussing matters concerning cultural heritage and looting. If cultural identity on the part of former colonies is at stake, one of the underlying questions concerns the right of one group to speak authoritatively about the life-ways of another. As Michael F. Brown puts it, "conflicts over the control and representation of heritage have become especially impassioned when the communities in question are indigenous ones, that is, comprising descendants of the earliest inhabitants of the New World, Asia, Africa, Australia, Oceania, and isolated corners of Europe. The comfortable assumption that experts from the metropole are qualified to speak or write about indigenous cultures is being challenged everywhere".[19]

What to do – is there a way out of this battle over control of cultural heritage, a way to mediate between the two fronts? In his seminal article, "The Nation and the Object", John Henry Merryman "attempts to add a second dimension to the traditionally one-dimensional discussion of cultural property policy".[20] He does so by means of suggesting that we stop focusing so much on 'nation' and instead turn our attention toward the 'object(s)' involved. Until now, what Merryman calls 'the basic position' has pretty much been the international norm. This is a position which is "summed up in international law in the concept of national sovereignty and in the related principle that the authorities of one nation will not enforce the public laws of another. Nations may agree by treaty to enforce one another's export controls, but there are few such treaties. In their absence, the importation of illegally exported cultural objects is legally permissible".[21]

Since the end of the Second World War, this position has been under attack by source nations and by people who are sympathetic to these nations and their problems with retentive cultural property export controls. Source nations argue from a position of cultural nationalism, as we have seen above; they claim that objects should stay within or be given back to the nations in which they were found and/or with which they are historically associated.

---

19 Michael F. Brown, "Exhibiting Indigenous Heritage in the Age of Cultural Property," in *Whose Culture?* ed. Cuno, 145–64, 146.

20 John Henry Merryman, "The Nation and the Object," (1995) reprinted in *Whose Culture?* ed. Cuno, 183–203, 183.

21 Merryman, "The Nation and the Object," 184.

They use one of two strategies, according to Merryman. They either enact legislation which declares cultural objects to be official state property and which turns illegal export from their respective countries into theft. Or they work toward the adoption of international treaties which will make it mandatory for countries to enforce other countries' cultural property export controls. "The centerpiece of that effort", writes Merryman, is the 1970 UNESCO Convention which "contemplates 'concerted action' by the importing nations in order to be effective".[22]

The understanding currently shown in intellectual as well as in political and activist circles toward the cultural nationalism premise and toward the demands for the 'repatriation' of cultural objects notwithstanding, Merryman's own sympathies go more in the direction of what he himself calls "an object-oriented cultural property policy". This is a policy in which

> the emphasis is on three conceptually separate but, in practice, interdependent considerations: preservation, truth, and access, in declining order of importance. The most basic is preservation: protecting the object and its context from impairment. Next comes the quest for knowledge, for valid information about the human past, for the historical, scientific, cultural, and aesthetic truth that the object and its context can provide. Finally, we want the object to be optimally accessible to scholars (for study) and to the public (for education and enjoyment).[23]

Today, the simpler, one-dimensional cultural nationalism premise has become the more familiar, but once people start paying attention to the actual object(s) involved they may well find that their faith in cultural nationalism as the bottom line of cultural property policy looks less attractive, suggests Merryman. There is in fact nothing new about the object-oriented approach; on the contrary, although it does contain some paragraphs which go in the direction of cultural nationalism, the Hague Convention on the Protection of Cultural Property in the Event of Armed Conflict of 1954 is a primarily object-oriented document, as we saw above. And it is, argues Merryman, but "a short step from Hague 1954, limited in application to the threat to cultural property during armed conflict, to a more general recognition of the importance of object-oriented values in international cultural property policy".[24]

That step, continues Merryman, has been taken with the UNIDROIT Convention on Stolen or Illegally Exported Cultural Objects from 1995. Writing in 1995, Merryman could not know that the UNIDROIT Convention would enter into force in 1998. He specifically points to Article 5 of

---

22 Merryman, "The Nation and the Object," 186.
23 Merryman, "The Nation and the Object," 187–88.
24 Merryman, "The Nation and the Object," 195.

UNIDROIT which contains certain "novel provisions" with an "emphasis on preservation and truth".[25] Thus, Article 5 (3) states that,

> The court or other competent authority of the State addressed shall order the return of an illegally exported cultural object if the requesting State establishes that the removal of the object from its territory significantly impairs one or more of the following interests:
> (a) the physical Preservation of the object or of its context;
> (b) the integrity of a complex object;
> (c) the preservation of information of, for example, a scientific or historical character;
> (d) the traditional or ritual use of the object by a tribal or indigenous community, or establishers that the object is of significant cultural importance for the requesting State.[26]

These novel provisions have, Merryman writes, met with a mixed reception, especially on the part of source nations. It is interesting, therefore, that one part of Article 5 which he quoted in his 1995 article from what was at the time a Preliminary Draft of UNIDROIT was changed in the final document. Whereas Article 5 (2) in the draft version of 1995 required a state's request for the return of an illegally exported cultural object to "contain all material information regarding the conservation, security and accessibility of the cultural object after it has been returned to the requesting state"[27] – Article 5 (2) now reads:

> A cultural object which has been temporarily exported from the territory of the requesting State, for purposes such as exhibition, research or restoration, under a permit issued according to its law regulating its export for the purpose of protecting its cultural heritage and not returned in accordance with the terms of that permit shall be deemed to have been illegally exported.[28]

All talk of "the conservation, security and accessibility of the cultural object after it has been returned" seems to have disappeared in the meantime and one cannot help wondering whether this is a testimony to the current success of the cultural nationalism premise. Whether or not one approves of this development is ultimately a question of intellectual and (cultural) political preference. "Applicable policy, ethics, and law are, in their present states, crude and incomplete", as Merryman concludes his 1995 essay; hence it is import-

---

25 Merryman, "The Nation and the Object," 196.
26 The UNIDROIT Convention on Stolen or Illegally Exported Cultural Objects from 1995 is available at http://www.unidroit.org/english/conventions/1995 culturalprop erty/1995culturalproperty-e.htm – last accessed on January 12, 2011.
27 Merryman, "The Nation and the Object," 195.
28 UNIDROIT Convention – see note 26.

ant that the dialogue concerning the international movement of cultural objects be carried on by academics as well as by professionals and politicians.

In the following, I shall continue this dialogue by looking at a Danish case study. The Director of the Royal Danish Library, Erland Kolding Nielsen, has just published a highly interesting article on "'Jyske Lov' [Jutlandic Law] as spoils of war. A myth is created, exploited and falls".[29] I shall use this recent piece of Danish historical research as a point of departure for a discussion of how wrong things can go if or when notions of cultural nationalism fall into the wrong hands, as it were.

2. The Jutlandic Law as Spoils of War

Jyske Lov (Jutlantic Law) was proclaimed by King Valdemar the Conqueror in Vordingborg, Denmark in March 1241. At some point during the late fourteenth or the beginning of the fifteenth century, it came to be viewed as merely a regional law for the Jutland-Funen area, but recent research has shown that it was originally considered to be a national law. The original document has been lost and until recently, historians believed that the oldest existing manuscript containing a surviving version of the Justlandic Law dated from approximately 1350. In 1977, Danish historian Thomas Riis published a dissertation in which he re-dated the oldest parts of the so-called *Codex holmiensis 37* (hereafter C 37), which does contain a transcript of the Jutlandic Law, to around 1276, however, thus making C 37 at least 25 and perhaps up to 50 years older than the later surviving version, which had previously been considered the oldest one. For the past close to 300 years, C 37 has been a part of the collection of the Swedish Royal Library in Stockholm.

How it was that this first Danish national law came to be in Swedish possession, and how this has become a politically hot issue for the Danish right-wing party, the Danish People's Party, over the past fifteen years or so, Kolding Nielsen's summary in English outlines for us:

> In 1996, the newly-founded national conservative Dansk Folkeparti [Danish People's Party] proposed in Parliament, for the first time, that the Danish state and government should demand that Sweden returns the spoils of war taken during the Dano-Swedish Wars in the 1600s. The demand has since been repeated six times in the Danish Parliament and at the Nordic Council in the last nearly 15

[29] Erland Kolding Nielsen, "'Jyske Lov' som krigsbytte. En mytes opståen, udnyttelse og fald" ('Jyske Lov' [Jutlandic Law] as spoils of war. A myth is created, exploited and falls), in *Fund og Forskning i det Kongelige Biblioteks Samlinger* (Findings and research concerning the collections of the Royal Library) 49 (Copenhagen: The Royal Library, 2010), 435–509.

> years. The demand included return of the *Jyske Lov* manuscript from 1241. The background was the notion that Sweden possessed what was called the "original edition". This was the origin of the myth that the Swedes were in fact unaware that it was in their possession, and this was reinforced, in its moral expression of the demand for return, by the view that the manuscript constituted spoils of war from 1658–1659.[30]

As Kolding Nielsen's own research as well as the research done over the past few years by other Danish historians has shown, C 37 was in fact not spoils of war; it was either purchased or bequeathed to the Swedish Royal Library in the 1720s. This important discovery has made it possible for Kolding Nielsen "at the express political wish of the Danish government in 2009" to approach his Swedish colleague at the Swedish Royal Library about possibly doing an exchange "on a voluntary, reciprocal, non-prejudicial" basis of C 37 "with a corresponding Swedish law manuscript containing Swedish provincial law, *Södermannalagen*, New Royal Collection 2237, n. 4, that presumably arrived in Denmark in the second half of the 1700s".[31] In June 2010, a draft exchange agreement was drawn up between the two Royal Libraries and in March 2011, the actual exchange took place.

What is of particular interest to us in this context is the way in which the Danish People's Party for a number of years misunderstood or refused to acknowledge the new historical research done by Kolding Nielsen and his colleagues. Instead, members of this party have put together their own version of the myth of the Jutlandic Law as spoils of war and in so doing have succeeded in using it for their own cultural-political ends. "Only rarely has Danish historical research concerning the Middle Ages had such direct political impact with such directly 'politically useful' results as in this case", as Kolding Nielsen dryly comments.[32]

It seems to be a Swedish amateur historian who is the source of the myth. A former policeman now dabbling in local history, Uno Röhndahl published a book in 1981 on the history of Scania (Skåne) which was highly critical of that part of Swedish history which led to the takeover of Scania from the Danes back in the 1600s. This book and the many talks Röhndahl gave at the time made him a cherished member of local groups such as the Danish-Sca-

---

30 Kolding Nielsen, "'Jyske Lov' som krigsbytte. En mytes opståen, udnyttelse og fald," 509.

31 Kolding Nielsen, "'Jyske Lov' som krigsbytte. En mytes opståen, udnyttelse og fald," 509.

32 Kolding Nielsen, "'Jyske Lov' som krigsbytte. En mytes opståen, udnyttelse og fald;" 439. My translation from the Danish – the following quotes from Kolding Nielsen's article are my translation from the Danish.

nia Society and the Society for the Future of Scania. The latter, which had a Danish sister organization by the same name, saw it as a "key issue to ask for the return to Denmark and Scania of cultural treasures which were taken by the Swedes during the wars of the 1600s". Repeated appeals to the Swedish and Danish UNESCO commissions, the Swedish and Danish governments as well as to the Nordic Council to look into this issue were unsuccessful. In a letter from August 1991, the Danish ministry of culture answered that "Denmark has no legislation about the restitution of cultural values that relate to situations of war; neither has Denmark ratified international agreements concerning this issue. It is our understanding, moreover, that Sweden has gained a prescriptive right to the cultural artifacts in question and that there is much cooperation going on between Swedish and Danish museums concerning these artifacts, for instance in relation to lending and exchanging them".[33]

A piece in one of the local Scania journals in 1996 seems to have inspired the political spokesman of the newly formed Danish People's Party to raise the issue of Swedish looting in the Danish parliament, thereby triggering the first major debate among Danish politicians and in the Danish media concerning the politics of cultural heritage since the debates on the Icelandic sagas, with which Mia Rendix deals in her contribution to this volume. Much like the debates about the sagas, the issue under discussion this time involved another Nordic country, but the cultural discourse had by now become somewhat more international.

What the political spokesman of the Danish People's Party wanted to know in 1996 from the minister of culture was whether "anything has been done from our side to make Sweden accede to the 1983 UN declaration about the restitution of cultural property". He furthermore wished to know "what initiatives the Danish government may and will take in order to further a dialogue with Sweden concerning the restitution of Danish cultural artifacts according to the 1983 UN declaration". In general, the Danish People's Party wished to ascertain the government's attitude as to whether or not the UN declaration "is a reasonable declaration", the matter at hand not simply being a question "between Denmark and Sweden; this question may also benefit third world countries as it concerns the cultural artifacts from these countries too".[34] Among the members of parliament who contributed

---

33 Kolding Nielsen, "'Jyske Lov' som krigsbytte. En mytes opståen, udnyttelse og fald," 465.

34 Kolding Nielsen, "'Jyske Lov' som krigsbytte. En mytes opståen, udnyttelse og fald," 469.

to this particular debate was Per Stig Møller, the later Danish minister of culture and member of the Conservative Party. Møller declared himself to be in sympathy with the views of the Danish People's Party and drew a parallel to the return of the Icelandic sagas. In the end, decisions on these issues were "political decisions" and Møller concluded by referring to the decision by the European Council of January 1996 according to which "the Russians must return a lot of stuff that they dragged back from the Baltic countries and from Germany in 1945. There is a new political decision in Europe on the restitution issue".[35]

For the next ten years, the Danish People's Party would continue to bring up the matter of the Jutlantic Law and other important Danish cultural artifacts with changing Danish governments. Having realized that the issue might have to be phrased or presented in a different way to meet with a more positive response, members of the Party now no longer talk about demanding the return of these artifacts by the Swedes, but instead suggest that a mutual exchange of cultural artifacts take place in the spirit of UNESCO's various declarations on cultural restitution. In addition, the Party has by now really appropriated the cultural nationalism discourse so in vogue, as we saw, with source nations. "We live in a globalized day and age", a member of the People's Party said in 2008, for example, "in which we are strongly influenced culturally by others. It is therefore important that we know about our own history and identity. The time is ripe, moreover, for an exchange of cultural artifacts. The Swedes must be convinced that just like other civilized nations, they must participate in international cooperation and exchange". The reason why Denmark should get back these artifacts, of which C 37 is one of the most important, is that "these Danish artifacts contain an invaluable part of Denmark's history, soul and identity. They consequently really do belong in Denmark".[36]

Another member of the Danish People's Party followed this up by emphasizing that the present suggestion of an exchange of cultural artifacts between Sweden and Denmark "is a really quite simple and straightforward one. We are only doing what the UN and UNESCO are also doing – we are saying: Let us do an exchange of those artifacts which are the result of unjust theft right up until today".[37] This would, he magnanimously added, also

---

[35] Kolding Nielsen, "'Jyske Lov' som krigsbytte. En mytes opståen, udnyttelse og fald," 470–71.

[36] Kolding Nielsen, "'Jyske Lov' som krigsbytte. En mytes opståen, udnyttelse og fald," 496.

[37] Kolding Nielsen, "'Jyske Lov' som krigsbytte. En mytes opståen, udnyttelse og fald," 502.

mean that Denmark should be prepared to hand back to other nations cultural artifacts that for one reason or another have ended up in the country but do not belong there.

Kolding Nielsen tells a fascinating story. His article runs over many pages and is obviously based on some very thorough historical research. Here, I have only been able to touch on but a very small part of it – the part that deals with my concern in this article: cultural looting. In one sense, the Danish People's Party got it their way in the end – whether or not they still believe in the myth of C 37 being the original Jutlantic Law which was looted by the Swedes in the 17th century, their proposed exchange deal between the two national libraries of Sweden and Denmark has now taken place. However, it is worth noting that this only happened when members of the Party started making use of a cultural political discourse which is currently gaining more and more ground at the global level. In another sense, therefore, this is a cautionary tale – a tale of how a very right-wing political party can appropriate for a number of questionable patriotic ends a particular cultural political discourse. The Danish People's Party is the party behind Denmark's increasingly tough immigration laws, for example, and with this issue of cultural looting they have found the perfect symbolic fight for their beloved Danish values and culture. "For historical research it does not play much of a role where these manuscripts are stored, but at a symbolic level this case has had a great impact in Denmark", as Kolding Nielsen concludes.

3. Concluding Remarks: Cultural Looting and Global Security

In addition to issues involving cultural and national identity, another reason why the question of who owns culture and cultural heritage has become such a hotly contested political one is that there is a lot of money involved in the illegal international trade with cultural artifacts. Concrete figures are hard to come by, but according to a 2006 estimate by the Archeological Institute of America, contractors pay looters in Iraq $10 million to $20 million each year for artifacts that fetch upwards of $100 million on the black market.[38]

In a very interesting article on "Cultural heritage in danger", Blythe Bowman argues that organized criminal groups operating on a global scale are becoming more and more involved in the theft and export of illicitly-ob-

---

38 See Laura de la Torre, "Terrorists raise cash by selling antiquities," *GSN: Government Security News* 4 (2006) – available at http://www.savingantiquities.org/pdf/GSNarticle.pdf (last visited on March 10, 2011).

tained antiquities and other cultural property, thereby increasingly posing a threat to our global cultural heritage:

> The drastic increase in the current market values of antiquities has precipitated an infiltration and monopoly of the black market by organized criminal syndicates. Plunder of ancient objects has become a thriving industry for these groups. While organized criminal groups are not the only figures involved in the business of looting, their presence in this illicit business makes plunder a particular threat to both cultural heritage and national security.
> The looting of archaeological sites is one of the most alarming and destructive types of cultural property theft. When criminal groups are involved, it can be especially damaging.[39]

Criminal syndicates have, it would seem, become very adept at recruiting locals to scour the countryside for archaeological treasures in economically depressed areas, where people need the money and therefore have a lowered resistance to getting involved in such illegal activity. Once found and excavated – often at the cost of extensive damage to the archeological sites themselves – such treasures are provided with forged provenance and export documents and smuggled over the border, only to end up on the international market. And it is the fact that these treasures have been stolen and then smuggled out of their countries of origin which is the problem. In and of themselves, art and antiquities are not illegal. When they have been properly, that is legally, excavated and when their archaeological context is preserved, then such objects can give us a lot of valuable information.

Reports from around the globe indicate that organized criminal groups who deal in drugs and arms often also tend to deal in stolen cultural property. Such black-market activities tend to go together, that is, and while they are often used as a means of money laundering on the part of these criminal groups, they also seem to further a thriving business in copies, fakes and forgeries.

Most often, the illegal activities of organized criminal groups is not confined to just one country. The fight against such activities and the protection of cultural property consequently, it is increasingly recognized by international organizations such as INTERPOL, Europol, and the United

---

[39] Blythe Bowman, "Cultural heritage in danger: Plunder of antiquities, a crime of global proportions," in *SAFE/Saving Antiquities For Everyone* (available at http://www.savingantiquities.org/crime.php). Bowman also refers to one study, United Nations Global Report 1999, in which the annual trade in illicit antiquities was estimated at around 7.8 billion dollars, ranking behind drugs (160 billion) and arms (100 billion) as the most profitable black market. The following paragraphs build on Bowman's article.

Nations, requires coordinated international efforts. This realization is a start, but much more needs to be done, argues Bowman:

> While organized criminal gangs may have infiltrated the global looting industry, not enough time, human resources, and transnational police efforts have been devoted to tracking, stopping, and prosecuting their illicit activities. However, there is growing recognition of plunder as crime among scholars, researchers, and practitioners from all sorts of agencies and institutions around the world. Such increased interest, cooperation and coordination of research and enforcement efforts is certainly an encouraging sign.[40]

After 9/11, moreover, cultural looting has sometimes been connected to terrorism – thus truly turning it into both a national and a global security issue. In an article from 2006 for *GSN: Government Security News*, Laura de la Torre claims, for example, that "terrorist organizations may be financing their deadly activities partly by dealing in the illicit trade of art and antiquities which come out of the Middle East and wind up in the homes of collectors who pay top dollar for ancient artifacts".[41] De la Torre refers to an article in the German newspaper *Der Spiegel* in July 2005, which reported that Mohammed Atta had approached a professor at the University of Göttingen in 2000 or 2001 and asked about selling antique Afghan cultural artifacts. "He wanted to know where one could sell such artifacts", *Der Spiegel* quotes this German professor as saying.[42] The interpretation of the *Bundeskriminalamt* (roughly: federal crime bureau) was that Atta may very well have tried to finance the attack on the twin towers in New York on September 11, 2001 through such illegal art dealing.

Again, hard facts are difficult to come by on this issue, but Cindy Ho, one of the founders of the non-profit organization SAFE/Saving Antiquities for Everyone, which was founded after the looting of the National Museum of Iraq in Baghdad in 2003 in an effort to curb the illicit antiquities trade and to preserve the country's cultural property, claims that "this story is not mere idle gossip, it was included in a letter to Congressman Clay Shaw [R-FL] of the House Ways and Means Committee by Archeological Institute of America (AIA) chairman James Wright".[43] Comparing current levels of loot-

---

40 Bowman, "Cultural heritage in danger: Plunder of antiquities, a crime of global proportions."

41 de la Torre, "Terrorists raise cash by selling antiquities," – available at http://www.savingantiquities.org/pdf/GSNarticle.pdf (last visited on March 10, 2011).

42 "Kunst als Terrorfinanzierung?" *Der Spiegel* (Ermittler), 29/2005, 20 – my translation from the German.

43 Cindy Ho, in de la Torre, see note 38.

ing to those of earlier periods, Ho concludes that current levels are much higher. For her, as for many other observers of and researchers into the issue, the thefts from Iraq have truly been a wake-up call to a problem that is becoming more and more severe.[44]

That this problem concerns all of us just means that we cannot and should not wish to shut our eyes to what is going on. For all kinds of good reasons – from identity to terrorism – plunder has truly become a crime of international concern. And with its both cultural-political and legal implications, it is a good and promising topic for scholars interested in law and humanities.

---

[44] de la Torre, see note 38. See also Brian Williams' article, "The restitution debate: The international fight over the world's most famous artifacts," at *DM/Damforst Museum, the Online Museum of Damaged, Forged & Stolen Art*, for a reasonably updated bibliography on this topic – available at http://damforstmuseum.org/stolen.html (last visited on March 10).

List of Contributors

Daniela Carpi is full professor of English Literature at the Faculty of Foreign Literatures, Department of English Studies, University of Verona, Italy. Her fields of research are: Renaissance theatre, critical theory, postmodernism, law and literature, literature and science, literature and visual arts. She collaborates with Longo publisher in Ravenna, with Ombre Corte in Verona, where she directs a section "Culture" devoted to comparative criticism and a section "Agon" on law and culture; with De Gruyter in Berlin, where she directs (together with professor Klaus Stierstorfer) a book series "Law and Literature". She is the Coordinator of the Doctoral Course in English Studies at the University of Verona. She is in the scientific board of the journals *Symbolism: a Journal of Critical Aesthetics* (New York), *Anglistik* (Heidelberg), *La torre di Babele* (Parma), *Law and Humanities* (Warwick) and *Cardozo Law Bulletin* (University of Trento). She has founded the journal *Polemos* which she directs with professor Monateri, and the Associazione Italiana di Diritto e Letteratura (AIDEL), which she presides. Among her most recent publications are *The Concept of Equity: an Interdisciplinary Assessment* (Heidelberg: Winter, 2007); *Practising Equity, Addressing Law* (Heidelberg: Winter, 2008); *Bioethics and Biolaw through Literature* (Berlin/Boston: De Gruyter, 2011).

Thomas Elholm is professor of Law at the University of Southern Denmark. His main field of research is criminal law, including comparative criminal law and criminal procedure. After graduating from Law School (LLM in 1997), he worked as a lawyer for a few years. In 2002 he published a PhD thesis on the relationship between national criminal law and EU law. Since then he has worked as a scholar, specialising in EU criminal law. He is President of the Danish Association of European Lawyers, co-founding member of the European Criminal Police Initiative, member of the editorial board of *European Criminal Law Review* (EuCLR) and chief editor of *Scandinavian Journal of Criminal Law and Criminology* (NTfK). In 2011–2012 he is a visiting professor at the Copenhagen Business School. For the last six years Thomas Elholm has been working closely with the Nordic Network for Law and Literature.

Jeanne Gaakeer holds a degree in English Literature from Utrecht University, the Netherlands (1980), a degree in Dutch Law (1990) and in the Philosophy of Law (1992, cum laude) from Erasmus University Rotterdam, the Netherlands. In 1995 she received her PhD from Erasmus University Rotterdam. Her dissertation is a study of the history and development of the *Law and Literature* movement, and the work of James Boyd White. She currently serves as a justice in the criminal law section of the Appellate Court of The Hague, the Netherlands, after having been a judge in the Regional Court of Middelburg for almost ten years. She is (extraordinary) professor of Legal Theory, more specifically in the field of literary jurisprudence, focusing on the bonds between law, language and literature, at Erasmus School of Law, Erasmus University Rotterdam, the Netherlands. Her research focus is on the relationship between law, language and literature, and on broader issues of interdisciplinarity involved in the interrelation of legal theory and legal practice. With professor Greta Olson (University of Giessen, Germany) she is the co-founder of the European Network for Law and Literature, www.eurnll.org. Jeanne Gaakeer's recent publications include: "The Future of Literary-Legal Jurisprudence: Mere Theory or Just Practice?", *Law and Humanities* 5.1 (2011): 185–196, "Law, Language and Literature: Their Interrelations in *Law and Literature*", in *Law and Method*, eds. B. Van Klink and S. Taekema (Tübingen: Mohr Siebeck, 2011), "Crises of Evidence, Crises of Truth", *Pòlemos* 2 (2010): 3–23, "Law and Literature in Europe: a first pragmatic inquiry", with 2 appendices, in *Teaching Law through the Looking Glass of Literature*, ed. B. Pozzo (Bern: Staempfli Publishers, 2010), 59–75 and 121–132.

HANS PETTER GRAVER, cand. jur. (J.D.) University of Oslo, Norway, 1980, dr. juris 1986, is professor and Dean of the Faculty of Law, University of Oslo. He specializes in administrative law, European law and legal theory. His main field of research for the past years has been rhetoric and law and legal arguments. His recent publications include *Alminnelig forvaltningsrett* [Administrative law] (3rd ed., Oslo, 2007), *Juridisk overtalelseskunst* [The Art of Legal Persuation] (Oslo, 2008) and *Rett, retorikk og juridisk argumentasjon* [Law, Rhetoric and Legal Argumentation] (Oslo, 2010).

MATTIAS KUMM is professor of Law at NYU School of Law, USA, and research professor for Globalization and the Rule of Law at the Social Science Research Center (WZB) and Humboldt University in Berlin, Germany. His research focuses on basic conceptual, doctrinal and institutional questions relating to Comparative Constitutional, European and International Law. Among his most recent publications are "How does European Union Law fit into the World of Public Law? Costa, Kadi and Three Models of Public Law," in *Political Theory of the European Union*, eds. Jürgen Neyer and Antje

Wiener (Oxford: OUP, 2011), "Internationale Handelsgesellschaft, Nold and the New Human Rights Paradigm," in *The Past and Future of EU Law: The Classics of EU Law revisited on the 50th Anniversary of the Treaties of Rome*, eds. Loïc Azoulai and Miguel Poiares Maduro (Oxford: Hart, 2010), "The Best of Times and the Worst of Times: Between Constitutional Triumphalism and Nostalgia," in *The Twilight of Constitutionalism*, eds. Peter Dobner and Martin Loughlin (Oxford: OUP, 2010) and "The Idea of Socratic Contestation and the Right to Justification: The Point of Rights based Proportionality Review," *Law and Ethics of Human Rights* 4.2 (2010).

SVEND ERIK LARSEN is professor of Comparative Literature at Aarhus University, Denmark. He is co-editor of *Orbis Litterarum*, member of ICLA Coordinating Committee and of Academia Europaea. His research interests include: literature and cultural history (urban culture, idea of nature, memory). Ongoing project: Forgiveness as a literary and cultural challenge. His latest book (in Danish) is *Literature and Globalisation* (2007). Recent articles: "Local Literatures, Global Perspectives" (2010), "Forgiving and Forgetting" (2010), "The mediality of Performance" (2010), and "Memory Constructions and Their Limits" (in print).

FIONA MACMILLAN is professor of Law in the School of Law at Birkbeck College, University of London, UK. At present she is a visiting professor at L'Università degli Studi Roma Tre, Italy. She is a member of the editorial boards of *Law and Critique* (Birkbeck Law Press) and *Law, Social Justice and Global Development*, *Media and Arts Law Review* (University of Melbourne) and of the advisory board for the series *Law and Literature*, published by De Gruyter (Berlin/Boston). She has a particular interest in interdisciplinary approaches to the study of copyright and has published widely in this area. Among her many publications may be mentioned 1) the monograph *The World Trade Organisation and the Environment* (2001); the edited volumes *New Directions in Copyright Law*, volumes 1–6; and *International Corporate Law*, volumes 1 and 2.

GRETA OLSON is professor for English and American Literature and Cultural Studics at the University of Giessen, Germany, and a general editor of the *European Journal of English Studies* (EJES). The author of *Reading Eating Disorders* (2003) and *'Criminal Animals' and the Rise of Positivist Criminology* (in preparation), she has edited *Current Trends in Narratology* (2011) and *9/11 – Ten Years After* (2011) and co-edited (with Monika Fludernik) *In the Grip of the Law* (2004) as well as a special issue of EJES on law, literature, and language with Martin Kayman. Her research interests are interdisciplinary and include

Law and Literature/Culture, punitivity, narratology, animal studies, and feminist and gender studies.

HELLE PORSDAM is professor of American Studies at the University of Copenhagen, Denmark. She teaches American history as well as the culture and history of human rights. She holds an MA in English from the University of Copenhagen and a PhD in American Studies from Yale University, USA, has been a Liberal Arts Fellow twice at the Harvard Law School, USA, and will be a visiting fellow at Wolfson College, University of Cambridge, UK, in the fall of 2011. Among her publications may be mentioned *Legally Speaking: Contemporary American Culture and the Law* (Univ. of Massachusetts Press, 1999), *From Civil to Human Rights: Dialogues on Law and Humanities in the United States and Europe* (Edward Elgar, 2009) and *Copyright and Other Fairy Tales: Hans Christian Andersen and the Commodification of Creativity*, which she edited for Edward Elgar in 2006. She is the Project Leader of CULTIVATE, a project on copyright, creativity and cultural heritage institutions which is funded by HERA (Humanities in the European Research Area, European Science Foundation), and which runs from 2010–2013 (www.cultivateproject.dk).

MIA RENDIX holds a PhD in Comparative Literature and is assistant professor at Saxo Institute, University of Copenhagen, Denmark. She is currently working on a two year-project, "Copyrighting Creativity," which is funded by the HERA (Humanities in the European Research Area) organization. Her research is centered around 1) the philosophical and literary implications and challenges of digitization and cultural heritage and 2) American literature and theater. One example is the article "The Enlightenment revisited: Digitization and the Right to Read," which she wrote together with Helle Porsdam. In addition, she has written several articles on tragedy and the tragic in American and British drama.

JAY WINTER, Charles J. Stille Professor of History, joined the faculty of Yale University, USA, in 2001. He taught at the Hebrew University of Jerusalem, Israel, from 1970 to 1973, and at the University of Warwick, UK, from 1973 to 1979. From 1979 to 2001, he was reader in Modern History and fellow of Pembroke College, Cambridge, UK. He holds PhD and DLitt from Cambridge. He is the author of *Sites of Memory, Sites of Mourning: The Great War in European Cultural History* (Cambridge: CUP, 1995) and editor of a collection of essays published by CUP entitled *America and the Armenian Genocide* (2003). In 2005 he published *The Great War in History: Debates and Controversies, 1914 to the Present*, written with Antoine Prost (Cambridge: CUP, 2005). In 1997, he received an Emmy award for the best documentary series of the year as co-producer and co-writer of "The Great War and the shaping of the twentieth century", an eight-hour series broadcast on PBS and the BBC, and shown subsequently in twenty-eight countries. He is one of the founders and a member of the comité directeur of the research centre of the Historial de la Grande Guerre, the international museum of the Great War, in Péronne, Somme, France.